Strength Down the Middle

THE STORY OF THE 1959 CHICAGO WHITE SOX

Strength Down the Middle

THE STORY OF THE 1959 CHICAGO WHITE SOX

RR Donnelley & Sons

During the course of my research on the 1959 Chicago White Sox baseball team, I had the privilege of contacting several of the players and coaches who were involved in the drama of that season. Through letter and telephone they shared their memories of the men and circumstances that made that team a success. I offer a special thank you to Jim Landis, Bob Shaw, Ray Berres, Al Smith, Gerry Staley, Don Gutteridge and Ray Boone for their time and patience. I also want to thank my editor Craig Adas for taking from his busy schedule the time and talent necessary to help give life to this effort. Laurie Parker provided the perfect finishing touch with the graphic design and artistic organization of the finished piece.

ISBN 0-9675109-0-2

Published by Mereken Land and Production Company, Fort Worth, Texas 76102

Photographs courtesy of National Baseball Hall of Fame Library, Cooperstown, NY, AP/Wide World Photos, New York, NY and UPI/Corbis-Bettmann.

Editor: Craig W. Adas
Book design: Laurie Parker
Cover photo: by Kaufmann and Fabry/Plastichrome® by Colourpicture, Boston, MA

Printed in the United States of America by RR Donnelley & Sons, Chicago, Illinois.

Table of Contents

Foreward

THERE IS SOMETHING SPECIAL ABOUT MAJOR LEAGUE BASEBALL THAT sets it apart from all other professional sports. While other major sports have their fair share of history and tradition, the tradition of grandfathers, fathers, and sons bonding through ballpark outings seems to hold a very unique place in American culture. Some of the earliest childhood memories of many men, myself included, involve trips to major league baseball parks with their grandfathers and fathers. These early childhood experiences often spark an enthusiasm and love for the game of baseball that is so great it becomes an integral and inseparable part of a true baseball fan's psyche.

In his book *Strength Down the Middle*, Larry Kalas pays tribute to the wonderful game of baseball by reliving one of his most memorable childhood experiences—the Chicago White Sox 1959 Pennant Race. Mr. Kalas captures the spirit of the 1959 season through player and coach interviews, detailed game research and recollection, and, most importantly, first-hand personal observations. He takes us on a wonderful and exciting journey back in time by immersing us in the 1959 White Sox season. For those readers who are seasoned White Sox fans, this book will be a trip down

Memory Lane, evoking memories and emotions that may have laid dormant for decades. Younger fans will be treated to a baseball history lesson and a glimpse of Chicago life in the late 1950s. Regardless of your age, background or knowledge of baseball, I'm certain you will find the pages that follow to be both informative and highly entertaining.

Mr. Kalas carefully dissects and analyzes for us the White Sox 1959 season through the eyes of a child. For historical perspective, he includes interesting public events that occurred during the White Sox 1959 season. And to finish out the book, Mr. Kalas adds a personal touch by sharing many of his childhood experiences— some pertaining to baseball and some to those other events in life that serve as little more than distractions to baseball.

Despite growing up 15 years later than Mr. Kalas and hundreds of miles from Chicago, in reading this book, I found striking similarities between our childhood experiences, especially in the area of baseball. Mr. Kalas's description of his progression through Little League, the method of choosing teams in a pickup game, the importance of selecting the perfect baseball glove, and the countless visits to grocery and drug stores to purchase trading cards could quite accurately describe my childhood, with only a few minor changes to the descriptions. While some of the similarities may be coincidental, I suspect that most are attributable to the pure traditions imbedded in the game of baseball; traditions that are subject to no geographic boundaries and that become stronger with the passing of each generation.

Although the decade of the 1990s has seen its share of unsavory events and developments in professional baseball, including the 1994 season-ending players' strike, skyrocketing ticket prices, juiced ball theories, and the resignation just this year of several National League umpires due to a labor dispute, the basic elements and rich traditions of the game and the game-watching experience have remained largely unchanged throughout the decade and the century. It is this consistency that creates an environment that is conducive to bridging the gap between generations and allows people of all ages to enjoy the game and grow closer together through sharing a love for the sport.

As we rapidly approach the new millennium and all of the uncertainties that accompany it, we can find comfort in the fact that children will continue to fall in love with baseball, just as we did, and will pass along the traditions of the sport to their children. We can only hope, however, that those children will not have to wait another forty years to see an American League pennant flying over Chicago's south side.

Craig W. Adas

A Love Affair

THE PORTAL TO COMISKEY PARK FRAMED A PICTURE THAT IS AS VIVID to me today as it was on that warm summer day in 1957. My prior exposure to major league baseball had been limited to watching our small black and white Stromburg-Carlson television set or listening to the old Farnsworth radio. I was unprepared for the incredible mixture of sight, smell and sound that greeted me. The emerald green grass and brilliant blue sky framed the impressive grand stands. The odor of the nearby stock yards could not dull the senses enough to cover the distinct aroma of popcorn and hot dogs. The scent of stale beer, spilled by generations of White Sox fans, permeated the stadium. Vendors hawked everything from souvenirs to score cards to popcorn, hot dogs, soft drinks and candy. The Boston Red Sox were in town to challenge our beloved Chicago White Sox. As the White Sox—led by Nelson Fox, Sherman Lollar, Larry Doby, Minnie Minoso and Billy Pierce—took the field, I knew that I was experiencing an event that would be forever etched in my mind.

Growing up in Chicago in the south side neighborhood of Mount Greenwood in the late 1950s presented a young boy the opportunity to fall in love. Like many of my peers I fell madly in love with

American League baseball. Before we were old enough to understand, our grandfathers and fathers passed this legacy of love onto us.

My maternal grandfather was a son of Swedish immigrants who
settled in the Armour Square neighborhood of Chicago in the early
1900s. Armour Square was located just east of the Bridgeport
section of the city at 34th Street. The strong work ethic of the community was attributable to ancestral tradition as well as necessity
for survival in this new land. Athletic activity, including baseball,
was encouraged and dominated when residents of Armour Square
were not working. In 1909, Charles A. Comiskey—sometimes
called the old "Roman" because of his distinct profile—selected
the site of an old cabbage patch adjacent to Armour Square to build
the majestic temple of baseball to be known as Comiskey Park. My
grandfather was a daily visitor to the construction site. Upon com-
pletion of the ball yard in 1910, he found employment shagging
foul balls that landed on the roof of the Park as well as other clubhouse duties. Until his death in 1995, my grandfather passed on
recollections of the game and the players from his era, including
tales of the exploits of the 1919 Chicago "Black Sox." The 1919
Chicago White Sox were tabbed with that infamous moniker
following the greatest scandal in baseball history. A total of eight
players on the 1919 team were accused of throwing the World
Series to the Cincinnati Reds. These men were acquitted of all
criminal charges but were banned by the Commissioner of
Baseball from participation in professional baseball for the rest of
their lives. The most recognizable name in the ostracized group
was "Shoeless" Joe Jackson. The other tarnished players accused
were Oscar "Happy" Felsch, Fred McMullin, Charles "Swede"
Risberg, Buck Weaver, Arnold "Chick" Gandil, Eddie Cicotte and
Claude "Lefty" Williams.

That visit to Comiskey Park in 1957 became a tradition for

several years to follow as my grandfather would take me and my brother on the tour of his old neighborhood—topped off with an afternoon baseball game at Comiskey Park. My father also loved baseball. However, as a Chicagoan transplanted from Thompsonville, Connecticut, he for reasons only known to him and God was a Detroit Tiger fan. Dad would make it an annual practice to take us to Comiskey Park for a Detroit Tiger or New York Yankee game. During those years I would spend countless hours either watching my baseball heroes on television by day or listening to their exploits on the radio by night.

In hindsight the most memorable season of all was 1959, when the Chicago White Sox captured the American League pennant from the hated New York Yankees. This would be the first and the last time since the scandalous 1919 Chicago "Black Sox" team that the American League flag flew over Chicago's south side. As a partial payment for the life-long memories that the 1959 White Sox provided for me, I write this book as a humble tribute to those men, that team and that year.

THIS BOOK IS DEDICATED TO THE MEMORY OF AND THE LOVE I HAVE for my grandfather, Lawrence Orn, and my father, Tony Kalas. In addition, I could not have accomplished this project without the love and support of my wife, Debbie, my daughters, Meredith and Kendall, and my mother, Winifred Kalas. I hope you enjoy the story and the step back in time.

CHAPTER ONE

The Feel of a Well-Oiled Glove

IN 1959, "SPRING TRAINING" WAS A TIME OF METAMORPHOSIS for most ballplayers. Year round nutritional and conditioning programs were decades from being common practice. The majority of professional ballplayers had to take advantage of the off-season to make money. Many of the player wages in this era were equivalent to that of a factory hand or a low level white collar employee. Accordingly, winter months were consumed by either playing winter ball or pursuing an occupation away from the baseball diamond. Younger players seeking to improve their skills earned extra dollars by playing baseball in tropical places such as Cuba or South America. By playing year-round they could support their families, maintain playing condition, and heighten their chance of sticking with a major league club. Older, more established players often found themselves working in factories or offices to make ends meet. These players used spring training to shed extra weight accumulated during the sedentary winter months and to knock the rust off of their game. The Chicago White Sox trained in Tampa, Florida. The warm confines of Florida hammered their bodies into competitive shape and resurrected their collective baseball skills.

Mount Greenwood, the neighborhood where I grew up, was also

coming to life after a long winter. The community lies within the city limits of far southwest Chicago. During my childhood years, the blue-collar working class neighborhood was a melting pot of immigrant groups including Irish, Dutch and Eastern Europeans. There were many factory workers, firemen, policemen, other government employees, independent businessmen, and a few bankers and lawyers just getting started with their careers. Most shared the American dream of working hard to provide a quality education and a better life for their children. Family units typically were close knit and consisted of a stay-at-home mother, a father who often held down more than one job, and several children. Five or more children in a single family was not uncommon. Homes were situated on small lots, side-by-side. These shotgun type homes were either brick or wooden framed with many having basements. Houses were small and included two or three bedrooms, one bath and a kitchen. Living conditions often were crowded, but at the time no one really seemed to notice. Most families were either first or second generation Americans. Oftentimes family unit households included a grandparent who had been born and raised in Europe and spoke little or no English. The culture of their mother land was usually maintained and passed down in part to their grandchildren. These circumstances and surroundings promoted a relatively simple life, steeped in tradition, in which the magnificent American game of baseball flourished as a favorite pastime.

As the club broke camp and moved north for the opening of the 1959 campaign, the neighborhoods and school classrooms of Chicago's south side buzzed with anticipation as well as doubts. In my particular case the unbridled anticipation was for the coming baseball season and the doubt was related to my academic survival. I found the public school system rewarding as well as challenging. However, the educational process seemed to intrude on my single-minded focus on baseball in the spring and early summer. The Board of Education of the Chicago Public School System knew in their infinite and unquestioned wisdom how to work an out-of-condition student into playing shape. I attended the Mount Greenwood Branch of the Chicago Public School System on 11109 South Homan Avenue. Teachers have always, as a matter of course, provided parents updates on the ongoing academic conditioning of their children. The General Superintendent of Schools, Benjamin C. Willis, utilized Form #EL 118-38 as the "Report of Pupil Progress" for this purpose.

In late January of 1959, I had progressed to the 4B level of education, which constituted the first half of the fourth grade. The half year was divided into four reporting periods. Each period covered approximately five weeks. Each student was evaluated on "Areas of Learning" which included subjects, Social Habits, Work and Study Habits, and Health and Safety Habits. For each of eleven different subjects the student was evaluated by use of a letter grade. The other "Areas of Learning" were graded by a pass/fail system. A check mark received in any facet of these other categories was a strong indication of need for improvement. The letter grade system was designed to redefine your self image on a continual basis. The system went like this. "E-Excellent achievement was a mark given to a pupil who through industry and effective use of his abilities has produced an exceedingly high quality of work." You felt really good to receive an E, but not terribly bad if you didn't. The next lower grade on the scale was G. "G-Good Progress was a mark given to the pupil who has produced a good quality of work." This was an average grade which reflected the most common image of one's self esteem. The next lower mark was the dreaded F. "F-Fair or acceptable progress was a mark given to the pupil who has produced an acceptable quality of work, all factors considered." What did they mean, all factors considered? Did it mean that the teacher considered you as dumb as a sack full of hammers and, accordingly, anything you achieved was acceptable? I really didn't know how to interpret this. The academic "F" word struck fear in our hearts and frustration in the eyes of our parents. The lowest mark was a U. "U-Unsatisfactory was a mark given to the pupil who through lack of industry, of ineffective use of his abilities, or absence has failed to produce an acceptable level of work." At least this mark recognized on an objective basis that you were either lazy or didn't attend class.

My manager, or teacher, in 4B was Mrs. Murphy, a stern gray-headed disciplinarian who, by her very nature, intimidated everyone. My 4B Spring Training was a disaster. The first quarter results of my progress were abysmal. I was graded in nine different subjects and, like the 1958 White Sox, I had started the year very slowly. All factors considered, I was sent to the dugout with an "F" four times. Apparently manager Murphy didn't appreciate the quality of my abilities in composition, handwriting, social studies and science. In reading, spelling, arithmetic, art and music I had elevated my game to a "G." Based upon overall results, I should have been returned to the minors. I prodded myself through the second quarter of the semester with the belief that the game was not over until the last out. While the whole academic process was somewhat daunting, my mind was on something far more important than my grades. The Chicago White Sox were going to open the 1959 season, and after all, I knew with unwavering certainty that I truly was smarter than a sack full of hammers.

The temperature hovered at the 37-degree mark at Briggs Stadium on April 10, 1959, as 38,332 shivering fans witnessed the Detroit Tigers and Chicago White Sox commence the chase for the 1959 American League pennant. Chicago manager Al Lopez and pitching coach Ray Berres selected Billy Pierce, fresh from a 17 win, 11 loss record in 1958, for the opening day assignment for the

Pale Hose. As he strode to the mound the left-handed hurler was once again returning to Detroit, the place of his birth. Born April 2, 1927, Walter William Pierce signed a contract with the Detroit club and reported to the Tiger camp in 1945 as a fire-balling 18-year-old. Pierce was impressive as a youngster appearing in 27 major league games and throwing 65 innings with Detroit during a brief call up in 1945 and a full season with the parent club in 1948. The baseball gods smiled on the south side faithful when on November 10, 1948, Frank Lane, White Sox general manager, on the advice of Paul Richards, the Sox manager, obtained Pierce and $10,000 from Detroit in exchange for Aaron Robinson. Robinson, a catcher with a lifetime .260 batting average, would remain in the major leagues for three more undistinguished seasons. Pierce became a decade-long mainstay of the White Sox staff. Pierce led the league in earned run average with a 1.97 mark in 1955, led the league in complete games from 1956 to 1958, and posted back-to-back 20 victory seasons in 1956 and 1957. Pierce was being counted on to join Early Wynn and Dick Donovan to form the nucleus of Chicago's starting rotation in 1959.

His mound opponent on this blustery afternoon was hard throwing right-hander Jim Bunning. Bunning was a rookie sensation in 1957, leading the league in wins with 20 and innings pitched with 267. As he approached the mound that day he was anxious to overcome his 1958 sophomore jinx when he slipped to a 14-12 won-loss record. The Tigers were led by Al Kaline, Harvey Kuenn and Charlie Maxwell. In addition to Jim Bunning, their pitching staff included Frank Lary, Don Mossi and Paul Foytack.

The opening day crowd was treated to a drawn-out battle that lasted four hours and 25 minutes. In an apparent effort to keep warm, some well lubricated fans tossed whiskey bottles and other projectiles onto the field hitting Chicago rookie Johnny Callison in the head as he patrolled left field. Callison remained in the game sporting a knot on his left temple. The fourteen inning affair saw several lead changes. Al Kaline stepped to the plate in the first inning and immediately got to Pierce. Kaline opened the scoring with a home run in his first at bat of the new season. That lead stood until the fourth inning when Chicago rookie Norm Cash singled and later raced home on an infield out by Pierce to even the score. Jim Landis, the White Sox speedy center-fielder, gave the Sox the lead with a two-run shot into the left center field bleachers in the fifth inning. The advantage, however, was short-lived as the Tigers came roaring back in the bottom of the inning to score three times on two singles and two doubles to take a 4-3 lead. In their half of the seventh frame the Sox scored four runs to push the lead to 7-4. The main contributor to this onslaught was Detroit left fielder Larry Doby who bungled pinch-hitter Billy Goodman's pop fly into a three-run error. The fourth run was tallied on a single by Nellie Fox. This would be little Nellie's fourth but not last hit of the day.

The battle continued as Charlie Maxwell slammed a three-run pinch hit homer off of Chicago reliever Ray Moore in the bottom of the eighth to even the contest at seven all. Gerry Staley, the sixth of seven Sox pitchers on the day, came on in relief in the 10th inning and pitched four and 2/3 innings of shutout ball. Staley was rewarded for his efforts with the victory. Sammy Esposito, Chicago native and valuable utility infielder, cracked a two-out single in the top of the 14th inning. Nellie Fox followed Esposito's single with a two-run blast off Don Mossi that traveled 340 feet to the lower deck in right field providing the final two-run margin in the 9-7 opening day win. The dramatic blast by Nellie was his first home run since 1957. The only disappointment in the day's activity for Chicago was that Al Smith struck out four of the five official times he went to the plate.

The cool temperature persisted the following afternoon. The Sox, however, remained hot as the normally light-hitting South Siders slammed three home runs in an eight hit attack which resulted in a 5-3 victory. Early Wynn, another mainstay of the staff, pitched a complete game, seven-hit performance as he notched his 250th career win. That victory total placed Wynn ahead of all other active pitchers in the major leagues at the time. Sherman Lollar, the veteran catcher, put on an offensive display slamming two solo home runs in addition to his first inning RBI single. Shortstop Luis Aparicio hammered the game-winning home run off Ray Narleski in the seventh inning. Fox at second base and Aparicio at shortstop were a sterling keystone combination for the South Siders, recognized primarily for their defense and speed. They were now adding a new dimension to their game, as they each had provided game winning home runs to propel their team to victory in Chicago's first two contests.

Veteran right-hander Dick Donovan took the mound against Detroit's famed Yankee killer, Frank Lary, in the closing stanza of the three-game set. The game was played before a sparse crowd of only 1,228 fans. It was business as usual for the Sox as rookie Norm Cash ignited a two-run rocket into the seats in right field in the first inning. The key blow, however, was a triple by Jim Landis in the sixth. Landis scored as Lollar singled for the game-winning hit. Both Al Smith, with two hits and an RBI, and Sherman Lollar, with two hits and two RBIs, turned in solid offensive performances. Donovan earned the 5-3 victory with relief help from Rudolfo Arias, Turk Lown, Don Rudolph and Bob Shaw. Shaw, the young right-hander, finished the game with one and 2/3 innings of scoreless relief.

The opening series of the 1959 season in Detroit saw major contributions from several key ingredients to what manager Al

Lopez believed would be his recipe for winning. Historically, strength down the middle was a necessity for team success in baseball. The Sox possessed a unique combination of youthful talent and seasoned veterans in those key positions. Behind the plate Sherman Lollar, an excellent handler of pitchers, had finished the 1958 campaign as an All-Star achieving career highs in home runs (20) and RBIs (84) while appearing in 127 games. Young Earl Battey and John Romano provided the White Sox with excellent depth behind the plate. At shortstop, Luis Aparicio hit .266 in 1958 and led the league in stolen bases for the third consecutive year with 29. Aparicio was considered one of the best defensive shortstops on the circuit. Nelson Fox was also coming off a 1958 All-Star year. Fox led the league in hits with 187 and compiled a .300 batting average while playing in 155 games. Fox's determination and on-field leadership were recognized by all. Aparicio and Fox provided the South Siders with outstanding offensive and defensive production in the middle infield. Jim Landis was an outstanding defensive center-fielder. In 1958 his batting average rose to .277 as he hit 15 home runs and knocked in 72 runs. The White Sox pitching staff included veterans Billy Pierce, Early Wynn, Dick Donovan and Ray Moore in starting roles with Turk Lown and Gerry Staley as veteran relievers. Youngsters Barry Latman, Don Rudolph, Rudolfo Arias and Bob Shaw were being counted on to fill out the rotation and to provide help in relief. In all, a splendid assortment of talent down the middle.

It seemed that almost every kid on the block was an American League fan and eternally had their hopes pinned on Chicago's chances in the new season. The season opening series in Detroit provided the fuel for our 1959 fire. Organized and sandlot baseball and softball games filled an important role in our daily lives during the spring, summer and early fall. Family planning in our predominantly Irish, Catholic neighborhood must have been dictated by the lords of sandlot baseball as there were many warm bodies to engage in spirited pick-up games. The Tracys, Dorans, Fitzpatricks, O'Connors, Shaughnessys, and Dignans all had boys close to the same age. This group of families formed the nucleus for our sandlot games. As the major league campaign became a reality, we all eagerly retrieved our baseball gloves from their winter resting places. They were recovered from the basement or the garage still bound securely with heavy duty string and a baseball firmly embraced in the pocket. The molded and sometimes moldy specimens could become a bit brittle from the cold and dry conditions of winter. Accordingly, the leather extension of our catching hand had been liberally caressed with oil prior to being placed in winter hibernation. The first course of action in the spring was to determine if the biological changes which had affected one's body during the winter months had also changed the size of one's glove hand. If a new baseball glove was in order, this became a very serious proposition. Our parents appreciated the hard earned value of a dollar. However, if a new glove was truly required, our fathers would join us in an exhaustive search for a fine and lasting specimen. The first and ultimately last stop would be the local sporting goods store in the village of Mount Greenwood. In my entire childhood, those searches produced only two baseball gloves of which I would be the original and only owner. All of my other gloves were well worn hand-me-downs. My first new glove was a MacGregor "Jim Landis" model. My second new glove, a few years later, was a Wilson A2020, Nelson Fox model.

As I said, almost every kid was a White Sox fan with the exception of Bud Tracy, who was a staunch Chicago Cubs follower. I believe the genesis of his unfortunate affliction stemmed from the fact that his father grew up on Chicago's north side. The north side was as predominantly National League "senior circuit" Chicago Cubs as the south side was American League "junior circuit" Chicago White Sox. That's just the way it was.

The Sox were on a winning streak and I was still on a downward academic spiral. Second quarter progress reports had been released and academically I was still struggling to catch up to the level of pitching I was experiencing in fourth grade. I did manage to slip in one "E" in arithmetic. I also managed a total of five "Gs." Unfortunately, I still performed like a bench-warmer in composition, science and handwriting. This time I really missed a sign in a crucial game situation by getting an "F minus" in handwriting. Generally my parents were strict but understanding. But this was too much! My performance earned me daily sessions of extra batting practice. I was required to show up at the kitchen table every day after school. There I would practice my handwriting until "my stroke" returned. It was going to be a long year.

The Sox on the heels of their opening series sweep of the Tigers returned to the south side of Chicago for their 1959 Comiskey Park debut. The home opener three-game set was scheduled against the Kansas City Athletics. The A's had finished the disappointing 1958 season one place ahead of the cellar-dwelling Washington Senators and had opened the 1959 campaign with two losses.

This would be the first home opening date in the history of the Chicago White Sox franchise that the Comiskey family did not have complete control and ownership of the American League team. The unwinding of the Comiskey dynasty actually started with the death of Lou Comiskey, son of founder Charles A. Comiskey, in 1939. Lou's wife, Grace Comiskey, fought off attempts by the trustees of Lou's estate to sell the franchise. Grace assumed the role of president of the club until her death in December 1956. For a number of reasons Grace Comiskey made provision in her will that a 54 percent ownership interest in the club would go to her daughter Dorothy, while the remaining 46 percent ownership would be allocated to her son Charles A. "Chuck" Comiskey. Grace clearly wanted her daughter to have the opportunity to have a deciding influence on the future of the franchise. But by the time 1958 had rolled around Dorothy was interested in removing herself from the day-to-day responsibility and pressure of running a major league baseball franchise. She was also weary of the family rift that had developed with her brother Chuck over control and management of the ball club. She was intent on selling her interest in the Chicago White Sox.

In order to establish a fair market value for her share of the franchise, Dorothy and her advisers, who included her husband Bill Rigney, a former White Sox pitcher and current Sox vice president, quietly sought expressions of interest from third parties. It appeared to be Dorothy's intention to establish a price for her share in the club so that her brother Chuck could match that value and keep the entire franchise under Comiskey ownership. At this point, Bill Veeck, former partial owner of the Cleveland Indians and St. Louis Browns, entered the bidding process. Veeck had a legacy in major league baseball in Chicago. While Bill was at the tender age of three his father, William Veeck, Sr., became president of the National League Chicago Cubs, serving in that capacity until his death in 1933. Bill Jr. had learned the game of baseball while a young man under his father's tutelage. A number of books have been written both by and about Veeck, who was an extremely talented baseball man as well as a prime time entertainer. He was the ultimate friend to his players and a self-proclaimed and sincere champion of the paying clientele. He strove to put a quality product on the field and in doing so he always attempted to ensure that the fans had fun. His exploits in the area of promotion and entertainment are legendary. Many of his philosophies on enriching the atmosphere and entertainment value of the baseball product for the fans followed patterns established by Mr. Larry MacPhail, baseball's great innovator, and former general manager and owner of the Cincinnati Reds, Brooklyn Dodgers, and New York Yankees. Veeck's use of promotional giveaways, fan and player participation in game-day contests, fireworks, circus acts and animal acts were combined with solid club promotional activities as an effective means of inducing fans to come to the ballpark and enjoy the product on the field. Many of these promotional gimmicks flew in the face of the so called baseball purists, resulting in Veeck being characterized by some members of the establishment as a clown and by others as a genius.

In 1958, Mr. Veeck obtained an option to acquire Dorothy Comiskey Rigney's 54 percent ownership interest in the Chicago White Sox. In spite of numerous legal actions initiated by Chuck Comiskey against Dorothy, their mother's estate and ultimately the Veeck ownership group, Veeck prevailed in purchasing Dorothy's 54 percent interest in the team. Chuck was given the opportunity to match the offer of the Veeck group but failed to do so. The relationship between the Veeck group, which included the legendary Hank Greenberg, and the Comiskey group could best be described as somewhat of an awkward peaceful coexistence. The interaction between Veeck and Comiskey would continue to provide an interesting backdrop to the on-field events of the 1959 season. Legal action continued on an intermittent basis.

By opening day Veeck had assumed practical control of the day to day activities of the club and later obtained control of the Board of Directors and was formally installed as club president. As his initial act of showmanship, Bill made a valiant attempt, with the aid of his Cuban-born relief pitcher Rudolfo Arias, to invite the recent emancipator of Cuba, Fidel Castro, to participate in opening day ceremonies at Comiskey Park. Castro was generally considered by many in this country as a nationalist and had not at that time bought into communism and the economic support of the Soviet Union. Castro made his first trip to the United States in April 1959, but due to a very busy calendar he graciously declined Veeck's invitation. Will Harridge, immediate past president of the American League, was scheduled to throw out the first pitch in Chicago's home opener. To the surprise of all present, Harridge gave way to the antics of Veeck by allowing Veeck to throw out the first ball to the receiving hands of Chuck Comiskey in a symbolic show of camaraderie.

Showmanship aside, the White Sox opened the home season on April 14, 1959 under pleasant sunny skies to a crowd of 19,303 enthusiastic fans. The atmosphere was perfect as a freshly painted ball yard decorated in ceremonial bunting provided a colorful backdrop to the new pin striped home uniforms of the local favorites. The fans roared their approval as the debris from the introductory fireworks display drifted onto the field and temporarily delayed opening play. On the field, Billy Pierce was given the assignment of stopping the Kansas City Athletics. The Kansas City club included the likes of Bill Tuttle, Hector Lopez, Bob Cerv, Dick Williams, and a young Roger Maris, who had been obtained from the Cleveland Indians in the off season. Their pitching staff boasted Bud Daley, Ned Garver, Johnny Kucks and Bob Grim. Pierce battled the A's and in rather easy fashion finished the day with a complete game, six-hit shutout. The shutout was the 32nd of Billy's career. Luis Aparicio led the Sox attack with three hits. The key hit of the game was Aparicio's two-run single off of young Ralph Terry in the bottom of the fifth inning. John Callison opened the fifth with a walk and Bubba Phillips chased him to third with a ringing double high off the left field wall. After another walk to Billy Pierce, Aparicio smashed his game-winning hit off the glove of Hal Smith as Callison and Phillips stormed home.

The Sox were off to a 4-0 start. This fast start coupled with the Sox strong finish in 1958 had management and players alike excited about their 1959 pennant chances. Commencing in June 1958, the Sox had played .588 baseball through the remainder of the season, winning 60 while losing only 42. During that same period of time, the New York Yankee's won 57 and lost 42 games. The Sox had finished in second place in 1958, ten games behind the pace of the champion New York Yankees. Sox skipper, Al Lopez, contended throughout spring training that the Yankees could be beaten in 1959.

In the second game of this three game set with Kansas City, Al Lopez sent Barry Latman to the mound. Latman, a six-foot, three-inch Californian, had an outstanding major league debut as a 1958 late season call up from Indianapolis. He finished 1958 with a 3-0 record in thirteen appearances, including a three-hit shutout of the 1958 version of Kansas City's club. The 22-year-old right-hander had an exceptional fastball. Both Al Lopez and pitching coach Ray Berres were counting heavily on Latman to move into the position of fourth starter in the rotation. The small crowd of 4,713 eagerly anticipated the Sox effort at a fifth victory in as many starts. Unfortunately, young Latman was rocked for eight runs on five hits in two and 2/3 innings. The fatal blow to Latman was a grand slam home run by Kansas City starter Bob Grim in the top of the third inning. On a bright note, the Sox received excellent relief pitching from Bob Shaw, Rudolfo Arias, Gerry Staley and Turk Lown. The bubble had burst as the White Sox were trailing 10-1 in the eighth inning. Giving the fans something to cheer about, Chicago rallied for seven runs in the bottom of the eighth keyed by Aparicio's two-run double. This splurge was not enough, however, to overcome the Kansas City lead as the White Sox fell to 4-1 on the season absorbing this 10-8 thrashing.

The rubber match of the three game set with Kansas City pitted Chicago's Early Wynn against Ned Garver. The day was bright and sunny, but only 3,211 fans showed up to see Wynn drop his first decision of the season. The Sox were shutout 6-0, as Wynn served up a second inning two-run home run to Frank House and a seventh inning two-run shot to Bob Cerv. The White Sox managed only five singles on the day.

The Sox next hosted the Detroit Tigers in a three game set to close out their brief six-game homestand. Under generally overcast skies and drizzle the South Siders' struggling starting rotation failed to produce results as Chicago split the series with the Tigers. The final game of the three game set was postponed due to inclement weather. In the opener, Dick Donovan was battered for nine hits and four runs in five and 2/3 innings. However, Chicago reliever Rudolfo Arias salvaged the game and gained his first major league win as Chicago rallied in the eighth for a 6-5 victory. Key hits for the Sox were Norman Cash's three-run homer off Frank Lary in the fourth and Jim Rivera's two-run game-winning double in the eighth. The following day Ray Moore, attempting to establish his spot as the fourth man in Chicago's starting rotation, pitched six and 1/3 innings in a 5-2 loss. Moore gave up seven hits and four runs as he was charged with his first loss of the season. The normally adept Sox defenders committed four errors in the losing cause. Promising rookie left-fielder John Callison continued to struggle at the plate, mired in a slump which saw him produce only one single in the first seven games of the season. Callison, a native of Bakersfield, California, signed a contract with Chicago in June 1957. The 18-year-old slugger had an outstanding season with Bakersfield in the California league in 1957, slamming 17 home runs while hitting at a .340 clip. Callison continued his success hitting 29 homers while with Indianapolis in 1958. After a successful late season call up to the parent club in 1958 he seemed ready for the 1959 season. Callison continued his production by leading the club with 13 RBIs in spring training, and Al Lopez rewarded him by slotting him into the opening day lineup for the 1959 campaign.

The Sox commenced their second road trip of the season, which took them to Kansas City for two games and Cleveland for four. On Tuesday, April 21, Billy Pierce was the starting pitcher for the Sox. His opposition was Bob Grim for the A's. The trend of mediocre starting pitching continued as Pierce departed the game in the third inning trailing 5-0. The Sox defense contributed to their demise by committing three errors (two by Nellie Fox) and many other lapses in the 8-3 loss. Al Lopez's work with Callison during the recent homestand paid off as Callison slammed his first round tripper of the year. The Sox received another strong relief performance from Bob Shaw, but Al Smith remained deep in a zero for 15 slump as his average shrunk to .167.

Al Smith was obtained by the White Sox from Cleveland in a package deal with Early Wynn on December 4, 1957. In exchange, Frank Lane, general manager of the Cleveland Indians, received Minnie Minoso, one of the original 1951 go-go White Sox, and Fred Hatfield, a reserve outfielder. Smith had played a key role in Cleveland's record-setting romp (111 victories) to the American League flag in 1954. That year the versatile Smith played in 131 games splitting time between the outfield, third base and shortstop. During the 1954 campaign Smith went to the plate 481 times, compiling a .281 batting average while stroking 135 hits, including 29 doubles, six triples and 11 home runs. Since coming to Chicago the strong-armed Smith had been hampered by a leg injury. Smith appeared to be fully recovered from his injury but not the negative reaction of fans who blamed Smith for the departure of their hero Minnie Minoso. Smith's slow start in 1959 only added to the growing chorus of jeers. Explaining his injury, Al Smith articulated "I slid into the plate in Detroit in 1957 and hurt the ankle. I developed a bone spur and the ankle would continue to swell up. It took a long time to heal completely but finally came around in the middle of 1959. When your leg bothers you it looks like everything is bothering you. Unfortunately, that is what the fans saw when I first came to Chicago."

Mayor Richard Joseph Daley, the 39th mayor of the city of Chicago, delivered his inaugural address at 8 p.m. on April 21, 1959. Mayor Daley defeated Republican Benjamin Adomowski in the April 7 general election to win a second term as mayor. Mayor Daley reflected upon the strength of the character of the citizens of Chicago as he reviewed the achievements of his first term in office. The focal point of his first four years at work for the city included an aggressive capital spending program for city roads and infrastructure. Chicago's gigantic new jet airplane terminal, O'Hare Field, and the expansion of Chicago's freeway system thrived under Daley's leadership. He noted Chicago's national leadership and the quality of the city's services and social programs. Daley challenged all citizens to continue to support programs that would fuel the city's growth, social responsibility and prosperity. Mayor Daley, an ardent White Sox supporter, would serve Chicago as mayor until his death on December 20, 1976.

As the series with the A's resumed, the South Siders won the second game 20-6. Early Wynn started for the Sox but was shellacked for eight hits and six runs in less than two innings. Wynn left the game in the second inning trailing 6-1. Bob Shaw's star continued to shine brightly as he earned his first victory of the season with seven and 1/3 innings of three-hit, no-run relief. Shaw's effort placed him as a candidate to move into the starting rotation. To this point in the season, starters Ray Moore and Barry Latman had been disappointingly inconsistent. To support Shaw's victory, the Sox scored single runs in the second and third innings, a three spot in the fourth on Aparicio's three-run home run, a single run in the fifth, and two runs in the sixth to put Chicago in front by a score of 8-6. In an incredible seventh inning the Sox scored eleven runs while hitting only one single. The generous Athletics issued 10 walks and contributed three errors as 11 Chicago runners scored. Fox led Chicago's 18 hit attack with five RBIs and four base hits. His mid-field partner Aparicio had four RBIs on three hits. Goodman, Lollar, and Rivera added two hits apiece.

As a final note to the day's activities, Washington Senators' president, Calvin Griffith, reported that he turned down an offer by Bill Veeck in which Veeck proposed that the Sox receive power-hitting Roy Sievers, right-handed pitcher Pedro Ramos and catcher Clint Courtney in exchange for $250,000 cash and various unnamed players. Rumors had abounded since spring training concerning a deal of this nature. Veeck had contended steadfastly that he did not believe that the White Sox had the manpower to take the American League flag away from the Yankees. Veeck's contention was somewhat of a distraction to the players but possibly motivated the players to prove Veeck wrong. On the other side of the argument however, Chuck Comiskey, architect of the current White Sox team along with Vice President Bill Rigney and field general Al Lopez believed that the current roster was strong enough to win the pennant.

The White Sox headed to Cleveland for a four-game set with the streaking Cleveland Indians. The Indians were in first place with a nine and one record, two and 1/2 games ahead of the third place Chicago club. Cleveland had a powerful and exciting lineup, including Minnie Minoso, Billy Martin, Rocco "Rocky" Colavito,

Jim Piersall and Vic Power. Their pitching was a blend of experience and youth featuring Cal McLish, Jim "Mudcat" Grant, Herb Score, Jim Perry and Mike Garcia. In the Friday night opener, the red-hot Tribe continued their winning streak by administering a 6-4 whipping of Chicago. Dick Donovan pitched well as his Sox jumped out to a 4-1 lead. Donovan tired after seven, however, and was relieved by Turk Lown as the Indians pulled even at four all. Gerry Staley was charged with the loss as Cleveland won their tenth game in eleven tries with two runs in the eighth inning. The loss lowered Chicago's record on the year to six and five.

On Saturday, Chicago ended Cleveland's winning streak with an 8-6 victory. The Sox overcame a 5-3 deficit with a five run ninth inning rally. The rally was aided by three Cleveland errors and Earl Torgeson's game-winning, three-run, pinch-hit home run. Callison also hit a two-run homer in the seventh for the Sox. Barry Latman out dueled Cal McLish through six innings but tired in the seventh after giving up four runs. Latman was relieved by Turk Lown who recorded the victory. Bob Shaw pitched the ninth inning for the save.

Sunday's doubleheader at Cleveland's frigid Municipal Stadium provided the White Sox with a prime opportunity to close the three game gap that separated them from the first place Indians. Al Lopez selected his two veteran aces, Early Wynn and Billy Pierce, to go to the mound and brave the 40-degree temperature. Both hurlers responded with their second victories of the season. The doubleheader sweep brought Chicago to within one game of first place. Wynn won the opener 6-5 but needed four innings of relief help from Staley before it was over. The White Sox scored all of their runs in the fourth inning with the key blows being Wynn's two-run double and Jim Rivera's sacrifice fly that scored the deciding run. Pierce went the distance in the nightcap winning 5-2, allowing eight hits. Pierce had three hits on the day including a triple and a

19

game-winning two-run double in the second inning. The White Sox were moving in the right direction.

The opening of their two-game home series with the New York Yankees was postponed until Wednesday due to inclement weather. Many players took advantage of their unexpected off day by attending the movies. There were many splendid choices of film releases including *Some Like It Hot*, starring Tony Curtis, Jack Lemmon and Marilyn Monroe. Other great features included *Gigi*, *Imitation of Life*, *The Sound and The Fury*, *The Shaggy Dog*, *Compulsion* and Walt Disney's *The Grand Canyon* and *Tonka*.

When play resumed on Wednesday, Ray Moore, the veteran right-handed pitcher, took the mound for the Sox against Bob Turley. Moore was greeted by Mickey Mantle's two-run home run in the first inning and never recovered. Moore lasted through the fifth inning and gave up four runs on five hits as he lost his second decision of the year without a victory. Moore's performance left Al Lopez still searching for one more effective starter. The Sox mustered nine hits, four by Nellie Fox, but could only push across two runs in the 5-2 defeat.

In the second game of the set the White Sox got another strong pitching performance from Billy Pierce, as the little left-hander went a full eleven innings to earn a 4-3 triumph. Pierce's third victory of the season was secured when Al Smith turned jeers into cheers with a bases-loaded single in the bottom of the eleventh inning to end the contest. Chicago's 13-hit attack included three singles by Aparicio and a Sherman Lollar home run.

The Sox completed the first month of the season with a record of 10 victories and six losses, positioning them in second place, one game behind the front running Cleveland Indians. Baltimore and Kansas City were tied for third place, two games behind Cleveland. The New York Yankees were tied with Washington and

Boston for fourth place, three and 1/2 games off the pace. And the Detroit Tigers were mired deep in the cellar as their miserable two victory and thirteen loss start took them eight and 1/2 games behind the league leaders. On the offensive front for the White Sox, Aparicio and Rivera had provided two game-winning RBIs apiece in the month of April. Fox, Torgeson, Pierce and Smith each had one game-winning RBI. Pierce led the starting pitching staff with three victories against only one defeat. Wynn followed with a 2-1 record and Dick Donovan was victorious in his only decision. Latman and Moore were winless, losing three games between them. The bullpen posted four wins against only one loss as Staley, Shaw, Lown and Arias each recorded one victory.

The start of the 1959 season for Chicago was in sharp contrast to their start in 1958 when the club was effectively (if not mathematically) eliminated from the pennant race during the first two months of the season. Manager Lopez recognized that in 1958 he had allowed the veteran players to slowly work their way into top playing condition so that they would not be worn down in August and September. This strategy unfortunately put them in such a deep hole that they couldn't dig out, despite their league-leading .582 winning percentage after the 1958 All-Star Game. Lopez worked the players much harder in the Spring of 1959 and the new strategy appeared to be paying off.

CHAPTER TWO

The Perfect Throw

AS THE YOUNG SEASON SPILLED INTO MAY, BOSTON MADE ITS FIRST appearance of the year in Comiskey Park. Boston's pitching staff was anchored by Ike Delock, Bill Mombouquette, Frank Sullivan and Jerry Casale. Ted Williams was on the injured list but the line-up remained formidable with the likes of Pete Runnels, Jackie Jensen and Frank Malzone. Early Wynn thrilled the crowd of 13,022 on Friday night, May 1, with a sparkling one-hit, complete game shutout. Wynn rose to the occasion as he struck out 14 BoSox en route to his third win of the year and 252nd of his 19-year major league career. Despite the victory, Wynn kept the home crowd on the edge of their seats with his wildness as he walked seven batters throughout the evening. The only hit off Wynn was a single by Pete Runnels in the top of the first inning. The game was scoreless until the White Sox came to bat in the bottom half of the eighth inning and Wynn lofted a towering fly ball to left that bounded off the outstretched glove of Bill Rena and into the seats for the game-winning home run. This was the type of gritty performance that manager Lopez was looking for when the White Sox acquired Early "Gus" Wynn, along with Al Smith, from the Cleveland Indians on December 4, 1957.

Wynn, born of American Indian heritage in Hartford, Alabama on January 6, 1920, began his major league career with the Washington Senators in 1939. The hard-throwing six-foot tall, 190-pound right-hander was acquired by the Cleveland Indians on December 14, 1948 along with Mickey Vernon in a deal that sent Joe Haynes, Eddie Klieman and Eddie Robinson to Washington. The trade, orchestrated by Bill Veeck when he was running the show in Cleveland, was a turning point in Wynn's career. In his nine-year stint with Cleveland, Early won twenty or more games in four different seasons and compiled 163 victories against only 100 defeats. In Cleveland's pennant drive in 1954, Wynn led the league with 23 victories while losing only 11. He pitched a league-leading 270 innings in his 36 starts and completed 20 games. Early struck out 155 batters and maintained an earned run average of 2.73 during the 1954 season. In 1957, Wynn experienced his first losing season in a decade when his record fell to 14 wins and 17 losses. After coming over to the White Sox in 1958, he finished below break even again with 14 victories and 16 losses. In spite of that record, Wynn led the league in strikeouts and pitched more than 200 innings for his ninth consecutive year, proving that he still had stamina and arm strength. Wynn's quick start in 1959 began to convince the Chicago brain trust that he still had some outstanding days ahead of him.

In a continuing attempt to add some much-needed power to their lineup, Chicago acquired veteran National League slugger Del Ennis from the Cincinnati Redlegs. Ennis, a 33-year-old, six-foot tall, 200-pound, right-handed hitter had clouted 286 home runs and driven in over 1,300 runs during his thirteen year career. The White Sox gave up 27-year-old, left-handed pitcher Don Rudolph in exchange for Ennis. As a part of the overall transaction the Sox sold reserve outfielder Lou Skizas to Cincinnati's Cuban affiliate ball club in Havana.

On Saturday, May 2, as Tommy Lee edged Sword Dancer and First Landing in the 85th running of the Kentucky Derby, the Sox dropped the second game of their series to Boston, 5-4. Barry Latman took the loss, lasting only three innings and giving up six hits and three runs. The ChiSox made the game respectable by scoring two runs in both the eighth and ninth innings, highlighted by Aparicio's two-run home run in the ninth.

Dick Donovan pitched eight strong innings against Baltimore on Sunday but retired with no decision and the score tied two all. Turk Lown, in relief of Donovan, was touched for home runs by Billy Gardner and Chico Carrasquel in the 10th inning and was charged with his first loss of the season. The Sox fell two and 1/2 games behind Cleveland with the loss. Johnny Romano slammed a tremendous shot to the upper deck in left center field for the first home run of his major league career. In the losing cause, Ron Jackson cracked his first home run of the season, a solo shot in the second inning.

In another move to provide left-handed power in the lineup, the White Sox acquired 33-year-old Harry "Suitcase" Simpson from the Kansas City Athletics for Ray Boone. Boone, sick with the flu, indicated that he was considering retirement rather than reporting to the Athletics. The 35-year-old veteran was experiencing knee problems and was weary of being shipped from one destination to another. Boone recounted that in 1958 Al Lopez brought him to Chicago to be an everyday ballplayer. However, despite playing regularly in 1958, Boone's age and recurring knee problems had relegated him to a utility role in 1959.

The Washington Senators moved into town on Tuesday, May 5, to face the South Siders for the first time in 1959. The Senators had finished last in the league in 1958. Their power-packed roster included Roy Sievers, Harmon Killebrew, Bob Allison and Jim Lemon. Washington's mound corps was anchored by Camilo

Pascual and Pedro Ramos. Billy Pierce received the starting assignment for Chicago and was no match for the Senators. He lasted only three innings in the 8-3 loss. The loss, coupled with Cleveland's 9-1 triumph over Baltimore, relegated Chicago to a three-way tie with Baltimore and Washington for second place.

Early Wynn lost a 6-4 decision to Washington the next day. Rookie Bob Allison's seventh inning grand slam home run provided the deciding margin. The loss was the fourth consecutive for the Sox as their season record slid to eleven and ten.

To wrap up Chicago's 11 game homestand, the Cleveland Indians arrived for a four-game set. The Friday night opener pitted Chicago's Dick Donovan against Cleveland's Cal McLish. McLish had been pivotal in Cleveland's early season success opening up with a 3-0 record. Donovan pitched a respectable game, giving up three runs on three hits in six innings. Donovan's work, combined with no-hit, no-run relief pitching by Shaw and Staley, was not enough to prevent the fifth consecutive White Sox defeat. The 3-1 loss was forged by Rocky Colavito's three RBI night which included a two-run home run off Donovan in the sixth. Jim Landis broke out of a prolonged slump by hitting a fourth-inning solo homer for Chicago's lone run. The sagging Sox record slipped to eleven and eleven as they sunk to fourth place in the standings, four and 1/2 games off the pace.

The White Sox were slipping and slipping fast. They had to find a way to stem the tide and reverse the extended losing streak. Barry Latman was handed the ball to start the second game of the series. Chicago jumped off to an early lead. The decisive inning of the game was the third as the Pale Hose scored five runs highlighted by Bubba Phillips' ground rule double driving in the deciding run. Latman contributed a two-run single to complete the third inning scoring. He faltered in the fourth inning and departed the game with a 8-4 lead. Ray Moore took over and pitched five and 1/3 innings of one-run relief for his first victory of the season. The season's longest losing streak was over.

Lopez sent Billy Pierce and Early Wynn to the mound for the twin bill to close out the Cleveland series on Sunday, May 10, the same pitching combination that found success in the April 26 doubleheader sweep of Cleveland. Pierce toed the rubber in the opening tilt before a Mother's Day crowd of 28,293. Mothers were granted free entry to the game by producing a picture of their children. Pierce struggled the entire contest giving up 13 hits and four runs during the course of the eleven inning two hour and 59 minute struggle. Al Smith contributed three hits to the Chicago attack but the hitting hero of the day again was Bubba Phillips. Phillips tied the game in the eighth inning with a leadoff home run, his first of the year. After Cleveland surged ahead in the top of the eleventh inning, Phillips once again came through with a long single driving in Earl Torgeson with the second and final run of the inning for the Sox 5-4 victory.

The nightcap of the twin bill was dominated by Early Wynn as the veteran hurled a complete game, four-hit shutout for his fourth victory of the season. A single by Nelson Fox in the first inning drove in Aparicio with Chicago's first and deciding run. Ennis hit his first home run in a Chicago uniform and the 287th of his career in the fourth. The Sox added one more run in the seventh and two runs in the eighth to close the book on Wynn's 5-0 dismantling of the Tribe.

Baseball players like Early Wynn became our real life heroes. Over the course of the season we followed the exploits of these men through radio and television broadcasts and newspaper accounts. The process of collecting baseball cards was another means of expressing our adoration for the men and the game. Collecting baseball cards was a religious experience. Any time that one could scrape together a nickel, it would be invested in baseball cards. There were at least four small retail establishments in our immediate neighborhood that sold bread, milk, soft drinks, baseball cards and such. These small neighborhood stores were able to stay in business in large part due to our baseball card purchases. The store in closest proximity to our house was "Dirty Shirt Andy's" and as the name implied the proprietor of the establishment was not a slave to personal hygiene or cleanliness. The "Little Store" was our favorite because it seemed they consistently were the first to get each new series of Topps baseball cards upon release. Dressel's and Greco's were other stores that fit into the category of family-owned and operated small businesses. The proprietors and their families lived in the back, or on the second floor of the store building. Normally the operation of the store was the sole income generator for the family. We earned our nickels in many different ways. I mowed grass, pulled weeds, collected empty soda bottles and ran errands for family and neighbors in hope of attracting enough cash for a bottle of pop and a few packs of baseball cards. I would scour the streets, alleys, and vacant lots of the neighborhood to collect discarded pop bottles. Regular bottles were redeemable for two cents apiece and quart-sized bottles fetched a nickel. These bottles would have one thing in common-they were absolutely filthy after spending days, months or even years laying in the dirt and weeds. The store clerks receiving these filthy bottles always looked at us quizzically, but I'm confident they remembered their own youthful experience of attempting to raise money and would complete the transaction.

It was an interesting experience to purchase the cards. I engaged in serious deliberation before selecting exactly which store would provide the best return on my investment. I kept mental note of the time and location of my premium card purchases. Luis Aparicio,

Mickey Mantle and Hank Aaron came from "Dirty Shirt Andy's." Greco's seemed to consistently produce team cards. Lollar, Fox, Ford, Koufax, Drysdale, Spahn, Landis and Berra were purchased at the "Little Store." Each destination had its own tendencies—real or imagined. Once the purchase was made, I would go to a quiet place and spread my unopened packs of baseball cards before me. With optimism I attempted to visualize which cards would be mine as the packs lay unopened before me. I would slowly open each package and gently remove the slab of bubble gum and immediately start to chew. Then very deliberately I would turn over each card and proceed with the chant "got'em, got'em, got'em, don't got'em, got'em, don't got'em." Clearly one's looking for the don't got'ems, but as the season wore on they would become fewer and farther between.

Once acquired, the trading of these cards was a glorious experience in barter. The key element to the trading process was to select a trading partner possessing either a large inventory of desirable cards or a limited inventory of knowledge concerning their value. Each party to the trade would thumb through the stack of cards that the other person was offering for consideration, examining the cards for overall quality, color, gloss, sharpness of focus and wear. The chant of "got'em, don't got'em, got'em" would linger in the air as the stack of cards was evaluated. These trading sessions took place among the lads in the neighborhood on a regular basis. It was a badge of honor to obtain a complete set of cards by season end.

After a travel day on Monday, May 11, the White Sox arrived at Fenway Park in Boston to face the Red Sox. The BoSox had the great Ted Williams in the lineup for the first time on the season, returning from an injury. Dick Donovan took the mound against Boston's Ike DeLock. Donovan helped his own cause with a two-run homer in the second inning. Donovan gave up one run in the Boston half of the second, but held that one run margin until he departed in the seventh inning with the bases loaded. Donovan was left with yet another no decision as reliever Gerry Staley walked Jackie Jensen to force in the tying run. More damage was averted as Jim Landis cut down Gary Geiger at the plate with a fine throw earlier in the inning. Turk Lown followed with three innings of shutout relief. Al Smith had his first hit of the day with the eventual game-winner, slamming a two-run homer in the top of the 12th inning off Boston reliever Murray Wall for the 4-2 lead. Arias entered the game to pitch the 12th inning and proceeded to give up a solo home run to Jackie Jensen before securing his second victory of the season by a final 4-3 margin. The extra-inning game lasted four hours and 25 minutes, the second longest of the season for the ChiSox.

The throw by Chicago center-fielder, Jim Landis, in the seventh inning to cut down Gary Geiger at the plate represented perhaps the most exciting play in the game of baseball. Nothing could beat the thrill and anticipation of a long throw from the outfield as ball and runner converged. Safe or out, the play would bring even casual fans to their feet. I was highly motivated by examples such as this to develop my arm strength and throwing accuracy. To refine this particular skill every opportunity was taken to throw something, in an attempt to hit something else. You name it and we would throw it—assorted balls, snowballs, stones, apples, tomatoes and anything else that made sense. Distance combined with accuracy was the measuring stick for the quality of one's arm. Accuracy perhaps was most important. But the rare individual who could combine accuracy with distance and velocity, like Landis, was one to be admired by all. I enjoyed being challenged and challenging others to contests of throwing ability, but most of my throwing was accomplished on a solo basis.

Oftentimes the target and one's reaction to throwing at that target would be very spontaneous. Due to this spontaneity, little thought would be invested in the consequences of hitting or missing the intended target. I had a tendency to re-enact throws such as the one that Landis made that day. I would drift back under the imaginary fly ball, watching the man at third tag and break for the plate. I would simulate coming in on the ball, catching it head-high over my right shoulder and letting it rip for home in one smooth motion. In my fantasy on this particular day, I imagined Sherman Lollar's glove was located about two feet above the head of neighborhood tough guy, Fast Eddie. Eddie was walking about 120 feet in front of me and moving rapidly away. My objective was to make a perfect throw to nail the imaginary runner at the plate and in the process startle ole Eddie. Eddie was the typical tough guy of the day. He wore a black leather jacket, black jeans, black pointed shoes, a white T-shirt and white socks. As he combed his duck-tail haircut, an ever present cigarette dangled from his lips. The fingers of each hand were barely inserted into the corresponding back pocket of his skin tight jeans as he confidently strutted down the street. He walked the walk and talked the talk of toughness. On this day I attempted to execute my fantasy throw by substituting a tomato for the baseball. However, as the tomato left my hand and rapidly approached Lollar's glove it began to sink. In fact, it sank exactly two feet below its intended target and plastered Eddie in the back of his head. As the tomato exploded on Eddie's duck-tail, juice and pulp flew in all directions. The stunned tough guy gathered his senses and screamed that he was going to kill his assailant. Before he could turn, I quickly disappeared with the speed and stealth of Aparicio. Conflicting emotions of fear and pride swept over me. Fear sprung from the possibility that Eddie might have seen and recognized his unwitting assailant. Pride in the knowledge that I had gunned down the runner at the plate, as Lollar made an excellent grab of the throw at his feet.

To complement the prior week's acquisition of Del Ennis, the White Sox announced that they had reacquired Larry Doby from the Detroit Tigers for an amount slightly in excess of the waiver fee of $20,000. To make room on the roster for Doby, the Sox secured waivers on Ron Jackson for the purpose of optioning him to Indianapolis of the American Association. Jackson, a big right-handed hitting first baseman was given the opportunity to win the starting job in 1958, but was never able to make the grade. Although Jackson hit seven home runs in 1958, he had only come to the plate seven times in 1959, primarily as a pinch hitter.

Doby's previous stay in Chicago ended when he was dealt to Baltimore on December 3, 1957 along with Jack Harshman, Russ Heman and Jim Marshall in exchange for Tito Francona, Ray Moore and Billy Goodman. Moore and Goodman remained as solid contributors on Chicago's current roster. Larry Doby was the first black man to play in the American League and followed Jackie Robinson of the Brooklyn Dodgers as the second black ballplayer in the major leagues. Lawrence Eugene Doby was born in Camden, South Carolina on December 13, 1924 and joined Cleveland in 1947. Larry enjoyed a solid career with Cleveland and was instrumental in its drive to the 1954 American League title. In an attempt to bring power and pennant winning experience to the club, the Sox first acquired Doby on October 25, 1955. However, by 1957 the White Sox had not won a pennant and Doby's home run production fell to 14, his RBI total to 79 and his batting average to .288. Disappointed with his level of production, the Sox dispatched Doby to Baltimore. His return was pinned on the hope that he could provide pop to the lineup as an occasional starter and pinch hitter.

The second game of the Boston series saw Bob Shaw get his first start of the season. Beginning with the April 10 opener in Detroit,

Shaw had been outstanding in relief. He appeared in 14 games, pitching a total of 24 and 1/3 innings. During that time he gave up 20 hits and three runs, two of which were earned, struck out 13 and walked only six. He earned a victory in his only decision of the season by pitching seven and 1/3 innings of shutout relief against the Kansas City Athletics on April 22. Shaw didn't disappoint as he proceeded to toss a five-hit, complete game shutout against the fifth-place Red Sox. With his first career shutout, Shaw lowered his season earned run average to an amazing 0.82. Chicago accumulated 12 hits in the 4-0 victory, its fifth consecutive win. Del Ennis provided the game-winning hit in the first inning as his single scored Sherman Lollar.

On Thursday, May 13, the Sox stretched their winning streak to six as they dismantled Boston 14-6. The South Siders' 19-hit assault against four Boston hurlers was led by Ennis (two hits, one home run, four RBIs), Landis (two hits, one home run, two RBIs), and Fox (two hits, two RBIs). Early Wynn pitched seven and 2/3 innings to gain his fifth victory of the season, aided by relief help from Turk Lown. With the win, the White Sox season record climbed to 17-11 as they surged to within 1/2 game of the Indians.

The White Sox rolled into Yankee Stadium as talk abounded that major changes were in store for the club. With the acquisition of Larry Doby earlier in the week, speculation increased that Doby would be included in a major trade with the Washington Senators. Rumors had persisted that the two clubs would make a major multi-player deal that would bring power hitting Roy Sievers to the Chicago White Sox.

The Yankees were a formidable opponent. Yogi Berra and Hank Bauer were aging veterans on the Yankee roster. Mickey Mantle, Elston Howard, Bill Skowron, Tony Kubek and Bobby Richardson were the nucleus of New York's youthful, championship hardened team. Whitey Ford, Bob Turley, Don Larsen and Ryan Duren anchored the pitching staff. A rowdy Friday night crowd of 27,863 Yankee hopefuls showed up to see Billy Pierce duel Whitey Ford. Pierce rose to the challenge and pitched a complete game shutout, supported by six Chicago runs, for his fifth victory of the season. Pierce's performance stretched Chicago's winning streak to seven by holding the seventh-place Yankees to six singles while striking out seven. Lollar chased in Aparicio with the winning run in the first inning on a fielder's choice ground out to shortstop. Aparicio, Lollar and Phillips each had two hits with Bubba Phillips' two-run double in the sixth providing the only extra base hit of the day.

The White Sox winning streak was extended to eight with their extra-inning 4-3 victory over the struggling Yankees on Saturday. Ray Moore pitched well but departed after seven innings trailing 3-2. Solid relief work by Staley, Arias and Lown provided Chicago the opportunity to stay in the game. In the ninth, Chicago sent the game into extra innings as Fox scored on a Lollar single. Fox had reached third base as Mickey Mantle lost a fly ball in the glare of the sun and was charged with a three-base error. Del Ennis once again provided the margin of victory as he singled in the winning run in the eleventh inning. Ennis had driven in seven runs in the eleven games he played since joining the club. Lown retired the Yankees in order in the bottom of the eleventh, earning his second victory of the year.

The White Sox made their first stop of the year in Washington on May 17 as they faced the Senators in a Sunday afternoon twin bill. The surprising Senators were in fourth place due to the power hitting of Harmon Killebrew, Jim Lemon, Roy Sievers and Bob Allison. The Sox eight-game winning streak came to an abrupt end as Dick Donovan lost the opening game of the doubleheader, 4-2. Donovan was knocked out in the second inning as he absorbed his second loss of the season. Home runs by Jim Lemon and Reno Bertoia sealed Donovan's demise.

In the nightcap, Chicago's newly established starter, Bob Shaw, received his worst pounding of the season giving up 14 hits and six runs in 7 and 1/3 innings. In spite of his lackluster performance, Shaw was rewarded with his third victory of the year as the Sox outscored the Senators 10-7 to return to the win column. The South Siders were led by Nellie Fox with four hits and Sherman Lollar with three in the winning effort.

In the finale of the three game set, Chicago smashed Washington 9-2. The victory put Chicago in first place by 1/2 game as Cleveland was shutout at Baltimore. Early Wynn won his league-leading sixth decision with an impressive five hit effort. Wynn's earned run average dropped to 2.55 on the season, and his four strikeouts boosted his season total to 54. Del Ennis' first inning double scored Torgeson with the game-winning run, his fourth game-winning hit in Chicago's last six victories. Sherman Lollar slammed his fifth home run of the year, a solo shot in the third. Al Smith led off the seventh inning with his second homer of the year, a shot into the "beer garden" in left center field. Lollar remained hot at the plate, hitting .500 on the road trip.

To have a grasp of the finite statistics on each game and each player made us feel as if we were an integral part of the game itself. Our thirst for statistical information was unquenchable. It took hard work and long hours to have command of the statistical nuances of the game. The process was facilitated by daily digestion of the sports page of either the Chicago *American* or the Chicago *Sun Times*. The articles describing the exploits of the Chicago White Sox were the primary focus of my attention. I would relive my recollection of the radio or television accounts of the game and compare them to the accuracy of the printed word. The process only served to heighten the memory of victory or saturate my mouth with the foul taste of defeat. I would methodically dissect the box scores of all the major league ball games. Of course, the American League was my domain and the majority of my concentration was focused on those eight teams. Command of statistics clearly established one's baseball credibility in the neighborhood. Adolescents would even be invited to participate in adult conversations if they could engage in meaningful statistical discourse. My parents had to be perplexed as to how I could have so much intensity and zeal toward baseball statistics while having so little interest in my classroom performance. But I was making progress. The third period grades were in. I was starting to get my timing back. I now could claim two "Es", although one was in art. I pushed my "G" total to six. However, all the extra batting practice had not produced results as I still couldn't hit the breaking ball. An "F-" in handwriting still dominated the landscape of my progress report. More reps at the kitchen table were in order.

This had been perhaps my toughest academic campaign since beginning my educational career in 1955. In the fall of 1955, I became intimately familiar with the Chicago Public School System. My family home was about three doors away and on the opposite side of the street from the first public school I attended. The structure was located at 11109 South Homan Avenue. We called these simple structures the "Portables." I do not know where the name "Portables" initially came from. The buildings themselves were not readily movable. At the outset they must have been placed there on a temporary basis and thus the name was passed down. There were three separate clapboard buildings. Each building housed two classrooms separated at center by a common area containing rest rooms. The furnace room was also located in this area, but was accessible only from outside the building. The antiquated

36

furnace supplied the heat on cold winter days. Open windows supplied fresh air for those sweltering late spring and early summer afternoons. The three building complex was organized in a block T configuration. Two of the buildings parallel to each other and the third at right angles to the other two. A large man of Eastern European descent was responsible for the custodial maintenance of the complex. The man's name was Stanley and our paths crossed often as the years drifted by.

The complex contained a playground located east of the buildings that was adequate for pickup games of baseball and softball. The surface of the playground was a fine gravel of gray slag. The slag had a rough consistency that worked well in fashioning pots for marble tournaments. However, it also tended to tear a hole in a pair of blue jeans on contact. Of course the only time that that would happen was when brand-new jeans were worn. The school complex was surrounded by a 4-foot chain link fence on three sides—north, east and south. The northern boundary of the school yard was 111th Street, the primary east-west thoroughfare in the neighborhood. On the opposite side of 111th Street, the northern boundary was overwhelmed by the Saint Christina Catholic Church and elementary school complex. The eastern boundary of the complex was dominated by Gussies' hamburger joint, and the house and yard of its proprietors. Gussies' yard contained a large pen that housed their guard dog. The southern boundary of the complex adjoined the side of two houses. The west side of the complex was unfenced and provided general access to the property. In all, the six room classroom facility handled approximately 120 students at any given time. Grades ranged from kindergarten through fourth grade. This was my school home for the first five years of my earliest formal educational experience. It was also the scene of many classic softball games as we tried mightily to emulate our baseball heroes.

The Baltimore Orioles, Chicago's next opponent, were in third place behind both Chicago and Cleveland. This was Chicago's first encounter with the Orioles on the season. Paul Richards managed the Orioles as they sought to improve upon their 1958 record of 74-79, which was good for only a sixth-place finish. Baltimore had strong pitching with Hoyt Wilhelm, Billy O'Dell and Milt Pappas leading the way. Brooks Robinson, Gene Woodling and Gus Triandos were the mainstays of their everyday lineup. In the series opener, Billy Pierce's record fell to 5-3 as he lost a heartbreaking 2-1 decision. His mound opponent, Billy O'Dell, hit an unusual inside the park two-run home run for Baltimore's only runs of the game. The loss coupled with Cleveland's 5-2 victory over Washington dropped Chicago into second place, with Baltimore trailing Chicago in the standings by only one game. Aparicio drove in the Sox only run of the day. In the last seven games Aparicio had been on base and incredible 21 times.

Prior to breaking into the major leagues in 1956, Aparicio toiled for two seasons in Chicago's minor league system. In 1954, Aparicio hit .282 at Waterloo in the Class B, 3-I league. In 1955, Aparicio jumped to Double A, Memphis. Aparicio had an excellent year at the plate with a .273 batting average and led the Southern Association in stolen bases with 48. Luis Ernesto Aparicio was born in the oil rich province of Maracaibo, Venezuela on April 29, 1934. His father, Luis Ernesto Sr., was an outstanding shortstop with the Caracas club in the Venezuelan League. When he got on in years, his son replaced him at shortstop at the tender age of sixteen. Aparicio played second base that winter season in Caracas. His childhood idol and fellow Venezuelan, Chico Carrasquel, played beside him at shortstop. The five-foot, eight-inch, 155-pound, Aparicio already had the defensive skills of a seasoned veteran. In 1955 winter league play, the young shortstop hit .321 for the pennant winning Gavelines team in the Venezuelan Occidental League. Frank Lane, general manager of the White Sox at the time, pursued Aparicio vigorously when he heard that the Cleveland Indians were about to sign the youngster to a contract. Chicago's regular shortstop, Chico Carrasquel, played that position in his native Caracas in the winter season. Lane threatened Pablo Morales, President of the Caracas club, with the notion that Carrasquel would no longer be available to him if he didn't persuade Aparicio to sign with Chicago. The ploy apparently worked as Lane purchased Aparicio's contract for $6,000 and paid Aparicio an additional $4,000. In the winter of 1955, Lane, frustrated with Chico's lack of hustle, traded Carrasquel to Cleveland.

Aparicio came to spring training in 1956 in Tampa, Florida and immediately impressed everyone with his defensive skills. Marty Marion, the Chicago skipper at the time, was recognized in his playing days as the best shortstop in the National League. Marion was an immediate fan of "Little Looie." The smooth Venezuelan had prepared himself for this day by diligently studying the English language for the previous two years. Aparicio had great range and a very strong arm. He won the starting shortstop job in 1956. Aparicio batted .266 in 152 games and led the league in stolen bases en route to American League Rookie of the Year honors. He continued to improve all aspects of his game in 1957 and 1958 and led the league in stolen bases both years. Don Gutteridge, Chicago's infield coach, recalled that "Aparicio was the best shortstop that he ever saw. He made more plays than any other shortstop. He never made a mental mistake. Aparicio had a terrific arm. In fact, in 1959 he went out to take all relay throws from the outfield and Fox covered the base. His arm was that strong."

On May 20, Dick Donovan evened his record at 2-2 with a complete game 5-2 victory over Baltimore in the second game of the two-game set. With this victory in the books Donovan joined Wynn, Pierce and Shaw for a total of eleven complete game victories on the season. Sherman Lollar tallied the winning run in the fourth inning with a sacrifice fly ball. Aparicio led the Chicago attack with four singles, raising his season batting average to .290. Fox and Landis had two hits apiece.

The real story of the day however was the New York Yankees. The Yankees lost a 13-6 decision to Frank Lary of the Detroit Tigers to fall into last place. Not since May 25, 1940—19 years prior—had the Yankees been in the cellar of the American League. The Yankees demise was attributed to injuries to key personnel. Mainstays Mickey Mantle, Bill Skowron and Whitey Ford were seeing limited action due to injuries. The impact of these injuries was amplified by poor performances from aging veterans and an ineffective pitching staff. The perennial champions looked like they were dying, but they were only in mid-May and there was a long distance to go before the tombstone of the Yankees could be engraved for 1959. The New York club was not built by men who sat back and waited for it to come to them. They would not give up the throne easily.

The White Sox boarded a charter flight to Kansas City for the final leg of the 13 game road trip. Travel weary at this point, manager Al Lopez tabbed Bob Shaw to face Bob Grim in the series opener on Friday night, May 22. Coming out of spring training Shaw had been expected to fill the role of long relief and fifth or sixth starter. His first start of the season against Boston on May 13 was spectacular. He was roughed up in his second outing against Washington but the club outscored the Senators 10-7 to hand Shaw the victory. Shaw joined the White Sox on June 15, 1958. He came to Chicago in the same trade that brought Ray Boone from Detroit in exchange for Bill Fischer and Tito Francona.

Ray Berres, Chicago's longtime pitching coach, always had the habit of going out to the ballpark very early on game days. His intended purpose was to scout opposing pitchers so that he could obtain a personal perspective on the opponents mound talent. This process over the years provided a sound basis to evaluate talent for potential trade or waiver claims. Berres remembered the day he was at the ball yard and happened to observe Bob Shaw throwing on the side. Ray remembered "He seemed to be struggling with his control and in frustration he threw his last pitch in disgust. I said to myself, 'That delivery was it!,' I put that in my memory." When the White Sox dealt with Detroit in 1958 to obtain Boone, Berres as well as others convinced the Chicago brass to obtain Shaw as well. Detroit was scheduled to send Shaw to the minor leagues and he informed management that he would rather be traded. After being informed of the details of his trade to Chicago, Ray Boone told Tiger general manager McHale, "I can see why you are getting rid of a 35-year-old guy like me, but you're making a mistake by letting Shaw go." When Shaw joined the club in the summer of 1958, Lopez and Berres convinced Shaw to abandon his style of pitching side arm to right-handed batters. Shaw started pitching strictly over the top and finished the 1958 season with a record of 3-3. Shaw went on to play winter ball in Cuba to refine this new approach. He showed rapid improvement as he posted an outstanding earned run average of 1.90. Unfortunately, the winter season was interrupted by the Cuban revolution. Shaw was even more convinced that he did not want to return to the minors so he listened intently to the advice of Berres, Lopez and some of the veteran hurlers. Shaw worked diligently to develop the consistent mechanics that gave him command over his slider and his out pitch which was his sinker. Ray Berres' fundamental theory on pitching was employed effectively by Bob Shaw. Berres believed that "unless you have proper mechanics, you cannot practice theory."

Shaw needed it all against the Athletics that night. Bob Grim held Chicago to two runs. Aparicio scored in the first on Fox's single and again in the third as Fox's sacrifice bunt was turned into a game-deciding, run-scoring error. Shaw gave up four hits and a single run. Ray Boone playing first base for the Athletics scored their only run of the game as he came home on Bob Cerv's double in the sixth. In the ninth inning Shaw ran into trouble. Hector Lopez reached base on Jim Rivera's error. After two were out, Shaw gave up a single and a walk to load the bases, prompting manager Lopez to summon Turk Lown from the bullpen. Dick Williams, the next batter, greeted Lown with a screaming line drive to center field. Jim Landis, the Chicago center-fielder, broke for the ball at the crack of the bat. With two outs, all three runners were on the move when the ball was hit. The stadium erupted in anticipation of the game-winning hit, but Landis made a headlong dive, rolled and came up with the spectacular game-saving catch. The defensive gem preserved Shaw's fourth victory of the season.

The following day was a day that everyone in a Chicago uniform would like to forget. Kansas City handed Chicago its most lopsided loss of the season as they thrashed the South Siders 16-0 on a Saturday afternoon. Early Wynn lasted only four innings as he, Barry Latman, Gerry Staley, Rudolfo Arias and Ray Moore were pounded for 21 hits and 16 runs. Wynn was charged with his third loss of the year against six victories. The Sox managed only four singles, one of which extended Aparicio's hitting streak to 10 games. Fortunately, Cleveland fell to Detroit allowing the White Sox to remain a half game off the pace.

The rubber match of the series on Sunday took place before the largest crowd of the three-game set, 14,985. Billy Pierce absorbed the 8-6 defeat as his season record fell to 5-4. Pierce gave up seven runs on seven hits in one and 2/3 innings. Although not enough to overcome the Athletics, the Sox put on an offensive display of their own as their 12 hits resulted in six runs, highlighted by Sherman Lollar's two-run ninth inning home run. Meanwhile, the Cleveland Indians split a doubleheader with Detroit to increase their lead over the Pale Hose to a full game.

The extended road trip proved to be a tonic for the Chicago offense. In the 13 games since leaving home, Aparicio, Landis, Lollar, Torgeson and Phillips all saw significant improvement to their anemic batting averages. Aparicio improved his batting average by 45 percentage points to .299. Landis raised his average to .250 while knocking in eight runs. Lollar's average rose to .286, a remarkable 60 point improvement, combined with a team-high 12 RBIs during that span. Torgeson drove in 10 runs as his average improved to .266. And Bubba Phillips returned to form as he broke the .300 barrier. In spite of recent team results, Bill Veeck persisted in the belief that his team was playing over their heads. Veeck articulated that another significant trade would be necessary to make Chicago true contenders for the American League flag. The New York Yankees made a strong move to improve their club on May 26, as they acquired Ralph Terry and Hector Lopez from the Kansas City Athletics in exchange for Johhny Kucks, Tom Sturdivant and Jerry Lumpe.

The White Sox returned home to meet the Cleveland Indians for the third series of the season against this club. In its two previous four-game series, Chicago had prevailed in six of the eight games played. Chicago had won three out of four games in both Cleveland and Chicago. Early Wynn and Billy Pierce had won two games apiece as Chicago wrapped up both prior meetings with doubleheader sweeps. Dick Donovan took the mound on Tuesday night, May 26, before a crowd of 40,018 paying customers. The crowd represented the largest Comiskey Park turnout to that point of the season. Donovan and reliever Gerry Staley pitched well but Don Ferrarese, the Cleveland left-hander, was better. Ferrarese not only pitched four hit, no run ball, but also slammed three doubles and two RBIs, in his 3-0 shutout of Chicago. Aparicio extended his hitting streak to 12 games as he slashed two of Chicago's four singles. With the loss, the Sox fell two full games behind Cleveland.

The Bill Veeck show that evening called for four midgets dressed as spacemen to descend into the Park in a helicopter. Their mission was to capture Aparicio and Fox, Chicago's two mid-field mighty mites. The spacemen were led by none other than Eddie Gaedel. The 3-foot 7-inch Gaedel gained fame in 1951 when Bill Veeck first called upon his services. Veeck was running the hapless St. Louis Browns of the American League at the time. As a promotional stunt to celebrate the fifty year anniversary of the league and to placate the team's major broadcast sponsor, Veeck came up with the spoof of sending a midget to the plate during an actual ballgame. Under utmost secrecy, Veeck signed the diminutive Gaedel to a major league baseball contract for that intended purpose. The much maligned stunt took place in the second game of a doubleheader in St. Louis as Gaedel pinch hit for reserve center fielder, Frank Saucier. Gaedel came to the plate and proceeded to take his stance, presenting a strike zone of approximately two inches. Veeck threatened Eddie's life if he swung at any pitch. Gaedel followed orders and proceeded to walk on four pitches. On this night the fans once again enjoyed Gaedel's appearance, this time as a spaceman. Additional entertainment was provided by a post game fireworks display. However, the show on the field was a flop. The continuous stream of stunts and promotional events were meant to bring fans into the ballpark. Jim Landis observed that these stunts were effective, but on occasion the team felt like "God Almighty, let's just play baseball."

Nothing that happened on the field that night could match the drama that unfolded a few miles north in Milwaukee. The Milwaukee Braves battling for a repeat of the National League pennant faced the Pittsburgh Pirates. Harvey Haddix, the diminutive left-hander started the contest for Pittsburgh. Haddix proceeded to retire the first 36 Braves he faced. The Braves lineup included Hank Aaron who led the league in hitting at .443, and in RBIs at 44, and was second in home runs at 13. Eddie Mathews, the Braves third baseman, led the league in homers with 14. Johnny Logan and Bill Bruton were also among the league's top ten hitters. This power-packed lineup went to the plate and came back with nothing—no runs, no hits, no errors, no base runners through twelve frames. Unfortunately, despite 12 hits, the Pirates could not muster a run either. In the 13th inning a throwing error by Pittsburgh's third baseman, Don Hoak, allowed Felix Mantilla of the Braves to reach first base safely. Mathews sacrificed Mantilla to second base and Hank Aaron was then walked intentionally. Joe Adcock, the next batter, crushed the ball out of the Park for the game-winner. He was credited with only a double as in the excitement of the moment Aaron left the field as Mantilla scored and Adcock passed him on the base path. Haddix became only the eighth man in major league history to pitch a perfect game for nine innings, and the first to pitch more than nine perfect innings in one game. He was rewarded for his place in baseball history with a 2-0 defeat as the Braves prevailed.

On Wednesday the Sox closed the brief two-game series with Cleveland on a positive note as the South Siders won 5-1. Early Wynn notched his seventh victory of the season as he limited Cleveland to five hits through eight and 1/3 innings. Gerry Staley relieved Wynn with one out in the ninth and retired the last two Cleveland batters. Third baseman Bubba Phillips retired Rocky

Colavito on a spectacular play to end the game. Larry Doby singled in Nellie Fox with the game-winning run in the sixth inning. Torgeson followed Doby with a two-run homer in the sixth and Lollar connected on a solo shot in the eighth. With the victory, Chicago moved back to within one game of the lead.

Early in the morning on Thursday, May 28, the United States launched a Jupiter missile from Cape Canaveral, Florida. The successful launch carried two female monkeys on a journey into outer space. Able, a seven pound rhesus monkey, and Baker, a one pound squirrel monkey, were a vital part of this experiment designed to study the effects of space travel and reentry on living organisms. The 300 mile journey into space terminated upon reentry and touched down in the Atlantic Ocean. The experiment was a key step in the process of evaluating the potential of manned space flights in the future.

Detroit followed Cleveland into town for a three-game weekend series. The Thursday night contest was stopped after one inning as a heavy downpour drenched the 20,000 plus fans in attendance. Veeck continued his string of group promotional events by providing all bartenders in the city free admission to the game. The bartenders as well as the other fans enjoyed a spectacular fireworks display in spite of the rain. The game was rescheduled for Saturday as part of a doubleheader.

On Friday night, May 29, Bob Shaw dropped his first decision of the season as the Sox fell to Detroit 4-1. Shaw toiled seven and 1/3 innings giving up all of Detroit's nine hits and four runs. Shaw fell behind in the fourth as Al Kaline and Lou Berberet reached him for solo home runs. The loss kept Chicago a full game behind Cleveland. Due to the previous night's rainout, the bartenders were given another opportunity to attend a ballgame at Bill Veeck's expense and showed up 8,000 strong.

On Saturday, the Sox split their doubleheader with Detroit. Billy Pierce dropped the opener 4-2, recording his fifth loss of the season. The killing blow was struck by Gail Harris when he slashed a three-run home run to right center field in the second inning. The game was delayed for one and a half hours by rain in the sixth inning.

In the nightcap, Turk Lown was credited with his third victory of the season as the Sox battled back from a three-run deficit to win with a closing two-run rally in the ninth inning. Dick Donovan squared off with Jim Bunning for 7 and 1/3 innings, retiring with a 3-1 deficit. Lown was the beneficiary as Chicago scored a single run in the eighth and then two in the ninth. Doubles by Sherman Lollar and Nellie Fox produced the first run in the ninth inning and John Romano smashed a game-winning single off the glove of Coot Veal driving in Nellie Fox.

Chicago closed out the month of May by losing once again to Ned Garver and the Kansas City Athletics. It was no contest as the A's lit up Early Wynn and Barry Latman for all nine of their runs and all of their 12 hits in five and 2/3 innings. Wynn departed in the second and Latman was put out of his misery in the sixth after giving up a grand slam home run to first baseman Preston Ward. Earl Torgeson provided Chicago's only offensive punch with three hits including a first inning home run. The White Sox continued to struggle against the mediocre Athletics as Chicago lost for the sixth time in nine decisions on the year.

The Chicago White Sox were competing with other forms of entertainment during the early spring of 1959. The 1959 National Hockey League Stanley Cup Playoffs were now complete. In the first round of the playoffs, Toronto bested the Boston Bruins in seven games. In the other first round match, Montreal beat the Chicago Black Hawks, led by Bobby Hull, in six games. The Toronto club, coached by Punch Imlach, had a Cinderella season as they rebounded from a last place finish in 1958 to an appearance in the 1959 Stanley Cup Finals. The Canadians, coached by Toe Blake, won their fourth consecutive Stanley Cup as they turned back the Maple Leafs winning the best of seven series, four games to one. Claude Provost and Bernie Geoffrion provided the offensive heroics for the Habs in victory. The league consisted of six teams: the Montreal Canadians, Toronto Maple Leafs, Boston Bruins, Chicago Black Hawks, New York Rangers and the Detroit Red Wings.

Television produced a number of programs that drew much attention in 1959. We gathered around our black and white Stromburg-Carlson television set and were able to watch programs such as *Maverick* with James Garner, *Have Gun Will Travel*, *Gunsmoke*, *Wanted: Dead or Alive* and *Wagon Train*. In addition to these westerns, we were entertained by *Make Room For Daddy*, *Father Knows Best*, *Perry Mason* and *77 Sunset Strip*. Acclaimed dramatic and comedy series included *The Jack Benny Show*, *The Loretta Young Show*, *Dinah Shore Chevy Show*, *Alcoa-Goodyear Theater*, *Playhouse 90* and *The Hallmark Hall Of Fame. The Huntley-Brinckley Report* provided the nation with the nightly recap of news and current events.

Popular and rock 'n' roll music was incredibly dynamic as new, young recording artists appeared on the scene at a never ending pace. Hit songs during the first half of 1959 included *Dream Lover* by Bobby Darin, *Smoke Gets in Your Eyes* by the Platters, *Stagger Lee* by Lloyd Price, *Venus* by Frankie Avalon, *Come Softly to Me* by the Fleetwoods, *The Happy Organ* by Dave "Baby" Cortez and *Kansas City* by Wilbert Harrison. One significant tragedy touched the world of music on February 3. In a winter snow storm, a small aircraft en route to Fargo, North Dakota took off from a small airport. Shortly thereafter in a field near Mason City, Iowa the plane crashed killing passengers and pilot. The fateful evening saw three young rock 'n' roll recording artists lose their lives. This tragedy was memorialized in song years later as "the day the music died." Buddy Holly, age 22, recognized as a performing and song writing genius perished. His music would serve as an inspiration to generations of musicians. Richie Valens, age 17, with hits such as *La Bamba* and *Donna* also died in the accident. Valens had burst upon the music scene only a few short months earlier. The Big Bopper was the third musician killed in the crash.

The music industry created bad publicity for itself when reports surfaced that many disc jockeys may have taken money from record companies in exchange for playing their records. The most noted disc jockey accused in this payola scandal was Allan Freed of WABC in New York. Freed was ultimately fired because he refused to sign a statement denying his participation in the payola scheme. Adding further taint, Chuck Berry, a popular recording artist, served several months in prison following his conviction for transporting a minor across state lines for immoral purposes.

Chicago finished the month of May with 15 wins and 13 losses (25-19 on the season), which slotted them in second place, one game behind the Cleveland Indians. Baltimore held down the third position in the standings with an overall record of 25-21, two games off the pace, Kansas City followed in fourth place, four and 1/2 games out, and Detroit finished the month in fifth place 5 and 1/2 games back. The Tigers opened the season with a 2-13 record in April and on May 3 replaced manager Bill Norman with veteran Jimmy Dykes. Norman's record was a bleak 2-15 when he was released. The managerial change coincided with the Tigers' 18 win, 10 loss performance in May. New York was mired in sixth place, six games out. Washington and Boston were tied for the final spot, six and 1/2 games behind the league leader.

CHAPTER THREE

Like a Dog Nipping at Your Heels

THE WHITE SOX WERE IN THE SAME POSITION ENTERING JUNE AS they had been at the beginning of May—one game behind Cleveland. Even though Chicago was in second place, its record of 25-19 represented a winning percentage of only .568. During the decade of the 1950s, the average winning percentage for the team bringing home the American League pennant was .639. If the White Sox were to achieve this percentage, they would have to win a total of 98 games on the season—73 out of their remaining 110 games. Winning two out of every three games for the remainder of the year was a daunting task, especially given Chicago's performance to this point in the season.

As spring evolved into summer, baseball continued to dominate our thoughts and activities. The end of the tunnel was near for the school year, and as the weather turned consistently warm, opportunities for neighborhood pickup baseball games increased. Our game of choice was baseball, but due to the strict confines of the playing surfaces available, we would normally revert to playing softball. In Chicago, softball generally meant the 16-inch circumference sized variety, which is somewhat softer and larger than a standard softball. Our favorite spot for the pickup games was the playground at the "Portables." The field as laid out was almost perfectly square, with approximately 150 feet from home plate to the fences in left field and in right field.

Our equipment was simple. Bases were scratched into the surface of the playground with the heel of a shoe. Bats and balls were scarce commodities. We would scour our homes for remnants of the season past. Each year a parent or two would spring for a new softball and a new bat. We would play with these items until they literally fell apart, with the softball normally the first to go. It would start out as hard as a rock. The hardness of the spheroid produced many early season jammed or broken fingers, as bare-handed efforts often came up shy. As the ball was hammered on a daily basis, however, the seams of its cover would start to split. Once this process began, the cover would be gone in a matter of minutes. The yarn which composed the mass of the ball would become less firm and very compressible, resulting in many spectacular, one-handed, running and diving catches. It was almost like grabbing a sponge out of mid-air. At this stage of the process, home runs were few and far between.

The bat was truly one-size-fits-all. We really didn't have any choices. The bat was durable, especially in softball. The biggest hazard to the health of the bat was a direct function of the frustration of the batter. If one was experiencing a particularly bad hitting slump, it seemed sensible to break the curse by whacking the bat against a tree or concrete sidewalk. I am certain that this barbaric ritual affected the premature demise of many a stick. Cracked bats, depending on the severity, often could be mended temporarily with electrical tape or nails. Regardless of the setback, the game would somehow continue.

Culture is created by people. Webster's New Collegiate Dictionary defines culture as "the integrated pattern of human behavior that includes thought, speech, action, and artifacts and depends upon man's capacity for learning and transmitting knowledge to succeeding generations." The nuances of baseball culture are intriguing in their evolution. The ritual of choosing sides was a fascinating and telling aspect of baseball culture. Most often the two best ball players would be selected as captains and choose up sides. First choice was determined by the toss of a bat from one captain to the other. The bat would be caught firmly in the palm of the hand. The tosser would place his hand around the bat directly above that of the tossee. They would alternate hand over hand until there was no longer room for a full hand to be placed around the bat. The last person would then clutch his hand around the top of the knob of the bat extending his fingers as far down as the other person's hand. This could result in anything from a fingertip hold on the bat, to a good grip with the knob pressed into your palm and fingers well extended on the shaft of the bat. The other person was in a losing position, but had one more bite at the apple. He would have one chance to kick the bat from the winner's hand. If he succeeded, he would have first choice of players for his team. If he failed, he would have second choice. This system, when compared to the flip of a coin, was cumbersome but it seemed to have the desired result. Players would then be selected, one by one, as each captain revealed his choice. The captains would survey the candidates and slowly select either the best player available or in some instances their closer friends. It was mortifying to be the last player selected. After all selections were made the game would begin.

The games lasted for hours. Ground rules were most often determined by the number of players participating in the game and the idiosyncrasies of the particular field. When playing pickup games on the playground of the "Portables" we only had one significant problem. Retrieving home run balls pulled directly down the left field line presented a test of our overall athletic ability and an even more daunting test of our manhood. Gussies' hamburger joint was on the other side of the fence in foul territory. However, the big vicious mongrel dog that guarded the premises at night was housed in a fenced pen, approximately 10 feet behind the left field fence in fair territory. Between the fence and the dog pen was a compost pile. When a home run settled in the dog pen someone would have to retrieve it. This happened at least once every other game. The drill went like this. The dog would have the softball at his feet and would bark menacingly, fangs exposed and drool lathered on his face. The ball must have tasted like a pork chop, as the beast would chew it and slobber over it like it was his next meal. The person who pitched the ball had the responsibility of getting the dog's attention and distracting him. This required a degree of creativity. The dog may have been ugly, but he was still a very quick study and was not fooled by the same old tricks. The person who hit the home run would pick his spot, decisively leap the fence, recover the saliva-soaked ball and retreat before the dog could attack. I had my share of home runs, and I must brag that my standing vertical leap would have made Jesse Owens proud by season's end.

The White Sox were like that dog nipping at the heels of the front running Cleveland Indians. Both Chicago and Cleveland opened the month of June with losses. Cleveland dropped a 3-1 decision to the Tigers in Detroit. The White Sox fell once again to Kansas City as Bud Daley outdueled Ray Moore 3-1, lowering Moore's season record to 1-3. The Sox had now lost seven of their last nine games. Joe Demastri led the Athletics attack with a triple and a home run.

The surprising Baltimore Orioles arrived in town for a three game series and promptly laid into the White Sox. Bob Shaw lost his second consecutive start at home on Tuesday evening, June 2. Baltimore sent Hoyt Wilhelm to the mound and he proceeded to post his eighth consecutive triumph, outlasting Shaw 3-2. Shaw pitched eight and 1/3 innings, giving up 12 hits as he was charged with all three Baltimore runs. Baltimore's victory pushed the South Siders into third place, one game behind Cleveland (who lost to Washington 3-2) and 1/2 game behind second-place Baltimore. In Chicago's last 10 outings, its starting rotation had produced only one victory. In dropping eight of ten ball games during that stretch, Early Wynn's 5-1 decision over Cleveland on May 27 was the only victory posted by the rotation of Wynn, Pierce, Donovan, Shaw and Moore. Turk Lown earned the other victory in relief of Dick Donovan in Chicago's 4-3 victory over Detroit on May 30. Manager Lopez needed his veteran starting rotation to step it up a notch.

On Wednesday, June 3, Lopez sent Billy Pierce to the hill against Baltimore to stem the tide of losses. Pierce proved to be the stopper as he held Baltimore in check for nine innings, finishing with a complete game 6-1 victory. Pierce gave up eight hits while walking two and striking out three. Aparicio and Fox combined to drive in three fifth inning runs, with Fox's two-run triple the game-winner. Aparicio and John Romano had two hits apiece in Chicago's nine-hit attack. Meanwhile, Cleveland dropped another decision to Washington 4-0. Chicago was now tied for first place with the Cleveland Indians, but had a slightly lower winning percentage, and Baltimore was 1/2 game off the lead, in third place.

On Thursday, June 4, I was scheduled to spend the night at my grandparents' home. My grandparents had a large room upstairs in the attic of their 1930s vintage frame home. The room contained three beds and served as my bedroom when I spent the night. The room was the ultimate hideaway for a young boy. Books of fiction and fact lined shelves and were available to pass the time and spark the imagination. The old photo albums were in the desk. It was a recurring pleasure to study the old photographs of family members past. During the summer, the sounds of the street drifted in through the open dormer windows providing a soothing backdrop on sultry nights. The breeze, if any, was the only comfort from that heat. My favorite radio was nestled on a low shelf adjacent to the largest bed.

The highlight of the evening was the opportunity to tune in the radio and listen to the mellow tones of Bob Elson. Baseball truly is a game that is best absorbed through listening on the radio. During 1959, Bob Elson, the long time radio voice of the Chicago White Sox, created vivid images of the game that will live forever in my memory. His knowledge and passionate command of the subject enhanced the listening audience's envisioned picture of the on field events. Because of my in depth exposure to the radio announcers of that era, today I continue to prefer listening to a baseball game on the radio over watching it on television. I believe that by capturing the essence of the game of baseball in word, these men helped to create the loyalty to and respect for the game shared by generations of fans who grew up during the 1930s, 1940s and 1950s.

As I settled into bed that Thursday evening, the White Sox took the field against the Baltimore Orioles at Comiskey Park. Little did I realize when the game started that I would still be intently listening four hours and 37 minutes later. This marathon battle raged for 17 innings. In the bottom of the 17th inning, Earl Torgeson came to bat with no runners on and two outs. Baltimore relief pitcher Jerry Walker worked the count to one ball and one strike. The next pitch was a knee-high fastball on the inside part of the plate. The left-handed first baseman strode into the ball and hit a rocket into the right field seats, giving Chicago the win. The victory put Chicago in first place, 1/2 game ahead of Cleveland and one and 1/2 games in front of third-place Baltimore. The Sox had summoned Dick Donovan, Barry Latman, Gerry Staley, Rudolfo Arias, Turk Lown and eventual winner Bob Shaw to the mound. Latman and Shaw were the most effective of the group. Bob Shaw pitched the final five innings yielding four hits and one run in earning his fifth victory of the year. The White Sox accumulated 14 hits off three different Baltimore pitchers as they squandered numerous scoring opportunities. Lollar and Torgeson led the offensive charge with three hits each, as Fox and Doby accounted for two apiece. The 6-5 victory represented the longest game in the major leagues to that point in the season.

Torgeson, according to infield coach Don Gutteridge, was a very fiery guy who was up and at them all the time. Earl arrived in Chicago on June 14, 1957 in a trade that sent White Sox veteran outfielder Dave Philley to Detroit. Torgeson, a six-foot, three-inch, 180-pound left-hander was born on New Year's Day in 1924. The Snohomish, Washington native began his major league career in 1947 with the Boston Braves of the National League. Torgeson moved to the Philadelphia Phillies in 1953 and on to Detroit in mid-1955. Earl appeared in 96 games for Chicago in 1958 as a part-time player. In his 188 plate appearances, he had fifty hits, including ten home runs. In limited playing time, Torgeson gave the White Sox much needed left-handed power in the lineup.

Boston was the next opponent on the slate for the White Sox. The fourteen game homestand would conclude with this series. The scheduled starters for Chicago were Early Wynn, Ray Moore, Dick Donovan and Billy Pierce. In the Friday night opener, Early Wynn worked seven strong innings and departed after loading the bases with no one out in the eighth inning. Wynn had given up six hits, walked six and struck out five to that point. Gerry Staley toed the rubber in relief of Wynn and was the victim of Earl Torgeson's error which allowed the tying run to score. In the bottom of the eighth, the White Sox loaded the bases on a single by Torgeson, an error on a bunt by Al Smith and an intentional walk to Jim Landis. Harry "Suitcase" Simpson pinch hit for, and made a winning pitcher out of, Gerry Staley. Simpson plated all three runners with his game-winning double to right center. The score remained 5-2 as Rudolfo Arias closed out the ninth with no additional damage.

On Saturday, June 6, the White Sox and Ray Moore lost to Ted Willis, Boston's rookie left-hander, by a score of 4-2. In another great promotional scheme Veeck created honor student day and 2,596 Chicago land school children joined 10,301 paying customers to witness the loss. Unfortunately, I was not among the students so honored. Moore's record tumbled to 1-4 on the season as he gave up seven hits and all four Boston runs in his seven inning stint. Moore had been counted on as Chicago's fifth or six starter coming out of spring training. The Sox acquired Moore on December 3, 1957 along with Billy Goodman and Tito Francona from the Baltimore Orioles in the trade that sent Larry Doby and Jack Harshman packing. At that time, Al Lopez tabbed Moore as one of the fastest pitchers in the league and slotted him in as both a reliever and a starter. In 1958, Moore appeared in a relief role early in the season and then competed as a starter to finish with an overall record of 9-7. Ray pitched a total of 136 innings on the year. The six-foot tall, 190-pound Moore, nicknamed the "Farmer," was an off-season tobacco farmer.

At the beginning of the day on June 7, the American League race was about as tight as it had been all season. Three and 1/2 games separated the top six teams in the league. Chicago was in first place, one and 1/2 games ahead of both Cleveland and Baltimore. The streaky Cleveland club had lost seven in a row. Kansas City was third and New York and Detroit were tied for fourth place, only three and 1/2 games off the pace. The Sox closed out their homestand splitting a Sunday doubleheader with the BoSox. The White Sox won the opener 9-4 as Dick Donovan got the necessary run support to even his record at 3-3. The White Sox went ahead to stay with a six-run second inning highlighted by singles by Callison, Phillips, Rivera, Donovan, Aparicio and Fox. The game-deciding run scored on Earl Torgeson's sacrifice fly. Jim Rivera, in his first start since returning from a rib injury, had two RBIs, two runs scored and two hits including a third-inning home run. The Red Sox prevailed in the nightcap 4-2 behind the outstanding pitching of Frank Sullivan. Billy Pierce took the loss for Chicago as his record slid to 6-6. Latman and Lown pitched four and 2/3 combined innings of two-hit shutout relief. Ted Williams, the Boston legend, continued to struggle as his batting average slipped to .185.

Between games, the Red Sox and White Sox players staged a "Dairy Farm Day" milking contest where Chicago's Ray Moore, Early Wynn and Nellie Fox lost to the Boston trio of Gary Geiger, Jim Busby and Pete Runnels. Also as a surprise element to the between game activities, Early Wynn rode into the Park on a horse posing as the masked "Only Stranger." He surprised the fans as he performed riding and roping stunts. Bill Veeck provided the carnival atmosphere as the crowd of 25,844 was rewarded with baseball, the carnival and free milk.

On Monday, June 8, Chicago departed on a scheduled twelve game Eastern road trip which would take them to Washington, Baltimore, New York and Boston. The White Sox had lost eight out of fourteen games in the just completed homestand. Despite that record, they moved into first place one game ahead of the pack. Looking back to 1958, at the same point in the season, the White Sox were fourteen games behind the eventual World Champion Yankees. The South Siders were hopeful that they could finish the 1959 campaign as strongly as they did in 1958, when they had the best second-half record in the league.

Bob Shaw faced off against Bill Fischer in Washington's Griffith Stadium on Tuesday night to open the three-game series with the Senators. The two pitchers dueled in a see-saw battle through seven innings to a 4-4 deadlock. Rookie Bob Allison was Shaw's nemesis as he slammed two home runs. After Shaw departed, Washington scored three runs off Turk Lown in the eighth inning to lift the Senators to their final 7-4 margin of victory. The White Sox aggregated 12 hits on the day but could only manage four runs. The loss dropped the White Sox into a tie for first place with Baltimore who had beat Cleveland 7-3 that same day.

On Wednesday, June 10, the White Sox moved into sole possession of first place as Early Wynn pitched a complete game five hitter for a 4-1 victory over Washington. In doing so, Wynn held the power-laden Senators without a home run and struck out seven in the sweltering 90-degree heat. Al Smith led off the White Sox scoring as he hammered a drive to right center field plating Luis Aparicio in the first inning. In a daring move to stretch his triple into an inside the park home run, Smith continued to the plate and scored with a hard slide that jarred the ball from the glove of catcher Hal Narragon. Fox, Smith, Lollar and Wynn each had two hits in Chicago's 10-hit attack. These campaign-hardened veterans continued to provide the Pale Hose with steady clubhouse leadership and on field focus.

The most significant offensive display of the day took place at Baltimore's Memorial Stadium. The Stadium was built for pull hitters with both the left and right field foul poles being only 309 feet from home plate. The center field fence was 450 feet in distance. Cleveland's incredible young slugger, Rocky Colavito, put on a power display that hadn't been duplicated at the major league level in twenty-seven years. Colavito slammed four consecutive home runs in Cleveland's 11-8 triumph over Baltimore. The feat accomplished by Colavito tied a major league record for consecutive home runs in the same game last attained by Lou Gehrig of the New York Yankees on June 3, 1932.

The following day, Washington fell victim to the White Sox as Billy Pierce hurled a one hit, one run masterpiece for a 3-1 Chicago victory. While the Senators managed only a third inning double the White Sox accumulated nine hits. The victory did not come easily for Pierce. The game was tied as Camilo Pascual matched Pierce in runs allowed through eight innings at one each. In the top of the ninth inning, however, Jim Landis lashed a two-run double for the game-winner. The one hitter was the fourth of Pierce's thirteen-year major league career. Prior to this performance, Pierce's last one-hitter was against this same Washington club on June 27, 1958. In perhaps the finest game of his career, Pierce was only one pitch away from hurling a perfect game. The no-run, no-hit, no-walk, no-error effort in perfection eluded him when Ed Fitzgerald slapped a two base hit with two out in the ninth inning of that game in Chicago.

The Friday night series opener between Chicago and Baltimore was lost to a rain storm. Dick Donovan and Hoyt Wilhelm dueled through the third inning when the game was suspended due to rain with the score 1-0 in favor of Baltimore. My brother and I took advantage of the night off and scheduled the opening game of our 1959 pinball summer series. In this confrontation, the pseudo Chicago White Sox squared off against the pseudo New York Yankees. I, of course, functioned as the stick man for Chicago and my older and wiser brother took the helm of the New York Yankees. We went to battle on an authentic, tabletop pinball game fashioned with a baseball theme. This electric, glass-topped, wood-encased model provided one more imaginative gateway to the game. The painted surface of the game replicated a ball diamond with appropriately positioned fielders. Small steel ball bearings were propelled by a spring assisted launcher to simulate a ball being hit by a batter. The spheroid would find its destination after proceeding through a maze of bumpers, cushions and flippers. The final destination was influenced by the player's touch with the launcher and his ability to caress the flippers as well as the machine itself. Tolerance and finesse were a must as the game had a tilt control. Balls, strikes, singles, doubles, triples, home runs, errors, hit batters, ground outs, fly outs and sacrifices were all potential results. In keeping with the rules of our game, we utilized the current major league team rosters to establish our game day lineup. In 1959, our league consisted of only two teams and a 50 game schedule. We played 25 games at home and 25 games on the road. We maintained meticulous statistical records for the entire season. Daily box scores and cumulative player statistics were published for our own benefit. Even though we were playing against a machine, we attempted to use every managerial strategy that the game situation would dictate. This competition played out over the entire summer. I'm certainly glad that we got a good game of baseball in on the pinball playing field that evening because the White Sox tumbled to Baltimore the next day.

This was the 56th game of the season for the South Siders. Al Lopez summoned Bob Shaw to take the mound. In a futile attempt to improve upon his 5-2 season record, Shaw lasted only two and 1/3 innings. It was not Shaw's day as Baltimore battered him for four runs on five hits. Shaw was spared the loss when Nellie Fox clubbed an eighth inning three-run homer to deadlock the game at four. Barry Latman kept Chicago in the contest with four innings of shutout relief. Gerry Staley came on to pitch to Baltimore in the eighth inning and was charged with his second loss of the season when Bob Boyd connected to put Baltimore ahead to stay 6-4.

Landis and Fox each had two hits for Chicago in the losing cause.

The Sox began Sunday's doubleheader against Baltimore with a 1/2 game lead over Cleveland in the standings. Early Wynn and Dick Donovan were slated to throw against Baltimore's Jack Harshman and Billy O'Dell. Wynn pitched eight and 1/3 innings allowing six runs on seven hits as Chicago prevailed 9-6. With the victory, Wynn ran his season record to 9-4. Nellie Fox went on another rampage driving in four runs on three hits. Fox's third hit on the day, a single in the eighth inning, drove in Early Wynn with the game-winner. Wynn, an excellent hitting pitcher, had four hits to support his own cause. Wynn's battery mate Earl Battey also had three hits.

Dick Donovan duplicated the success of Wynn in the nightcap winning 3-2. Donovan pitched nine and 2/3 innings to earn his fourth victory in seven decisions. Arias was credited with the save as he came in to get the final out of the game. Al Smith's second hit of the contest, a single in the top of the 10th inning, scored Aparicio with the winning run. The performance by Dick Donovan was the fourth strong performance from a starting pitcher in the last five outings. Donovan was considered by Al Lopez to be one of his "Big Three" starters, together with Billy Pierce and Early Wynn.

Richard Edward Donovan was born December 7, 1927 in Quincy, Massachusetts. Donovan, recognized as an excellent infielder, attended North Quincy High School where he became a pitcher in his senior season. The six-foot, three-inch, 190-pound right-hander started his major league career in the National League with the Boston Braves organization. In brief stints with the parent club from 1950 through 1952, Donovan appeared in 56 innings losing four ball games. He pitched a few innings with Detroit of the American League in the early days of the 1954 season before Detroit gave up on him and sent Donovan to its Atlanta farm club. There Donovan established an excellent 18-8 record in 1954. Donovan's contract was purchased by the Chicago White Sox after the 1954 season. While Donovan was in Atlanta he developed a good slider that contributed greatly to his success in 1954 and his ticket to the major leagues. In 1955 Donovan finally established himself as a major league starting pitcher in Chicago. During the four year span from 1955 through 1958, he averaged more than 14 victories per season against an average of 10 losses. He started an average of 31 ball games per year and pitched in excess of 220 innings per season. He had a slow start in 1958 but finished very strong with a 12-4 record after the All-Star break. The strong finish enabled Dick to win 15 games while losing 14. Teammate Bob Shaw remembered Dick as having a very dry "Boston" sense of humor and as a fierce competitor who was very focused when he pitched. Donovan also possessed idiosyncrasies in that he didn't want anyone to touch him or talk to him when he pitched. Donovan's leadership and competitiveness were contagious on the 1959 team.

The doubleheader sweep pushed Chicago's lead over Baltimore to three games. The sweep was necessary to maintain Chicago's half game lead over Cleveland. Minnie Minoso, the Cleveland Indian left-fielder, led his resurgent club with nine RBIs as the Tribe pummeled Washington 9-5 and 12-6 to sweep both ends of their Sunday twin bill.

At a stockholders' meeting held on Monday, June 15, Bill Veeck officially gained control of the Board of Directors of the club. Veeck, Hank Greenberg, A. C. Allyn Sr., Chuck Comiskey and Frank Curran were elected to the expanded five member board. Veeck, Greenberg and Allyn were longtime associates and significant members of the group that acquired Mrs. Rigney's 54 percent ownership interest in the team. Mr. Curran was Chuck Comiskey's father-in-law. Veeck's day lasted long into the night as he and Greenberg attempted to hammer out the long rumored trade that would bring Roy Sievers, the Washington Senator slugger, to Chicago. As the trading deadline ended at midnight, Calvin Griffith turned down Veeck's offer of $250,000 in cash and five Chicago players for Roy Sievers and two other Senators. The "other players" on both sides of the proposed transaction were unnamed. In addition, a deal that would bring Minnie Minoso to Chicago from Cleveland died when Minoso had his nine RBI day. Frank Lane, Cleveland's General Manager, couldn't make the four player for four player trade after Minoso's sterling performance. The rumors and speculation of those trades, as well as Veeck's persistent theme that the club was not good enough to seriously challenge for the pennant, were a distraction to the players. With the trading deadline now past, the team could better focus on their jobs on the field. In other player related transactions, Norm Cash returned from his service commitment and his roster exemption terminated. To make room on the major league roster for Cash, the White Sox waived Del Ennis. Since coming to Chicago from Cincinnati, Ennis was directly responsible for four of Chicago's mid-May victories.

Chicago took the field against the New York Yankees on Tuesday night, June 16, having fallen from first place. Cleveland's 5-1 triumph over Boston on Monday inched the Tribe percentage points ahead of the Sox. Billy Pierce started for Chicago and lasted seven innings yielding four of the five Yankee runs. Despite opening the scoring in the first inning, the White Sox were shut down by Art Ditmar on four hits in the 5-1 defeat. Norm Cash returned to the starting lineup and had two of Chicago's hits. The loss to the Yankees coupled with Cleveland's seventh win in a row, a 4-1 beating of Boston, shoved Chicago a full game out of first place.

Cash had been a surprise in spring training and was inserted into the starting lineup as the opening day first baseman. Norman

Dalton Cash, born on November 10, 1934, grew up in the cotton farming community of Justiceburg, Texas. The six-foot tall, 185-pound power hitter didn't play baseball until he was 19 years of age. He attended Sul Ross College where he starred in football. Norm was an excellent football player and was selected by the National Football League Chicago Bears in the 13th round of the amateur draft. Cash signed a baseball contract with the White Sox and played for its Waterloo farm team in 1956 finishing the year with a .334 batting average. After serving time in the Armed Forces, he played sparingly at Indianapolis in 1957. A season in winter ball improved his game significantly. Until the last days of spring training in 1959, Cash's entire career had been spent in the outfield. Impressed by Cash's bat, but unimpressed with his defensive play in the outfield in spring training, manager Lopez had Cash work out at first base so that he could get Cash's potent bat in the lineup. Cash was another outstanding example of the young talent that was developed in the Chicago farm system under the guidance of Bill Rigney and Chuck Comiskey.

While in New York, the nation's business capital, players were able to take note that the Dow Jones Industrial Average hovered at 628.05 points. The overall trading volume for the day's activity on the New York Stock Exchange was 2,850,000 shares. The use of computers, relatively new to Wall Street, was being escalated by the larger brokerage firms led by Merrill, Lynch, Pierce, Fenner & Smith, Inc., Bache & Co. and E. F. Hutton & Co. Industry veterans observed that computer processing was necessary to combat the increasing number of daily transactions, speculating that the volume of shares traded could reach five to ten million shares per day. Technological advancements in computer data processing had been achieved by Radio Corporation of America and International Business Machines. While computer technology was leading the way in the business world, other breakthroughs were also taking place. Laser technology was conceived by Bell Labs. This process of light amplification by stimulated emission of radiation revolutionized several industries including communications, medicine and optical scanning. The computer microchip was also invented during the year. The Xerox Corporation developed full scale manufacture of plain paper copiers. The General Electric Corporation developed the electronic recording machine system for the banking industry, using magnetic ink character recognition technology. While major technological changes were taking place at a lightning quick pace in the fields of science and industry, only subtle rule and equipment changes were taking place in the game of baseball. The game itself remained much the same as it was 40 years earlier.

On Wednesday night, June 17, Ray Moore lasted less than two innings while losing his fifth game of the season against only one victory. Moore gave up six of the Yankees' seven runs including a three-run tape measure home run by Mickey Mantle in the second inning. The blast settled in the upper reaches of the third deck in right field traveling over 450 feet from home plate. The drive missed clearing the ornate facade on the face of the outfield roof by only inches. Mickey Mantle was legendary for such displays of raw power but had yet to hit one out of cavernous Yankee Stadium. Fox and Lollar each had two hits for Chicago. Bob Turley, with relief help from Ryan Duren, gained the victory. The loss put the Sox one and 1/2 games behind Cleveland.

Bob Shaw took the mound in the series finale for manager Al Lopez on June 18. Shaw's opposition that day was New York Yankees rookie Jim Bronstad. Looking to avoid a series sweep, Shaw built a 4-2 lead heading into the eighth inning. Fox and Aparicio had combined for four hits and three RBIs to give the ChiSox the lead. Shaw departed in the eighth inning as the Yankees rallied to tie the score. Mickey Mantle slammed a home run on the second pitch from reliever Gerry Staley in the bottom of the 10th inning to end the game at 5-4 and complete the Yankee sweep of the three-game set. The Yankees were now only two games behind the slumping White Sox and only three and 1/2 games behind the league-leading Indians.

The White Sox traveled to Boston on June 19 for the fourth and final leg of their Eastern swing. The opener was rained out giving both teams a much needed rest. Early Wynn and Dick Donovan were selected to pitch for Chicago in Saturday's doubleheader. Chicago's losing streak was extended to five games as Early Wynn dropped the opener 8-2. Wynn, Barry Latman and Rudolfo Arias were all ineffective in the outing. Wynn's record fell to 9-5 for the year. Sammy Esposito, substituting for Luis Aparicio who suffered an ankle injury in pre-game warm-ups, had two of Chicago's eight hits.

In the night game of this day-night doubleheader the Pale Hose were blanked 9-0. Gerry Casale twirled the three-hit complete game for Boston as he easily handled the light hitting White Sox. Dick Donovan lasted just two and 1/3 innings as he was hammered for seven hits and six runs. The loss dropped Donovan's season record to 4-4. The overworked relief corps once again was called upon for five and 2/3 innings of work. The doubleheader loss left the White Sox one and 1/2 games behind Cleveland as the Indians were beaten by the Yankees by a score of 10-2. Worse yet, the Sox dropped all the way to fifth place in this tightly packed race. Cleveland, Detroit, Baltimore and New York all were in possession of a better winning percentage than the Pale Hose. Veeck's prediction that Chicago's club did not have the forces to win the flag was now receiving some empirical support.

In an unrelated minor league transaction, the White Sox added another player to their strong farm system by signing Oklahoma State University's Joel Horlen. Horlen, the six-foot tall, 175-pound right-handed pitcher was placed at Indianapolis for evaluation and assignment. Horlen led the Oklahoma State club to the NCAA College World Series Championship as they defeated Arizona 5-3 on June 18. Horlen would become a Chicago standout in the 1960s as the big right-hander forged a twelve-year major league career highlighted by a 19-7 record in 1967. That year he led the American League in winning percentage with .731, shutouts with six and earned run average with 2.06.

On Sunday, June 21, in the last game of the road trip, Chicago defeated Boston 3-2 behind the pitching of Billy Pierce. The victory by Pierce stopped the current losing streak at five and vaulted Chicago into second place due in part to Cleveland's sweep of the Yankees in a doubleheader, Detroit's split of a doubleheader, and Baltimore's single game loss. The White Sox lost a half game in the standings but were able to move ahead of all teams except Cleveland. Pierce went the distance giving up just six hits. Sammy Esposito and Harry "Suitcase" Simpson hit back to back home runs in the second inning. Simpson, batting seventh in the order, also had a double in the fourth inning to set up the game-winning run.

Sammy Esposito was in the lineup for the third day in succession subbing for the injured Aparicio. Esposito began his career in the Chicago system when he signed a contract with the White Sox in 1952. A Chicago native, Sammy attended Fenger High School and then Indiana University. Esposito was born on December 15, 1931. He joined the major league club for good in 1956 and played in 81 games hitting .228, .207 in 1957, and .247 in 1958. He proved to be a valuable utility man during his major league career. Don Gutteridge, the White Sox first base and infield coach in 1959, characterized Esposito as a great utility man and outstanding third baseman. Gutteridge explained further that Esposito filled the utility role well in that after he was exposed to regular play for 10 consecutive games or so, his abilities would fall off. Esposito was considered one of the team's best defensive infielders.

On Monday, the White Sox and the cross town National League Chicago Cubs took advantage of their off day to play their annual charity game for the Boys Club. The crowd of 29,383 witnessed the Cubs top the Sox 3-2. The proceeds from the affair were used to purchase baseball equipment for Chicago area youth programs.

During the course of the day on Monday, I had made another error in judgment at school. On the playground, I had been tossing a ball with a friend and let the throw get away from me. My errant throw was about three feet too tall for my pal, Dave Aggen. Unfortunately, it was in a perfect spot to shatter a pane of glass in a nearby school room window. Immediately, Stanley, the custodial engineer for the school complex, rounded the corner. In a language I couldn't begin to understand, I knew I was being chastised for my error in judgment. I knew intuitively that I would never hear the end of it once word reached home of the broken window. With a quickness and grace that was incongruous with the size and look of the man, the debris was cleared away and the pane of glass replaced. To my shock and eternal gratitude I never heard another word of this incident. I remained uneasy for a few weeks knowing that any moment the hammer could fall. My concern soon passed. Stanley and I became friends, even though I couldn't understand a word he said. Judging the way he reacted to me it was clear he understood every word I said. His intelligence and wisdom were not tarnished by his inability to speak English.

On Tuesday, June 23, the Washington Senators arrived for a three-game series in Comiskey Park as the White Sox resumed the American League race. Early Wynn improved his record to 10-5 with a 4-1 complete game victory. Wynn struck out seven while yielding eight hits and three walks in nine frames. Earl Torgeson drove in Chicago's first two runs, the second of which was the game-winner in the fifth inning. Sherman Lollar connected for his eighth home run of the year, a two-run shot to the upper deck in left field. The White Sox outstanding defense cut off several Washington threats as they threw three runners out at the plate. Jim Landis turned the trick in the second inning and both Aparicio and Rivera duplicated the feat in the eighth inning.

The White Sox and Washington squared off again on Wednesday, June 24, but Chicago came up short, 4-2. Dick Donovan pitched a complete game but lost in the ninth as Washington scored three unearned runs. The runs came home on throwing errors by Earl Torgeson and Luis Aparicio. The Aparicio error put a taint on his day which included a brace of great defensive plays, an inside the park home run and his 21st stolen base of the season.

In the final game of the series, rookie Barry Latman won his first decision of the season, 4-1. Latman hurled a complete game as he shut down the powerful Senators on five hits. Latman followed Donovan, Wynn and Pierce with the fourth consecutive complete game from a starting pitcher. Latman's modified delivery, straight over the top, helped with his pitch location and ball movement. Latman helped his own cause when his sacrifice fly drove home Bubba Phillips with the game-winning run in the fifth inning. Phillips had previously tripled to drive in Jim Rivera for Chicago's first run. Earl Torgeson continued his timely hitting with a sixth inning two-run homer, his sixth of the campaign.

Only two games behind league-leading Cleveland and one behind second place Chicago, the fourth place New York Yankees moved into town Friday night for the opener of a four-game series. Billy Pierce took the mound against Art Ditmar for the second time of the season. A crowd of 37,909 came out to witness the rematch. Ditmar, with three-inning, eight-strikeout relief support from Ryan Duren, humbled the White Sox 8-4. Pierce was hit hard as he fell to his eighth defeat in sixteen decisions on the year. Turk Lown was grazed for the final two Yankee runs. Landis went four for four at the plate with two doubles and two singles. The loss dropped the Sox into a tie with the Yankees for third place, one game behind Baltimore and two back of Cleveland.

Another battle for a championship was taking place that evening. At Yankee Stadium in New York the heavyweight boxing champion of the world, Floyd Patterson, defended his title against Ingemar Johansson. The Swedish challenger knocked Patterson down repeatedly in the third round. The surprising Johansson was awarded the world title when the referee stopped the bout at 2:03 of the third round. Patterson's contract called for a rematch within 90 days.

On Saturday, Bob Shaw pitched eight innings of five-hit, two-run baseball to earn his sixth victory against only two losses. Shaw departed in the ninth inning for pinch hitter Norm Cash, and was trailing the Yankees 2-1. In the dramatic ninth inning, Harry Simpson pounded Bob Turley's offering into the upper deck in right field for the game-winning grand slam home run. Chicago executed perfectly the classic ninth inning, two-out, come from behind rally. Nellie Fox walked, Torgeson singled, Lollar walked and Simpson followed with his blast. New York did not go down easily as Seibern and Skowron hit ninth inning home runs off Rudolfo Arias. Gerry Staley was called upon and struck out Tony Kubek for the last out to end the game and preserve the 5-4 victory.

In a roster move that took place after the game, preseason rookie of the year candidate, and former bonus baby Johnny Callison was optioned to Indianapolis to allow him to play every day and regain his hitting stroke. To fill Callison's spot on the major league roster, right-handed hitting outfielder Jim McAnany was called up from Indianapolis.

As the White Sox were wrapping up the month of June, I finished my season in an academic sense. The school year ended on June 26 and my fourth quarter results were in. The final tabulation was three Es, in reading, spelling and art, and five Gs. I had even raised my handwriting grade from an F- to an F. I attributed my late season surge to inspiration provided by Aparicio, Landis and Fox. Hopefully I would be ready for the next level of competition in September. The good news was that I had been promoted to 4A. The bad news was that Mrs. Murphy was going to be my manager again next season.

My father had promised that if I pulled my grades up to a level of respectability he would take my brother and me to a White Sox game as soon as school was out. My brother never had a problem with respectable grades so my performance hung in the balance. I had squeaked by on my part of the deal and Dad came through like a champion. Dad informed us that he had purchased tickets for the three of us to the Sunday afternoon doubleheader with the New York Yankees. This would be my first doubleheader at Comiskey Park. We rose early on Sunday morning and prepared ourselves for a day at the ball yard. As we piled into the two-door Mercury with the windows rolled down and the fresh air blowing in our faces, we set out with joyful anticipation. We knew we were close to the ball yard as the smell of the stock yards became overpowering. As the light standards loomed on the horizon, we knew we were getting close. We parked the car in the yard of a coal supply company and made our way under the railroad tracks to the Park.

Our seats were in the second row of the lower right field bleachers. As we settled in, I couldn't help but think back to the first trip that my brother and I had made with my Dad to Comiskey Park. It was two years earlier, and at the age of seven I had a hard time sitting still despite my love for the game. On that disastrous day, we also had seats in the right field bleachers to watch the Sox take on the Detroit Tigers, my father's favorite team. The game was barely two innings old and I asked my dad if it was time to go home. My brother and I persisted with this inquisition for another two innings until my dad finally grew weary of our complaints and grabbed us up and headed to the car. He was so angry that the sweat was sizzling on his forehead as we silently made our way back to the car. To make matters worse, despite repeated warnings of danger, my fingers got slammed in the car door. The only sound in the car on the trip home was my pathetic little whimpers as I nursed my aching digits. Needless to say, all of that was in the distant past as we settled into our seats for the twin bill against the Yankees.

Early Wynn and Dick Donovan were called upon by manager Lopez to face the Bronx Bombers. Wynn received an incredible display of long ball support to secure his 10th victory of the season. Al Smith, Sherman Lollar, Earl Battey and Bubba Phillips all went deep in support of Wynn in his 9-2 triumph. Lollar's two-run shot in the sixth inning was the game-winner. Rookie Jim McAnany made a defensive impact in his first game with the parent club. His throw from left field gunned down Bill Skowron as he attempted to score the game's first run in the second inning. Al Smith had an opportunity to regain his position in the starting lineup and came up big with several solid at-bats. Commencing in early June, Al Lopez had inserted Jim Rivera into the outfield rotation. Smith began to play sparingly as Simpson, Doby and Callison received the majority of the playing time in the other outfield spot.

Dick Donovan won the second half of the doubleheader 4-2, as he went eight and 1/3 innings. The White Sox knocked Yankee starter Don Larsen from the game in the first inning as Sherman

74

Lollar once again displayed home run magic in his bat. Lollar drove in Fox and Torgeson with his three-run line shot for the game-winner. Donovan gave up a run in the eighth and another in the ninth before getting relief help from Turk Lown for the final two outs of the game. The White Sox had turned the Yankees lethal weapon-the home run-against them to win the last three encounters, giving the Sox a 6-5 edge in the season series. Once again, the South Siders needed the doubleheader sweep to stay within one game of Cleveland as the Indians followed suit on Sunday by beating Boston 5-4 and 1-0 to maintain their league lead.

The White Sox seemed to be hitting stride with timely hitting and improved starting pitching. Chicago began to look forward to a very important four-game series in Cleveland starting Tuesday. The opening match pitted Billy Pierce against Cleveland's new found ace, Cal McLish. McLish had previously started two games against the White Sox during the year with only one decision-a 3-1 victory over Dick Donovan at Comiskey Park on May 8. Pierce had defeated the Indians in the two prior encounters with them earlier in the season..

Tuesday night McLish was almost untouchable as he twirled a 3-1, four hit masterpiece before a crowd of 23,416 in massive Municipal Stadium. Pierce pitched well but his record slipped below .500 to a season worst 8-9. In the defeat, Pierce gave up a two-run inside the park home run to Vic Power and a solo shot to Rocky Colavito.

The loss completed Chicago's month of June at 14-14, enough for a second place spot two games behind Cleveland. Baltimore held the third position, three and 1/2 games behind. New York and Detroit were tied for fourth, four games out. Washington trailed in sixth place, eight games off the pace. Kansas City was fading, slipping to seventh place, nine games in arrears. And Boston was in the cellar, nine and 1/2 games behind the leader.

CHAPTER FOUR

Winning the Close Ones

THE DOG DAYS OF SUMMER WERE FAST APPROACHING. THE CHICAGO record stood at 39 wins against 33 losses. At the halfway point of the season Chicago's overall winning percentage of .5417, if continued for the remainder of the year, would project a total of only 83 victories. Unless there developed a complete collapse of the quality of play of the other leaders in the American League, Chicago would need to catch fire to make a serious run at the flag.

Chicago's club was built upon speed, pitching and defense. Al Lopez preferred that approach to the game and the brain trust of the team had aggregated players, via trade or development in the farm system, who fit that profile. Chicago's home playing field was conducive to that type of game as well. Comiskey Park, located at 35th Street and Shields Avenue, opened in 1910. The stadium was almost completely double-tiered in 1927, increasing its seating capacity to 46,550. The only part of the ballpark that did not have a second level of seating was the center field bleacher area. However, by 1959 the area above the bleachers was dominated by a massive scoreboard. This design resulted in a fairly well enclosed playing field in which prevailing winds were stunted by the stadium superstructure. Comiskey Park was symmetrical. The distance down each foul line, from home plate to the wall, was exactly 352 feet. The power alleys to the left and right of center field were 375 feet from the plate. The fabric and metal framed wall in dead center field was a distance of 415 feet. With the exception of the bullpen fence in center field, the outfield walls were eight feet high and made of concrete. There was no padding on the walls. The White Sox had excellent speed in the outfield. Jim Landis had developed into possibly the best defensive center fielder in the game. His instincts, speed and arm strength were perfectly suited to the cavernous center field area of Comiskey Park. Don Gutteridge likened Landis in this fashion: " He was like a race horse. When the ball was hit, it was like opening the gate and he would get to the ball." Pitching coach Ray Berres seconded that opinion and added "Landis was so fleet footed he would consistently hold doubles and triples to singles with his speed and his arm. Those things did not show up in the statistics but they made the difference in many ball games." Jim Rivera, Jim McAnany and Johnny Callison were excellent outfielders with speed as well. The infield grass was kept rather long, and the basepaths were fast. The first and third base lines were slightly tapered toward the center of the infield. The overall condition of the infield was tailored to Chicago's strengths both on offense and defense. The bat control and speed of Aparicio, Fox, Phillips and Landis took advantage of the slow infield grass and friendly foul lines. Once on base Aparicio, Landis, Phillips, Fox and Rivera were adept in going from first to third on a single, taking the extra base and in stealing bases. On the defensive front, the long infield grass would slow down ground balls which enabled Aparicio, Phillips and Fox to take advantage of their speed and quickness to make more plays. Quality arm strength would then allow them to finish the play. The stadium and the Chicago players were well matched.

The White Sox first game in July was the continuation of their brief two-game series with the Cleveland Indians. Chicago had dropped the opener, 3-1, on Tuesday and now had to beat the Indians to gain a split of the series. Jim "Mudcat" Grant went to the hill for Cleveland. Barry Latman started for Chicago. Latman had won his last start and was trying to make it two in a row. Latman pitched well through five innings, but was relieved by Gerry Staley after giving up a leadoff home run to Cleveland's Tito Francona in the sixth inning. Latman departed with a 5-3 advantage. The lead had been built on the strength of Aparicio's two-run triple to right center in the second, Lollar's bad hop single in the third, and Torgeson's seventh home run of the year in the fourth. The deciding run came home as Jim Landis scored Aparicio with a sacrifice fly in the ninth inning. After Cleveland scored two runs in the ninth, Staley was relieved by Turk Lown. Lown retired the last three Cleveland hitters on routine ground balls to preserve the 6-5 victory for Latman.

The next stop on the road trip was Detroit. The brief two-game series was scheduled for Thursday and Friday. The first game was a slugfest with Detroit scoring nine runs on nine hits and Chicago tallying seven runs on 13 hits. Chicago starter Bob Shaw was cuffed for four hits and three runs in four innings of work. Shaw was handed his third loss of the campaign as he departed trailing 3-0. The lethal blow to Chicago was Charlie Maxwell's eighth inning grand slam home run off reliever Rudolfo Arias. While the Sox managed a five-run, ninth-inning rally punctuated by Al Smith's grand slam home run, they could not overcome Detroit's lead.

In the second and final game of the series, on July 3, Early Wynn opposed Detroit's Jim Bunning in the battle of the All-Stars. Both of these right-handed aces would be representing the American League in the 1959 All-Star Game to be played in Pittsburgh the following week. Wynn was wild as he walked five Tigers and gave up four hits before departing in the sixth inning trailing 4-3. Gerry Staley relieved Wynn and was the beneficiary of single runs by Chicago in the seventh and eighth innings. Staley tired in the ninth as Jim Wilson reached him for a home run to deadlock the game at five. Turk Lown was summoned by Al Lopez and closed the door on Detroit. In the top of the 10th inning, Al Smith scorched a Tom Morgan full count offering to the farthest reaches of the left field upper deck for the 6-5 game-winner, giving Chicago their eighth win out of ten extra inning decisions on the year. Al Smith provided the game-winning hit in four of those victories. The Sox collected 12 hits on the day with Aparicio, Fox, Lollar and Torgeson collecting two apiece. Lollar and Torgeson also had two RBIs each. Turk Lown was credited with the victory.

Chicago's next stop was Kansas City for a three-game series beginning with a doubleheader on Independence Day. The Pale Hose won the first game of the big holiday doubleheader 7-4, but dropped the second 8-3. A crowd of 18,884 turned out to witness what turned into a long ball contest. A total of seven home runs left the Park in the twin bill, three by the White Sox and four by the Athletics. In the opener, Chicago's Dick Donovan was hammered and departed the game in the fourth inning trailing 4-2. Bob Shaw came on in relief. Shaw had pitched only four innings himself when he last appeared in a losing effort against Detroit on Thursday. But on this day he was untouchable, giving up only one hit in five and 1/3 innings. Shaw's teammates rallied for two runs in the sixth and three runs in the seventh to present Shaw with his seventh victory in ten decisions. Bubba Phillips and Johnny Romano went deep, back-to-back, in the sixth frame. Sherman Lollar's two-run homer in the seventh inning put Chicago ahead to stay. Chicago's 17 hit attack featured a five hit, one RBI effort by Jim Landis, and a four hit, two RBI game by recent call up Jim

McAnany. Every non-pitcher in the lineup got at least one hit. Nellie Fox's two hits gave him 104 on the year. Fox's .329 batting standard placed him fourth in the league in hitting behind Harvey Kuenn and Al Kaline of Detroit, and Pete Runnels of Boston.

Chicago was never in the second game as Billy Pierce went only two and 1/3 innings and collected his 10th loss of the year. Kansas City scored early and often, jumping out to a 5-0 advantage after three innings. Rudolfo Arias had another poor performance in relief as he was pummeled with back-to-back home runs by Dick Williams and Roger Maris in the fifth. Chicago managed only eight hits, three by Al Smith and two by Jim McAnany. The doubleheader split dropped the South Siders two games behind first-place Cleveland.

In the Sunday afternoon finale of the current road trip, Chicago prevailed over Kansas City, 4-3. Barry Latman had another decent start, departing after six innings trailing the Athletics 3-1. Aparicio homered in the eighth inning and Al Smith homered in the ninth to knot the score. In the 10th inning Aparicio singled for his third hit of the day. Luis stole second and scampered home on Nellie Fox's game-winning single. Turk Lown, who had relieved Latman in the seventh, completed four innings of one-hit, no-run baseball to earn the extra-inning victory, his fifth of the season.

Baseball shut down for the 26th mid-summer All-Star classic pitting the favored National League against the American League on Tuesday, July 7. The game was played at Pittsburgh's Forbes Field. Casey Stengel's American League contingent included three White Sox in the starting lineup: Nellie Fox at second, Aparicio at short and Early Wynn on the mound. Rounding out the starting lineup for the junior circuit was Minoso, Kaline and Colavito in the outfield from left to right. Harmon Killebrew was at third with Bill Skowron completing the infield at first. Baltimore's Gus Triandos was behind the plate. All-Star bench support for the American League included Sherman Lollar of Chicago; Ted Williams, Frank Malzone and Pete Runnels from Boston; Mickey Mantle, Yogi Berra and Gil McDougald from New York; Harvey Kuenn from Detroit; Roy Sievers from Washington; and Vic Power from Cleveland. The pitching staff was filled out by Billy Pierce, Whitey Ford, Ryan Duren, Jim Bunning, Hoyt Wilhelm and Bud Daley.

Fred Haney led the National League with Wally Moon, Willie Mays and Hank Aaron in the outfield. The infield starters were Eddie Mathews, Ernie Banks, Johnny Temple and Orlando Cepeda from third to first. The starting battery consisted of Don Drysdale pitching and Del Crandall receiving. National League substitutes included Frank Robinson and Vada Pinson from Cincinnati; Ken Boyer, Stan Musial, Bill White, Joe Cunningham and Hal Smith from St. Louis; and Dick Groat, Bill Mazeroski and Smokey Burgess from Pittsburgh. Roy Face, Don Elston, Johnny Antonelli, Gene Conley, Warren Spahn and Lew Burdette joined Drysdale on the pitching staff.

The game was broadcast over the National Broadcasting Company radio and television network. Radio coverage was handled by Curt Gowdy and Mel Allen. Television play-by-play was entrusted to Jack Brickhouse of Chicago and Bob Prince of Pittsburgh.

In a thrilling battle that left the fans hanging on the edge of their seats the National League prevailed. Its two-run, eighth-inning rally off losing pitcher Whitey Ford provided the final 5-4 margin of victory for the senior circuit. Don Drysdale pitched three perfect innings to open the contest for the Nationals. Drysdale was selected the game's "Outstanding" player by the sports writers. Willie Mays' triple over the head of Harvey Kuenn drove in the winning run. The 1959 season would be the first year that major league baseball experimented by scheduling two All-Star Games. The second game would take place in early August in Los Angeles, California.

In the White Sox first contest following the All-Star break, Billy Pierce faced off against Cleveland's Herb Score. The July 9, Thursday night game drew a crowd of 36,742. Pierce stopped his own personal three-game losing streak by stifling the Indians 4-3. The key hit for the White Sox was Bubba Phillips' home run in the bottom of the sixth inning. To that point in the season, the White Sox had won 17 out of their 21 one-run decisions. Pitching coach Ray Berres characterized 1959 as the "Nervous Stomach Season" because of all the tight games the South Siders experienced. The win allowed Chicago to pick up a game on Cleveland, reducing the Indians lead to only one game.

The second game of the series was under the Comiskey Park lights and drew an even larger crowd of 41,588. Early Wynn's record slipped to 11 and six as Cleveland pounded Wynn and relievers Staley, Lown and Shaw for 17 hits. Colavito and Francona each had three RBIs for the victorious Indians. The twice rain delayed contest lasted three hours and 20 minutes before Cal McLish was awarded the 8-4 victory, reinstating the Indians' two-game lead.

The South Siders' weekend plans included hosting the Kansas City Athletics with a single game on Saturday, July 11, and a Sunday doubleheader. In earlier meetings on the season, the seventh place Athletics gave the Sox trouble, winning eight of 13 encounters. Within a period of two weeks, I had the opportunity to make my second trip of the season to Comiskey Park to see the White Sox for the Saturday game. The trip was courtesy of Bill Veeck and the ball club as they sponsored one of several Little League days at the Park. It was a perplexing task, loading several hundred boys aged nine through twelve on buses and transporting them from the far south side of Chicago to Comiskey Park. I was looking forward to this event, as it was my first year to participate. I had visited the ball yard on other occasions, but never in uniform, and never with several thousand other uniformed lads from around the city. I glanced at the paper the night before and knew that Chicago was scheduled to start Barry Latman. This was the first time I would be able to see this rookie pitch. We loaded up on the buses and completed our journey to the Park without incident. I was proud of my uniform, even though it was several sizes too big for me. My team, the "Falcons", was emblazoned across my chest in block letters. The heavy wool uniform did come in handy as the day was rather cool and cloudy. We paraded in mass from the bus to the upper deck grandstand in left field. The crowd was not very large. As it turned out only about 17,705 walked through the turnstiles of which 7,346 actually paid to see the game. As I strolled around the Park that day with my friends, I was able to point out to them the childhood home of my grandfather. As we stood on the second deck catwalk near the scoreboard the neighborhood of Armour Square was less than a stone's throw away.

Little League baseball was the only organized sport available to the boys in our community. The league playing fields were located at 115th and Homan Avenue, approximately four blocks from home, and consisted of four rustic diamonds. Two of the fields were for the Little League, one for the Minor League and the other for Babe Ruth League. Little League was for boys aged nine through twelve. Minor League was for younger boys, age eight, and older boys aged nine through twelve who were baseball impaired. The Babe Ruth League catered to ages 13 through 15. The games were played throughout the summer on weekday evenings and on Saturday and Sunday. The Little League was divided into an American and National division, with six teams in each division. The fields were very crude. The infield was dirt, no grass and plenty of rocks and pebbles. The outfield was basically weeds with the occasional sprig of grass thrown in. The pitcher's mound was only slightly raised, barely enough to get leverage. For the 1959 season, the National Little League Association changed its rules and moved the mound distance back two feet, from 44 feet to 46 feet, in an effort to protect the players. The batter's box was atrocious. The box for right-handed hitters was depressed several inches from constant use, as the league was predominantly right-handed. Right-handed hitters were literally hitting out of a hole. The fields were quite typical of those in other parts of the city and were maintained by volunteer labor. In spite of their condition, these diamonds were the venue on which we established our love and understanding of the game. Each year players would tryout in the spring. Team managers would then draft their players for the upcoming season. At age nine, I was drafted by the Falcons.

The Falcons competed in the American division against the Wildcats, Owls, Panthers, Robins and Tigers. The Falcons stressed fundamentals. We practiced endless hours in the field, with each position player exposed to every conceivable game situation. Everyone was expected to learn the proper movement and positioning of every other player in all game situations. We learned how to hit the cutoff man, who to backup on all plays, what base to throw to in each situation-all the defensive fundamentals. From an offensive standpoint, however, our manager's philosophy was you were on your own. We rarely had batting practice and offensive output was a function of our own natural abilities and good fortune. Fortunately, most of us possessed an ample supply of both. Each year the champions of the American and National divisions would play a three-game series to determine our version of world champions. Annually an All-Star team was selected from each division and they attempted to climb the single elimination ladder of competition to the Little League World Series. In 1959 the competition for the crown was slightly less difficult as two-time champ Monterrey, Mexico was barred from the 1959 competition. The disqualification of the Mexican team was for their failure to comply with the rules that stipulated that only players from a predetermined geographical area could play on a team.

The game we attended that day proved to be well worth the trip. Barry Latman started and pitched his strongest game of the season. The rookie right-hander allowed only four Athletic hits in winning his third game of the year, 8-3. Latman also scored two of Chicago's eight runs and had three of their 12 hits. Aparicio and Fox continued their assault on American League pitching as they combined for four hits and five RBIs. Fox's fifth-inning double plated Latman and Aparicio with the deciding runs. Roger Maris drove in all of the Kansas City runs with a sacrifice fly and a double. The return bus trip home was a celebration of victory. I was impressed with Latman. It was hard for me to imagine that the stature of Aparicio and Fox could grow any further in my mind. The prominence of their role on this club exploded after witnessing firsthand their offensive and defensive magic. It was also the first time that I witnessed Roger Maris perform. I was impressed with the young left-hander's swing and his prowess in the outfield.

The White Sox made it three in a row on Sunday with a double-header sweep of the Athletics to even the season series between the two clubs at 8-8. In the opener, Chicago scored all five of its runs in the first inning off of Bud Daley, with Jim McAnany's three-run, game-winning triple highlighting the attack. Dick Donovan started for Chicago and was ineffective and departed in the second inning. Ray Moore took over and was awarded the 5-3 victory with the assistance of three no-hit innings of relief help from Gerry Staley.

Al Smith had three of Chicago's hits with Landis and McAnany responsible for two hits apiece.

In the nightcap, the White Sox scored four runs in the first. The barrage was capped off by Al Smith's two-run rifle shot to the lower deck in left field. McAnany again slammed a bases-loaded triple in the fifth inning pushing Chicago's lead to 9-0. McAnany's hit proved to be the game-winner as Kansas City rallied for seven runs in the final four frames. McAnany had been spectacular since his June 27 call up from Indianapolis. The rookie was hitting .387 with 11 RBIs. McAnany capped off his day by robbing Jerry Lumpe of extra bases in the eighth inning. The rookie's diving grab on the right field foul line prevented the winning runs from scoring. The White Sox scorched three Athletic pitchers for 13 hits, led by Lollar with three and Aparicio, Smith and Romano with two each. Lollar continued to be a run producer as he had three RBIs in the game. Bob Shaw left the game after six innings when he twisted his knee. Shaw claimed the victory, his eighth of season against only three losses. Lown and Staley, showing signs of overwork, permitted Kansas City five runs on seven hits over the final three innings.

Jim McAnany had a tremendous year in 1958 for the White Sox affiliate in Colorado Springs, Colorado. He appeared in 119 games and collected 175 hits, scored 108 runs and drove in 117. His .400 batting average, tops in the minor leagues, included 29 doubles, one triple and 26 home runs. McAnany, born September 4, 1938, was signed by Chicago after completing his freshman year at the University of Southern California. The California native proved to be a more than adequate replacement for the Sox other highly touted rookie outfielder, Johnny Callison.

The weekend sweep of Kansas City provided Chicago with an excellent send off on its seven game road trip. The short eastern swing was scheduled to take the South Siders to Boston for a three game set at Fenway Park and then on to New York for a four-game weekend series with the fourth-place Yankees. Cleveland was also scheduled to play the same two clubs in reverse order as they start out with New York before taking on Boston.

The boys in the neighborhood, including myself, took advantage of the White Sox day off on Monday. We scheduled our first meaningful intra-neighborhood pick up softball game of the season. The day was hot and our spirits were high, as we assembled on the school playground of the "Portables" for the battle. Stanley, the custodial engineer for the school, was responsible for maintaining the buildings and the grounds during the summer months as well. This man seemed to adjust to the rhythm of our activities and could sense when we were to play a meaningful game. As the teams took the field, I surveyed the landscape. The mongrel guard dog came to focus, as I calculated his demeanor for the day. Stanley's face appeared at a window. Our eyes met and he quickly attempted to act as though he were at a task. It was clear that he enjoyed our competition and appreciated the intensity and emotion that we invested in the game.

On this particular afternoon, our 1959 addition of the Trumbull and Homan Avenue warriors, the "Troman Terrors", were taking on the lads from 113th Street. We were able to muster our best players for the game that would decide bragging rights for the neighborhood. Rich and Jerry Doran, Dave and Tim Shaughnessy, Mickey O'Connor and myself were there. We were also able to entice my brother Tony, Bud Tracy and Billy Fitzpatrick, our more senior athletes, to join the fray. The day was sweltering and the time was high noon. The sun reflected off the gravel of the playing surface with the intensity of a furnace blast. Our competition was exceedingly difficult. The battle lived up to all expectations. Every pitch was important. During the course of the game, Dave

Shaughnessy, Bud Tracy and I made run saving fielding gems. Everyone on both sides was sacrificing their bodies on every difficult chance. Stanley was now watching unabashedly, cheering and encouraging our exploits on the field. The Doran brothers contributed several key hits to our attack, as did Bud Tracy and I. I ripped one into Gussies' dog pen to give us an early lead. It seemed that even the dog was caught up in the competition as he showed absolutely no aggression when we retrieved the ball. At the beginning of the game we had established the ground rules. Everyone in the region was familiar with my brother Tony's skill in baseball and softball. Accordingly, in important games such as this one, Tony was required to bat left-handed. Tony, a natural right-hander, could blast the ball out of any park from the right side. From the left side he was somewhat handicapped.

The game moved into the top of the final inning. As hard as we had fought, we found ourselves behind by two runs. The power of their lineup stared us in the eye. My brother made a diving stop at shortstop and fired the ball from his knees to nip the runner at first for the first out. The second batter slammed a double to right center field. Bud Tracy playing second base fielded a smash behind the bag to prevent a run from scoring. Runners were at first and third, with one down. The next hitter cracked a line shot to our pitcher Rich Doran. Two were down. The next batter scorched a line drive to the wall in left center field. I broke with the crack of the bat and as I hit the chain link fence in left center, I jumped and speared the ball in my right hand, ending the rally.

We still trailed by two runs, but the results from the top of the inning changed momentum in our favor. Bud Tracy led off with a single. Jerry Doran followed with a single. With no outs and two runners aboard, my brother Tony approached the plate from the left side. The drama of the moment couldn't have been more intense.

Tony quickly turned our two-run deficit into a one-run victory as he tagged the first pitch 50 feet over the right field wall. The home run sent us dancing with glee as the 113th Street gang was sent home with heads hung in defeat. I believe our personal experience in games such as these made us appreciate more intensely the season long drama that was unfolding at Comiskey Park.

The White Sox drilled Boston 7-3 to open the series on Tuesday July 14. The victory coupled with Whitey Ford's 1-0 shutout of Cleveland, pulled Chicago to within percentage points of the Indians. Billy Pierce lasted for 8 and 1/3 innings giving up ten of the 11 Boston hits and all three of their runs. Pierce evened his season record at 10-10 as Chicago overcame an early 2-1 deficit by scoring three runs in the top of the fourth inning to take the lead for good. The rally started with singles by Landis and Lollar. Landis scored as Boston third baseman Frank Malzone threw high to second on Al Smith's grounder, leaving both Lollar and Smith safely aboard. A sacrifice fly by Romano set the table for McAnany. McAnany's sharp single to center scored both Lollar and Smith with what proved to be the winning run. Chicago's 13-hit attack included two hits each by Fox, Landis, Lollar, Romano and McAnany. Fox extended his hitting streak to 11 games and Romano clubbed his third home run of the season. Sherman Lollar again started at first base. Manager Lopez wanted to have both Lollar and Romano's right-handed bat in the lineup.

Wednesday night's game with the Red Sox was scuttled as day long rain showers drenched Boston. The game was rescheduled for Thursday as part of a doubleheader. In the opening game of the doubleheader, Dick Donovan won his sixth game of the season as Chicago outlasted Boston 4-3. Donovan pitched seven strong innings while walking two and striking out four. Staley provided two innings of no-hit relief to earn the save. Jim McAnany continued his red hot streak, raising his batting average to .396 with three of Chicago's nine hits. Landis, Torgeson, Donovan and Lollar had RBIs. Lollar's eighth inning double drove in the game-winner.

In the second game of the twin bill, the BoSox ended Chicago's winning streak at five as they defeated Ray Moore, 5-4. Moore relieved starter Barry Latman with two out in the fifth inning. The White Sox climbed into a 4-3 lead in the sixth inning on a Phillips single, a Moore double, and Aparicio's sacrifice fly ball. Moore allowed a run in the sixth and the deciding run in the seventh as he was charged with his sixth loss of the season. Romano and Fox each had three hits in the losing cause. Fox ran his hitting streak to 13 games and his season batting average to .335 with his performance. Both Staley and Lown were called upon again in the final one and 2/3 innings.

The doubleheader split vaulted Chicago into first place by one game. Cleveland was swept out of the top spot for the first time in over a month as they dropped 7-5 and 4-0 decisions to New York. Mantle clubbed his 19th home run of the year to win the opener for New York in ten innings. Enos Slaughter and Hank Bauer home runs provided Bobby Shantz the support as he shutout Cleveland in the nightcap.

The White Sox rolled into the Bronx on July 17 for the 12th meeting between these two clubs on the season. Chicago had won the last three. A crowd of 42,020 was treated to a display of great pitching and spectacular defense from both combatants. Early Wynn held the Yankees to one Ralph Terry single through eight innings. Ralph Terry was even better as he held the Pale Hose hitless until Jim McAnany led off the ninth with a single to center field. McAnany was safe at second as he beat Terry's throw to the bag after fielding Early Wynn's bunt. An Aparicio sacrifice bunt and an intentional pass to Nellie Fox loaded the bases. Jim Landis then cracked the game-winner, a line drive single between first and second scoring McAnany and Wynn. The Yankees managed one more single off Wynn in the ninth. Spectacular defensive plays were made by Landis, Fox, Goodman and Torgeson. Landis robbed Mickey Mantle of extra bases in the fourth as he raced to the fence and made a lunging back handed stab of Mantle's long drive. With the 2-0 victory, the White Sox maintained their one game lead as Cleveland downed Boston.

Bob Shaw faced Don Larsen as the two clubs went toe-to-toe again on Saturday, July 18. Both pitchers performed exceptionally well as Shaw prevailed over Larsen in this 2-1 thriller. The Yankees had Shaw in trouble in the second inning as they scored their first run. An outstanding throw by Al Smith prevented further damage, as he nailed Hector Lopez at the plate when he attempted to score from second on a single by Bobby Richardson. Chicago amassed 11 hits, three by Smith and two each by Aparicio, Fox and Shaw. Jim McAnany's ground rule double scored Al Smith for Chicago's first run in the fourth inning. Bob Shaw chased Billy Goodman home with the second run of the inning on his single to left, which proved to be the game-winner. Shaw tired in the ninth and was relieved by Gerry Staley with two outs and the bases loaded. Staley threw one pitch, a sinker low and away, that Hector Lopez hit into a game ending, Fox to Aparicio to Torgeson, double play.

The win enabled Chicago to maintain its position in the standings as Cleveland edged Boston 7-5 in 13 innings. The White Sox were now seven and 1/2 games on top of the Yankees.

Chicago selected Barry Latman and Billy Pierce as its starters for a Sunday doubleheader as Casey Stengel countered with Whitey Ford and Eli Grba for the Yankees. In Latman's previous nine starts, Chicago had won six with Latman getting credit for three of those victories. Latman was tagged for a two-run home run in the first inning by 43-year-old Enos "Country" Slaughter. Latman gave up another run in the fourth and departed trailing 3-2. The Yankees scored three more runs including another two-run homer by Slaughter, to seal Latman's defeat. The 6-2 victory was the 10th of the year for New York's Whitey Ford as he allowed only six hits and two unearned runs.

Eli Grba won the second game of the doubleheader 6-4 before the crowd of 57,057. In the first win of his major league career, Grba gave up only three hits. The porous Yankee defense contributed to Chicago scoring four unearned runs, but Bauer and Mantle both went deep for New York to preserve the Yankee victory. Billy Pierce managed to last only four innings as his record dipped to 10-11 with the loss. The doubleheader loss coupled with Cleveland's doubleheader split with Boston dropped Chicago into second place.

Chicago returned home from its four win, three loss road trip, July 21, stinging from Sunday's double defeat at the hands of the Yankees. The White Sox were looking forward to a long home-stand with Boston, Baltimore, New York and Washington sched-uled to visit Comiskey Park. Dick Donovan took the hill for Chicago on Tuesday against the Red Sox. Donovan was on his game. Donovan gave up only six hits on his way to a 2-1 master-piece over Boston and Tom Brewer. The big right-hander won his third start in a row, bringing his season record to 7-5 with this complete game victory. Jim Landis blooped a seventh-inning sin-gle that scored Aparicio with the go-ahead run. The White Sox managed nine hits on the day, including three by Lollar and two each by rookies Cash and McAnany.

In the eighth inning of Tuesday's game, Vic Wertz pinch hit for Boston's shortstop, Don Buddin. Wertz reached base on a single. Manager, Billy Jurges, inserted Elizah Jerry "Pumpsie" Green into the lineup as a pinch runner for Wertz. Green stayed in the game to play shortstop in the ninth. Green had been called up that day from Boston's Minneapolis farm club. With his appearance, Green became the first black man to perform for the Boston Red Sox in a regular season game. This event completed the process of integration in major league baseball more than a decade after Jackie Robinson and Larry Doby became the first black ballplayers in the National League and the American League, respectively. The Boston Red Sox became the last major league team to have a black player on its roster. In April, Tom Yawkey, president of the Red Sox, had been called upon to respond to questions concerning charges of racial discrimination by the club. The Massachusetts Commission Against Discrimination had responded to charges made by the Boston chapter of the National Association for the Advancement of Colored People that the Red Sox had been guilty of racial bias in sending Green to the minors in the spring of 1959.

Chicago was getting contributions from nearly everyone on the roster. Pitching coach Berres properly characterized the team by saying "It seems different players would step forward and do things at the right psychological moment. Everyone pulled for one another." Don Gutteridge, the fiery first base and infield coach, said "Chicago had a great clubhouse in 1959. Players had respect for each other and camaraderie. Everyone knew what was expected of them. When one guy didn't get the job done someone else would step up." Bob Shaw echoed that judgment, " All the men were down to earth, regular guys who played hard every day." Landis highlighted the team's cohesiveness by stating the club's strength was " how hard we played as a group to win those tough ball games. The character of the team had just as much or more to do with our success as did our talent."

The man that set the tone for the team was the field general, Al Lopez. Lopez became manager of the Chicago White Sox on October 30, 1956, replacing Marty Marion. Lopez's major league managing career began in Cleveland in 1951. After managing effectively in the minor leagues for three seasons, Lopez took over Cleveland's helm and led the Tribe to 570 victories in a six year period. The "Senor's" overall winning percentage of .6129 with Cleveland resulted in five second place finishes and one record setting first place finish in 1954. In that year, Cleveland won 111 games as they took the American League flag back to the shores of Lake Erie.

Alfonso Ramon Lopez was born on August 20, 1908 in Tampa, Florida. His major league playing career commenced in 1928 with the Brooklyn Dodgers. The 5-foot 11-inch, 170-pound catcher had a career that spanned 19 seasons and a record setting 1,918 games behind the plate. Lopez played his entire career in the National League with Brooklyn, Boston and Pittsburgh except for 61 games in the 1947 season that he played with Cleveland in the American League. Lopez, a defensive wizard, accumulated 1,547 hits in 5,916 plate appearances for a career .261 batting average. He drove in 652 runs while scoring 613 times himself.

After he joined Chicago in the fall of 1956, Lopez led the club to a second place finish in both 1957 (90W-64L) and 1958 (82W-72L), finishing behind the New York Yankees on both occasions. Al Lopez was one of the most well liked and highly respected tacticians in the game. Lopez brought together a great combination of baseball knowledge and the ability to manage and motivate people. Ray Berres, Chicago's pitching coach before and after Lopez arrived, felt that "Lopez was always a step ahead of everybody in strategy. He had a great knowledge of the game. He also had a great knowledge of his players' capabilities and expectations. Lopez was all business when the game started. He was very strict with his pitchers. He played the game several innings ahead of all others." Berres indicated that Lopez had the final say on handling pitchers. Berres was also recognized as one of the best pitching coaches of his day. He had an outstanding reputation as a teacher of pitching mechanics. " I spent all of my time in the bullpen" said Berres. "I could see from that vantage point when pitchers would slip out of their groove mechanically. I maintained strict notes on each pitch and recognized when the pitcher's delivery started to go bad."

Lopez surrounded himself with a strong, experienced group of coaches. In addition to Ray Berres, Lopez had John Cooney as his bench coach, Tony Cuccinello as his third base coach and Don Gutteridge as his coach on first base. Al Smith, who played for Lopez in Cleveland in 1954 and again in Chicago, was a solid contributor in the 1959 season. Smith felt that "Lopez surrounded himself with coaches who knew the players and how to get the most out of them." Gutteridge commented that Lopez made certain that "Everybody knew what Lopez expected of them, coaches and players alike. Lopez would talk to his coaches and let them know if one of the players needed instruction. The coaches would then take the players aside and communicate with them privately about the problem." Jim Landis had a great deal of respect for his manager because, according to Landis, " [Lopez] knew how to handle me, he knew how to handle each character and how to treat them." Landis went on to describe a major reason why the 1959 club had such camaraderie and cohesion, "Lopez wouldn't permit troublemakers in the clubhouse. He could tolerate free spirits but not troublemakers." Landis also offered his observation on another factor that influenced the 1959 Chicago club: "Money was the least concern. Most of the guys were there to play and really wanted to play on a winning team. Money issues were really secondary." The 1959 Chicago White Sox had excellent leadership, strong technical advice and a group of hard-working ball players that were motivated by respect for each other and respect for winning.

On July 22, in the second game of this extended homestand, Early Wynn took the mound against Boston's Jerry Casale. Early Wynn pitched through the seventh inning and departed as his teammates tied the score at four all. Wynn gave up home runs to both Ted Williams and his mound opponent Jerry Casale. Chicago's winning run scored in the eighth inning as Sherman Lollar slapped a single to left field to drive in Nellie Fox. Both Fox and Lollar had three hits in Chicago's 13 hit assault. Turk Lown pitched the final two frames to earn his sixth victory of the season. The White Sox moved ahead of Cleveland by a full game as the Indians lost to New York by a count of 8-5. The final game of the three-game series with Boston was washed out by rain.

On Friday, July 24, the Baltimore Orioles arrived in Chicago for four games. The pitching lineup for Chicago had Pierce, Shaw, Wynn and Donovan scheduled to face Baltimore's Wilhelm, O'Dell, Portocarrero and Pappas. Prior to this series, Chicago had only faced Baltimore nine times on the season, winning five and losing four. Of those five victories over the Orioles, Donovan had two, with the others going to Pierce, Wynn and Shaw.

Playing before a Friday night crowd of 29,274, Billy Pierce evened his record at 11-11 with a seven-hit, complete-game outing. The White Sox had five hits, with Nellie Fox getting three of them as he raised his season batting average to .337. Baltimore's Hoyt Wilhelm held the South Siders scoreless until the eighth inning when McAnany worked Wilhelm for a leadoff walk and came around to score on Nellie Fox's long triple to right center field. With the game tied and one out in the last half of the ninth inning,

Al Smith crushed Wilhelm's first pitch into the lower left field seats for the game-winning home run. The 2-1 victory was Chicago's 22nd triumph in one-run games as it remained 1/2 game on top of Cleveland.

Cleveland continued to put pressure on the front running White Sox as they stomped Washington 8-1. Cal McLish improved his season record to 13-3 with his seven-hit complete game performance.

Saturday's crowd at Comiskey Park included free passes for strike-idled steel industry workers, honor students and Pony Leaguers, along with 12,562 paying customers. The White Sox and Orioles put on a four hour and five minute, 17 inning performance. Chicago trailed the Orioles 2-1 entering the ninth inning. Starters Bob Shaw and Billy O'Dell had been outstanding. Sherman Lollar sent the game into extra innings when he hit an O'Dell slider into the seats in left for his 13th home run of the year. With the game knotted 2-2, Turk Lown took over for Shaw and pitched six innings of three hit, shutout ball to earn his seventh win of the year. The White Sox loaded the bases in the 17th inning on singles by Landis and Lollar and an intentional walk to Al Smith. Pinch hitter Harry Simpson ended the suspense by hammering a long single to right field that drove in pinch runner Sammy Esposito with the game-winning run. Gerry Staley recently reflected that, "as a team, if we went into the late innings with the score tied or we were close, we felt we had the game in the bag. That was the type of mindset that we had." This was Chicago's 23rd one-run victory of the season.

As the White Sox were winning most of the close ones, it appeared the opportunity for democracy was slipping away in Cuba. The revolution in Cuba was drawing the country closer to socialism or communism. In March, the new government initiated the nationalization of the Cuban Telephone Company, an affiliate of International Telephone and Telegraph. Rates for phone service were immediately reduced. In May, Fidel Castro signed the Agrarian Reform Act, which prohibited foreign ownership of land and expropriated all farmlands over 1,000 acres in size. In June, Che Guevara, one of the Cuban revolutionary leaders, made first official contact with the Soviet Union during a meeting in Cairo, Egypt. Fidel Castro supporters in a gun wielding demonstration disrupted a baseball game on July 26 between the Havana Sugar Kings and the Rochester Red Wings. The game, in Havana, was halted as gunfire from the stands sprayed the field. The violence resulted in minor gunshot wounds to Havana shortstop Leo Cardenas and Red Wings coach Frank Verdi.

Early Wynn went after his 13th victory of the year in the opening game of a doubleheader on Sunday, July 26. Wynn proceeded to pitch a complete game, two hitter for the 4-1 victory over Baltimore. Al Smith hit a game-winning, three-run inside the park home run in the fourth inning. Jim Landis once again made a spectacular catch to save the victory. With runners on first and second in the ninth inning, Gus Triandos slammed an Early Wynn offering to deep center field. Landis raced back and, as he was crashing into the wall, reached over the fence to take a three-run homer away from Triandos. The catch was the most spectacular defensive play, in a crucial game deciding situation, that I had ever seen. As I watched on television, my shouts of triumph could be heard a block away.

The White Sox dropped the series finale on July 26 as young Milt Pappas shutout the South Siders on three hits, 4-0. Barry Latman made the start for Chicago replacing Donovan who had a sore shoulder. Latman took the loss, his fourth of the season against three wins. The Indians continued to dominate Washington.

They swept a doubleheader from the Senators 9-0 and 4-3 to move 1/2 game ahead of Chicago in the standings. The lead, however, was short-lived as the Tribe lost to Boston 4-0 on Monday to drop into a first place tie with the idle White Sox.

Tuesday night's matchup between Billy Pierce and the Yankees Ralph Terry drew a weekday crowd of 43,829. The White Sox took a 4-1 advantage into the ninth inning on the strength of Al Smith's two-run home run in the eighth. Smith drove in Fox, who had singled for his third hit of the day, with a rifle shot off of the lower face of the second deck in left field. The home run proved to be decisive as the Yankees rallied in the ninth inning. The Bronx Bombers scored two runs before Pierce struck out Bobby Richardson for the final out of the game. Pierce, winning for the fourth time in his last five starts, improved his record to 12-11 on the season. The victory combined with Cleveland's doubleheader split with Boston propelled Chicago into first place once again, 1/2 game ahead of Cleveland.

On Wednesday, July 29, New York and Chicago battled to a 4-4 tie as the game was postponed after six innings due to rain. The game was tied up when Yogi Berra blasted a two-run home run off Bob Shaw in the top of the sixth inning. The game was rescheduled to August 23. Despite the no-decision, Chicago's lead over Cleveland increased to one full game as Cleveland lost again to the BoSox.

Chicago drew 30,858 fans to the Thursday, July 30, finale of the series with the Yankees as the rains cleared. The afternoon crowd was treated to another sterling performance by the Chicago workhorse Early Wynn. Wynn won his 14th game of the season 3-1, once again going the distance and striking out nine Yankees. Lollar scored the winning run as he trotted home on a single by Billy Goodman in the seventh inning. Aparicio stole his league-leading

32nd base of the year. The loss dropped the Yankees ten and 1/2 games behind Chicago.

On Friday night, July 31, the Washington Senators provided the opposition for Chicago's league-leading White Sox as they opened their last weekend series in July. The White Sox were then scheduled to be on the road through August 16 as they would travel to Baltimore, Washington, Detroit and Kansas City. Barry Latman toed the rubber for Chicago against Pedro Ramos. Latman responded with a four-hit, complete-game victory. The 7-1 triumph was perhaps Latman's best start of the season as he struck out 11 Senators. The game was never in doubt as Chicago scored three runs in both the second and third innings. The defeat was the Senators' 13th in a row. Jim McAnany's single in the second inning drove in Earl Torgeson with Chicago's second run, which proved to be the game-winner. Torgeson, Landis and McAnany had two hits each. One of Torgeson's hits was his seventh home run of the year, a two-run blast to the right field bleachers in the third inning.

The White Sox closed out the month of July with an overall record of 59-40, good enough for first place in the standings. Chicago's spectacular record of 20-7 in July erased the two game lead that Cleveland had held at the end of June. Cleveland, despite its 19-12 record in July, trailed Chicago by one game. It clearly appeared to be settling into a two team race for the pennant. Kansas City was in third, 9 and 1/2 games back. Baltimore was in fourth place, falling 10 games off the pace. The Yankees appeared to be finished as they were in fifth place, ten and 1/2 games back. Detroit trailed by 11 and 1/2, Boston fell to 16 games back, and Washington was deep in the cellar, 17 and 1/2 games behind league-leading Chicago.

CHAPTER FIVE

The Knock Out Punch

CHICAGO OPENED THE MONTH OF AUGUST EXACTLY AS IT HAD CLOSED out July, with a victory over the hapless Washington Senators. Washington's seemingly endless downward spiral continued. The White Sox 2-1 victory represented the Senators' 14th consecutive defeat. Washington received an outstanding pitching performance from Camilo Pascual as the right-hander took a no hitter into the seventh inning before yielding a double to Billy Goodman. Pascual was unable to return to the mound to open the eighth inning due to a sore shoulder. His mound opponent, Ray Moore, pitched a great game for Chicago but trailed 1-0 when he was lifted for a pinch hitter in the eighth inning. Chicago rallied for two ninth-inning runs when Norman Cash and Earl Torgeson scored on a Jim Landis double. Gerry Staley pitched the ninth inning for his third victory of the season.

On August 1, the White Sox optioned Larry Doby to their San Diego farm club. Doby's demotion was a move necessary to provide a position on the roster for an additional starting pitcher. To fill that role, Ken McBride, a right-handed pitcher, was acquired from Chicago's Indianapolis affiliate. These moves were necessary because of Dick Donovan's continued shoulder problems.

Bill Veeck turned over every rock in his efforts to motivate his players. After the game with Washington, he presented Ray Moore with a small puppy as a reward for his efforts in the game. Veeck was certainly a players' owner. Al Smith remembered Veeck as "One of the best men you would ever want to meet. He was all business. If he told you he was going to do a certain thing he did it." Bob Shaw indicated that Veeck made a habit of rewarding players for good performances. After one of Bob's first good outings of the year, Shaw recalled that "Veeck sent me to Marshall Fields to buy a $50 shirt for myself. At that time, I only made about $10,000 a year. I had come from a pretty simple background. My dad was a school teacher and I didn't have a lot of money growing up. Instead of a $50 shirt, I bought five $10 shirts. A $10 shirt was a really nice shirt at that time. Veeck was really irritated that I did not get the $50 shirt." Apparently Veeck's irritation was short-lived as Shaw recalled that later in the season Veeck rewarded him with a $300 custom suit for pitching particularly well in a game. Gerry Staley confirmed Shaw's story, "Veeck was a nice guy to play for; if you had a good game he would send you downtown to get a new suit."

A basic maxim in sports is to hold your own against the good teams and really dominate the lesser teams. Chicago had another opportunity to fulfill the second portion of that maxim as they faced the Senators in a Sunday doubleheader on August 2. The contests would complete the four-game set and the homestand. Billy Pierce started the opener for the Pale Hose and pitched effectively. Pierce had given up only six hits and two runs, but was trailing 2-1, when he departed after eight innings. Fox had singled in Aparicio with the first run of the game in the first inning. Pierce gave up a Faye Throneberry home run in the third and balked in Harmon Killebrew in the fourth to set the stage for another

Chicago come from behind triumph. Turk Lown relieved Pierce and was spanked for three hits in the ninth. Fortunately, Washington did not do any more damage on the scoreboard. Aparicio led off the Chicago ninth inning with a single and scored the tying run as Fox's bunt single was thrown into right field for an error. Smith and Lollar were intentionally walked to fill the bases, setting up a force play at any base. Billy Goodman foiled that strategy, however, as he laced a single over the drawn in outfield for the game-winner. Lown earned his eighth victory of the season as the final score was Chicago three, Washington two.

The second game of the twin bill provided no relief for Washington as they were beaten 9-3 for their 16th loss in a row. Chicago scored three runs in each of the third, fifth and sixth innings as starter Bob Shaw cruised to his 10th victory of the year. Bubba Phillips connected for three hits and two RBIs. Al Smith had two hits and one RBI. The game-winner was Johnny Romano's two-run double in the fifth inning. Staley relieved Bob Shaw in the eighth and retired the final four Washington hitters.

The twin victories capped off an unbelievable homestand. Chicago was dominant as they won 11 games while losing only one and tying one. This surge increased their lead over Cleveland to three full games. At the conclusion of the homestand, Early Wynn, Sherman Lollar, Nellie Fox and Luis Aparicio made their way to Los Angeles for the experimental second All-Star Game of the season. With teams in both leagues focused on their pennant races, it was fair to say that players and managers were not excited about this second interruption of their schedules. Most clubs had settled into pitching rotations that were now being temporarily disrupted by the second All-Star break. The two All-Star Game per season system continued for four years. In 1960, the games were played in Kansas City and New York. In 1961, San Francisco and Boston hosted the affair. Washington and Chicago's Wrigley Field provided the venue for the 1962 All-Star Games. The dual All-Star Game format was deemed a failure by the 1963 season as the mid-summer classic returned to the single game format.

As Chicago battled Cleveland in the race for the American League pennant, the United States and the Soviet Union were in a struggle for supremacy in rocket technology and space exploration. Earlier in the year, the United States successfully launched Discoverer II. The National Aeronautics and Space Administration (NASA) announced the selection of its first group of astronauts. At the insistence of President Eisenhower, these men were drawn from a group of highly trained, well educated military pilots. From a universe of 508 applications received, seven were selected to pioneer our manned space flight program. The group of seven were dubbed the "Mercury Astronauts" and included Alan B. Shepard, John H. Glenn, Jr., Virgil I. Grissom, Donald K. Slayton, Scott M. Carpenter, Walter M. Schirra, Jr., and Gordon L. Cooper, Jr. Each player on the winning team in the 1958 World Series received a World Series bonus of $8,759.10, slightly more than the minimum level of annual compensation for the men being asked to risk their lives in pioneering the exploration of outer space. The initial guidelines for compensation for astronauts varied from $8,330 to $12,770 per year, depending upon the relative qualifications of the man.

On Monday, August 3, the American League defeated the National League 5-3 in the second All-Star Game of the year. The game was played at the Los Angeles Coliseum and drew a National League partisan crowd of 54,982 fans. Yogi Berra's two-run homer and solo shots by Rocky Colavito and Frank Malzone provided the firepower to fuel the junior circuit's victory. The National League received home runs from Frank Robinson and hometown favorite Jim Gilliam of the Los Angeles Dodgers.

The National League Dodgers moved to Los Angeles from Brooklyn in 1958, at the same time the Giants moved from New York to San Francisco. Walter O'Malley and Horace Stoneham conspired to bring major league baseball to the West Coast. This move changed the dynamics of the market penetration and market potential of the game of baseball forever. It would no longer be a game solely dominated by the region east of the Mississippi River. This move would provide the foundation for further American and National League expansion in the years to come. The City of Los Angeles opened its arms wide in support of the Dodgers. The Dodgers opened their inaugural 1958 season playing their games in the makeshift confines of the Los Angeles Coliseum. That stadium, when configured for baseball, had a seating capacity in excess of 90,000. As part of the original inducement to bring the Dodgers from Brooklyn to Los Angeles, the City agreed in part to provide land and infrastructure for a modern $12 million stadium to be located on land in the Chavez Ravine area of the City. A portion of the land in Chavez Ravine was acquired by the City via standard condemnation proceedings. In May, the City had one last legal obstacle to overcome. The last family in Chavez Ravine, the Arechigas, refused to honor the condemnation order to vacate their dwellings. This forced the City administrators to procure an eviction notice. Immediately after the family was formally evicted, bulldozers destroyed the remaining structures as Manuel Arechigas, 72, and his family and their dogs and chickens looked on. The Arechigas family was awarded $10,050 for their property in the condemnation proceedings. The Arechigas' claimed that the fair value of their property was $17,000 and refused the condemnation check. Legal wrangling continued, but the progress of the stadium moved forward.

The White Sox took off for Baltimore on the first leg of their 13 game, four-city road swing. Overall, Chicago had beaten Baltimore eight times earlier this season while losing only five. Chicago's record at Baltimore's Memorial Stadium was 3-2. With Dick Donovan sidelined due to lingering shoulder problems and Early Wynn unavailable because of his two innings of work in Monday's All-Star Game, Al Lopez selected recent call up Ken McBride to start the series opener. McBride, making his major league debut, held Baltimore to just four hits and one run through seven innings of play. The White Sox took the lead in the top of the seventh on the strength of Johnny Romano's pinch hit, two-run home run. Taking a 2-1 advantage into the eighth, McBride loaded the bases with one out. Relievers Turk Lown and Gerry Staley allowed two runs to score on a walk and an infield single. The unearned runs put Baltimore in the lead to stay as the Sox went down harmlessly in the ninth to lose 3-2. Meanwhile, Cleveland beat Washington 8-2 to climb within two games of Chicago.

In Wednesday's doubleheader with Baltimore, the White Sox won the opener 2-0 before dropping the nightcap 7-1. In the opener, Barry Latman twirled a complete game for his fifth win of the season. Latman gave up only three hits, struck out six, and walked one. Jim McAnany drove in Romano with a single for the game-winner in the second inning. Al Smith and Jim McAnany had two hits each. In the day's second game, Early Wynn failed to gain his 15th victory as he was removed in the fourth inning after giving up four runs. The game was a disaster for the White Sox as they walked eight Orioles and committed five errors. Torgeson had a miserable game in the field as he was charged with three errors.

In action Thursday night, August 6, Chicago and Baltimore battled for four hours and five minutes through 18 innings before they were stalemated by the curfew laws in Baltimore. Chicago scored a run in the third and Baltimore a run in the eighth and the marathon affair ended that way in a 1-1 tie. Billy Pierce pitched 16 marvelous innings for Chicago with Turk Lown going the final two. Billy O'Dell pitched the first eight innings for Baltimore with Hoyt Wilhelm going the final 10 frames. The Cleveland Indians picked up a half game in the standings as their 5-2 victory over Washington moved them to within 1 and 1/2 games of Chicago. The victory was an expensive one for the Tribe as they lost their fiery second baseman, Billy Martin, for at least a month. Martin was struck in the head by a pitch thrown by Washington's Tex Clevenger. The ball shattered Martin's jaw and cheekbone.

Chicago opened its scheduled three-game series in Washington's Griffith Stadium on Friday night. The Stadium, with a seating capacity of only 27,523, had non-symmetrical dimensions of 328 feet down the right field line, 405 feet down the left field line, 421 feet to dead center field and 457 feet to the power alley in right center field. Bob Shaw started for Chicago and won his fifth consecutive game. Shaw improved his record to 11-3 with the 4-1 triumph. The pathetic Senators, who had lost 20 of their last 21 games, managed only eight hits off of Shaw. Billy Goodman spear-headed Chicago's ten-hit attack with three safeties, each driving in a run in the first, third and fifth innings.

In a minor player move, Chicago purchased the contract of Joe Stanka from its Sacramento farm team. Stanka, the six-foot, five-inch right-handed pitcher, would report to Chicago at the end of his minor league season.

In another totally unrelated minor move, it was time to get my summer haircut refreshed. Growing up, we had a choice of hair-cuts: short, shorter and shortest. The spot where I had this outpatient surgery performed was John's Barbershop. John's Barbershop had three barber chairs, but for the most part only one barber. Of course, that was John himself. For a period of time his son had joined the business, but departed shortly thereafter for a much more glamorous career in police work. John wasn't much on style. During the summer, I had what was called a crew cut. Definitions of this type of haircut varied, but John's definition was the only one that mattered. In his terms, it meant that your hair was cut to within a quarter inch of your skull all the way around. Quite practical for summer activities. John's other two options were flat tops and the regular haircut. The flat top was about the same as a crew cut, with about a half inch of hair left on the top of your head. With the aid of wax, the hair would stand upright and give the impression of being flat on top. The regular haircut, differed only in that about three-quarters of an inch of hair was left on the top of your head. Just long enough, that it would lay down as it was brushed to the side. The haircut, your choice, cost $1.25. For real style, the older guys went to Frankie's Barbershop for their cuts. Frankie did it right. He had five barber chairs and five busy barbers. He could handle any style requested, but specialized in current favorites such as the duck tail.

After being rained out of Saturday night's game, Washington and Chicago met for Sunday's doubleheader on August 9. Gerry Staley earned the 4-3 victory in the opener for Chicago. Staley, in his 46th appearance of the season, relieved Ray Moore in the fifth inning with one out and the White Sox trailing 3-2. Moore had taken the mound in relief of starter Ken McBride. Staley pitched four and 2/3 innings of one-hit relief as the South Siders rallied for single runs in the seventh and eighth innings for the victory. Landis scored the game-winner in the eighth frame on Roy Sievers' errant throw of Johnny Romano's infield bouncer. Aparicio connected for his sixth home run of the season. Landis had three of Chicago's 10 hits as Nellie Fox collected two hits to break out of a minor slump.

To this point in the season, both Gerry Staley and Turk Lown had provided Chicago with consistent and reliable performances out of the bullpen. Gerald Lee Staley, born August 21, 1920 in Bush Prairie, Washington, was originally acquired by the White Sox on waivers from the New York Yankees on May 28, 1956. Staley began his major league career with the St. Louis Cardinals as a starting pitcher in 1947. From 1947 through 1953 Staley compiled a record of 82 wins against 63 losses. In 1954, his record slipped to seven and thirteen, while his earned run average ballooned to 5.26. On December 8, 1954, Staley and Ray Jablonski were traded to the Cincinnati Redlegs for Frank Smith. In 1955, after establishing a 5-8 record in 30 appearances for the Redlegs, Staley was placed on waivers. He was picked up by the New York Yankees on September 11, 1955. In his own words " The stay with the Yankees was not long enough to get a cup of coffee." After another trip to the waiver wire, Staley joined the White Sox. Ray Berres had noticed that Staley was relying almost exclusively on his knuckle ball. When he came to the Sox, he started to rely on his hard sinker. That pitch combined with his great control made Staley a critical part of Chicago's relief corps during the 1959 campaign. Berres characterized Staley as "Cool and calculating, he had ice water in his veins. He had a great sinker with good command. When he was right, they beat the ball into the ground all day long."

In the second game of the twin bill, Early Wynn dominated Washington with a 9-0, three-hit, shutout. The victory was Early's 15th of the year. Fox, Torgeson, Battey and Wynn each had two hits. Torgeson had three RBIs in this two-hour and 27-minute laugher. Meanwhile, Baltimore beat Cleveland 4-3 as Chicago's league lead grew to three full games. Chicago's record stood at 66 and 42, a winning percentage of .611.

The performance of Early Wynn, the 39-year-old veteran, had been an inspiration to his mates throughout the season. Wynn was noted for his toughness and hard-nosed approach to the game. Pitching coach Berres looked upon Wynn as a " very gutsy pitcher, at times very overpowering. He loved the competition and was basically a fastball pitcher who used the slider and the occasional knuckle ball effectively." Bob Shaw, Early's roommate on the road in 1959, recalled how Wynn taught him many things about baseball and about life. Shaw indicated that Wynn helped teach the younger pitchers by example. "Early demonstrated that you have to be tough-don't ever give in to the hitter. Wynn was very professional. He thought he, not the hitter, owned the plate. Early always used an example to illustrate the justification for a pitcher to throw the ball on the inside portion of the plate. He would say when a pitcher gets hit with a line drive, the batter never stops to ask him how he feels, he just keeps running to first base. If a batter gets hit with a pitch inside, I don't feel bad. I am just working my half of the plate." Wynn also showed young Shaw the ropes in other facets of life. "Wynn was very business oriented. I paid attention and became business oriented myself. Early was a pilot and I became a pilot as well. He was a good man to follow."

Wynn also knew how to have fun Shaw recalled, "Early didn't miss many bases. He would have his drinks but then he would put on that rubber jacket and run like a fool. He always came ready to play." Al Smith, Wynn's teammate with Cleveland and Chicago, paid Wynn perhaps the highest tribute, "If you had to win a ballgame, give the ball to him." Wynn led with his performance and was an example for the younger players. Outfielder Jim Landis recalled an example that illustrated Wynn's character, "I had goofed up a fly ball in center field one day that cost Wynn the ballgame. I felt really bad and was down on myself. Wynn came and sat next to me in the clubhouse after the game and 'said forget about it,' and then went out and bought me a nice dinner." The type of character that Early displayed on and off the field encouraged personal respect, team unity, and a sense of camaraderie. The 1959 club in many respects was like a family. They cared for each other like members of their own family. Al Smith remembered recently that the 1959 team "was one hell of a bunch of fellas. They were like my family. I can see those fellas in my mind like it was yesterday, even though some of them have passed away."

Family life strengthened the fabric of our neighborhood. By the summer of 1959, I had two younger sisters, as well as my older brother Tony. In 1959, my sister Martha was four years old. Monica, the youngest, had been placed on this earth about the time Early Wynn was losing to Ned Garver and the Kansas City Athletics on April 16 earlier this season. As was the norm for the day, my parents had a fundamental conviction that they would make any sacrifice required for their children to have a better opportunity in life. My Dad worked long hours in the factory. In the evening he had a second job, or two, at the gas station, grocery store or butcher shop. My mother dedicated most every moment of her time to maintaining the house, preparing meals and doing all things necessary to make her children functional and presentable. Even more fundamental than this was their love and acceptance of each child as an individual. My parents and grandparents nurtured and encouraged our strengths and did the best they could to help us understand and compensate for our weaknesses. They certainly made mistakes in the process, just as we did in responding to their tutelage. Fundamental character was taught by example. There was always a clear understanding of the difference between right and wrong. In most cases, the core families in the neighborhood shared these principles of child-rearing. My mother, Mrs. Tracy, Mrs. Shaughnessy and Mrs. Doran were saints and remain so to this day. The neighborhood fathers generally were hard-working and short on outward expressions of tenderness and emotion, as was typical for men of that era.

The Roman Catholic Church played a significant role in family and neighborhood life. Many of the families in the neighborhood were of Catholic faith. The parish, St. Christina's, and related elementary school touched everyone's life, regardless of one's faith. The church building itself had a dominant physical presence on 111th Street. It was located directly opposite the Mount Greenwood public school "Portables." The toll of the church bell could be heard periodically throughout each day. The priests and nuns of St. Christina were involved in the lives of most young people in the community—Catholic and non-Catholic. Many of my peers attended the Catholic Church and school. In spite of the fact I attended public schools, the nuns and priests recognized me and treated me as one of their own. Many of the nuns appeared to be firm disciplinarians and relish the opportunity to display their authority. Countless were the times that I received a cuff on the back of my head or a stern word, if I were perceived to be out of line by a nun. If a child did anything except pass them on the sidewalk, eyes straight ahead and a respectful greeting on his lips, he was deemed to be out of line. Such unacceptable behavior would be brought to one's attention swiftly. The added discipline certainly didn't hurt my development and perhaps served as sound reinforcement of the principle of unconditional respect for authority that was hammered into us at home. Respect, love, family, sound character and authority were active ingredients for a successful experience at home, as well as on the major league ball diamonds.

Manager Al Lopez sent Billy Pierce to the mound to oppose Jim Bunning in Tuesday night's opener at Briggs Stadium in Detroit. The Tiger fans got what they came for as Al Kaline smashed a

May 9, 1959—*Aparicio is out at home and out of the game in Cleveland for arguing too strongly with umpire.*

June 11, 1959—*White Sox southpaw Billy Pierce sets to deliver against Senators.*

Comiskey Park located at 35th Street and Shields Avenue on Chicago's south side.

Young Dodgers' fans, standing in the shadow of Ebbett's Field in Brooklyn, watch the 1959 World Series on a portable television set. The Dodgers abandoned Brooklyn in favor of Los Angeles, California in 1958.

June 17, 1959—*Chicago first baseman, Earl Torgeson, takes big cut at Yankee Stadium.*

June 11, 1959—*Sox fleet-footed center fielder, Jim Landis, and lefty Billy Pierce combine talents to lead a 3-1 victory over the Washington Senators.*

August 23, 1959—*"Old Sarge" Hank Bauer of Yankees eludes tag of Nellie Fox as Aparicio backs up throw.*

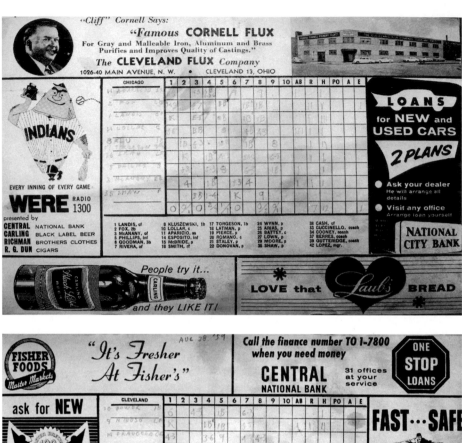

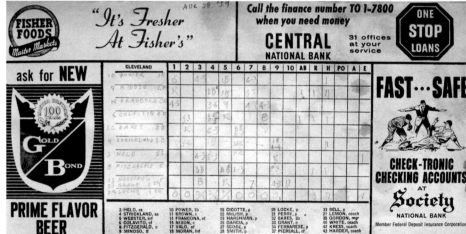

August 28, 1959—*Scorecard from Chicago's pivotal 7-3 victory over the Cleveland Indians in Cleveland's Municipal Stadium before a crowd of 70,398.*

Nellie Fox, Sox second baseman and 1959 ALMVP, makes the pivot and throw to complete another double play.

September 15, 1959—*White Sox MVP Nellie Fox in action at second base against Yankees.*

September 16, 1959—*Chicago field boss Al Lopez directs the Sox from dugout against Yankees.*

October 1, 1959—*Early Wynn delivers the first pitch of the 1959 World Series to Jim Gilliam of the LA Dodgers.*

October 1, 1959—*Chicago mound-ace Early Wynn in World Series first game.*

October 1, 1959—*Big Ted Kluszewski homers in first game of World Series.*

October 2, 1959—*Los Angeles' Johnny Podres and Chicago's Bob Shaw are selected to start the second game of the World Series.*

October 2, 1959—*Sherm Lollar of the White Sox is tagged at the plate by Dodgers' John Roseboro in pivotal play in the eighth inning in game two of the World Series.*

October 5, 1959—*Wally Moon of the LA Dodgers scores as Chicago's Sherm Lollar receives late throw to the plate in third inning of game four of 1959 World Series.*

October 7, 1959—*Chicago's big right-hander Dick Donovan closes out shutout of Dodgers in fifth game of the World Series.*

three-run first inning home run to put Pierce on the ropes early. Pierce departed after four innings, trailing 5-0. The White Sox mustered little offense as Jim Bunning prevailed 8-1, for his first victory over Chicago on the season. Luis Aparicio sat out the game with a minor leg injury. In addition, Al Smith injured his left elbow during the contest as he banged into the left field wall chasing Al Kaline's home run.

On Wednesday, August 12, Chicago reversed its offensive fortunes by scoring 11 runs on eight hits. The ineffective Tiger pitching staff contributed eight walks to the day's futility. The big blow for Chicago was Lollar's three-run home run in the fifth inning which proved to be the game-winner. Lollar had two hits and three RBIs on the day. Nellie Fox had two hits and three RBIs and Torgeson and Goodman each knocked in two. The White Sox pitching staff didn't fare well either as starter Barry Latman and relievers Staley and Lown were racked for 14 hits and six runs. But the Chicago offense carried the day as Gerry Staley earned the victory in the 11-6 route.

The White Sox beat the Tigers 9-0 in Thursday afternoon's rubber match of the three game set. Early Wynn notched his 16th victory with another strong performance in the three-hit shutout. The Pale Hose hammered 14 hits including five for extra bases. Jim Landis put the game winning runs on the board with his three-run, first inning home run, his fifth of the campaign. In addition, Phillips hit his fifth home run, Torgeson his ninth, and Lollar his 15th of the season. Lollar had a total of four hits and two RBIs. Nellie Fox continued his resurgent offensive output with three hits. Fox and Landis helped preserve Wynn's shutout with several run-saving defensive plays.

The White Sox next ventured into Kansas City's cozy Municipal Stadium for a weekend series with the Athletics. Municipal

Stadium had the second smallest seating capacity in the league at 30,726. With 60 feet of territory between home plate and the back-stop, the right and left field foul poles were only a distance of 320 feet from home. The center field wall was 410 feet from the plate. The White Sox had prevailed in the last five meetings between the two clubs. The sixth-place Athletics selected Johnny Kucks to oppose Bob Shaw. Kucks and Shaw pitched scoreless ball through six innings. However, in the top of the seventh, Landis reached first on a single and Sherman Lollar followed with the game-win-ner, a drive over the left field screen. Lollar hammered another two-run homer to left to cap off Chicago's three-run eighth inning. Shaw won his 12th game of the year against only three losses giv-ing up five Kansas City hits and a single eighth inning run. The 5-1 victory increased Chicago's lead over Cleveland to three and 1/2 games as the Indians fell to Detroit 11-1.

Chicago dropped a 2-1 decision to Bud Daley and the Kansas City Athletics on Saturday, August 15. The Sox also lost left-han-der Billy Pierce as he pulled up lame in the third inning. Pierce strained muscles in his back and ligaments attached to his hip. Latman and Lown finished the game in relief. With the score Kansas City 2 and Chicago 0 in the eighth inning, Al Smith slammed a Bud Daley offering into the seats to close the deficit to one. In the ninth, Chicago loaded the bases but failed to score as Jim Rivera was caught off third, missing the sign for a suicide squeeze bunt.

Lopez knew that the loss of Billy Pierce for any extended period of time could pose a severe obstacle to Chicago's hope for a pen-nant. Pierce had a sub-par year going by his standards, but his vet-eran leadership would be needed down the stretch drive. At the beginning of the year, Al Lopez would have cringed at the thought that two of his "Big Three" starting pitchers would be down for an extended period due to injuries. With the shoulder problems of Donovan and the back and leg injury to Pierce, other players would have to step up to fill the void. Wynn and Shaw had been dominating as starting pitchers. Staley and Lown had been outstanding in both long and short relief roles. These pitchers would have to maintain their peak performances with others showing improvement if the Sox had any hope of preserving their lead and taking the pennant.

On Sunday afternoon, August 16, the Athletics won the finale of the three-game series 7-2. Ned Garver pitched a complete game for the A's. Dick Donovan, in his first start after coming off the injured list, took his sixth defeat of the season. Six Chicago pitchers paraded to the mound as Donovan, McBride, Moore and Lown were touched for runs. The two hour and 54 minute contest was played before a crowd of 13,373. Aparicio had a successful return to the lineup for Chicago as he produced three hits out of the leadoff spot.

Chicago finished the 13 game road trip winning seven, losing five and tying one. Their overall season mark stood at 69-45, which gave them a three-game lead over Cleveland. That lead grew to three and 1/2 games on Monday as the Detroit Tigers edged the Indians 5-4.

On August 18 the Sox opened their next extended homestand against Baltimore. This would be Baltimore's last scheduled visit to Comiskey Park for the season. Washington, New York and Boston were scheduled to follow in the homestand. In the National League it appeared to be a three-way race as the San Francisco Giants led the pack with a 67-50 record. The Giants' west coast rival, Los Angeles Dodgers, were in second place at 65-54 and the 1958 National League Champion Milwaukee Braves were in third place with a record of 63-54. Pittsburgh, Chicago, Cincinnati, St. Louis and Philadelphia followed the leaders in the standings. The

Chicago White Sox record of 69-45 led all major league teams in winning percentage at .605.

The White Sox edged Baltimore Friday night, 6-4, as Gerry Staley won his sixth game of the season in relief. Chicago starter Early Wynn was removed in the fifth inning with the score 4-2 in favor of Baltimore. Ken McBride and Staley held the Orioles at bay over the final five frames. The Sox scored single runs in the fifth and seventh innings to tie the score at four. Then in the eighth inning, Gerry Staley started the Chicago rally by coaxing a walk from Bill Fischer. Aparicio followed with a sharp single to center. And Nellie Fox chased them both home with a bases clearing double to the wall in right field. On the evening, Aparicio had three hits, scored three runs and stole his 38th base of the year. Jim Landis also had two hits and two RBIs. The "Formal and Tuxedo" night crowd of 34,547 was treated to one more heart stopping thrill in the top of the ninth inning. With two outs, Baltimore's Willie Tasby leveled on a Gerry Staley hanging sinker and hit a rocket to the gap in deep left center field. The ball was headed into the seats. But Jim Landis raced back to the wall and made a tremendous, backhanded, leaping grab as he reached over the fence to take a home run away from Tasby. The Chicago lead in the American League race grew to four and 1/2 games as Washington once again thrashed Cleveland. The Senators handed the Tribe their fourth loss in a row, 11-4.

The next day Bob Shaw was denied his 13th victory as Baltimore drove him from the mound in the third inning. Billy O'Dell pitched the Orioles to the 3-1 victory as he mastered the South Siders for his seventh win of the year. Lollar's 18th home run of the year in the eighth inning, a solo shot, provided the only score for Chicago. On that same day, Cleveland sneaked by Washington 5-4 to pick up a game on Chicago.

On August 20, the Orioles handed Chicago its second loss in a row as they outlasted Barry Latman and six Chicago relievers, 7-6. The Sox fell behind by three in the first inning and never gained the advantage as Hoyt Wilhelm won his 12th game of the year. Jim McAnany had two hits and three RBIs for Chicago in the losing cause. Meanwhile, Cleveland cut another game off Chicago's lead as Jim "Mudcat" Grant beat Washington 6-1. The events of the day provided a poor backdrop to Al Lopez's 51st birthday.

On the evening of August 21, 37,986 fans turned up at Comiskey Park as Chicago honored Nellie Fox. Nellie, his wife JoAnne, daughters Bonnie and Tracey, and his parents, Mr. and Mrs. Jacob Fox, were also present as the club, his teammates and his fans rained gifts and expressions of thanks on the longtime Chicago favorite. Mayor Richard Daley, self proclaimed as the White Sox greatest fan, spoke at the ceremonies. Daley was a life long resident of the Bridgeport section of south side Chicago. Bridgeport is located a short distance west of Comiskey Park. Many Irish immigrants settled in the Bridgeport area at the turn-of-the-century. The Armour Square neighborhood, immediately north of the ballpark was the place of my grandfather's birth and was inhabited by many Swedish immigrants. In the 1910s and early 1920s, young men made a habit of establishing rivalries between neighborhoods. My grandfather entertained us as children with stories of his boyhood conflicts with future Mayor Dick Daley and the Bridgeport boys.

That night all attention was on Nellie Fox. Chicago's expression of affection for Nellie included two automobiles, a power boat and motor, an all expense paid vacation to Hawaii, a television set, two suits of clothes, and other assorted gifts of food, appliances and clothing. Jacob Nelson "Nellie" Fox was born in St. Thomas, Pennsylvania on December 25, 1927. Nellie signed a contract to play professional baseball with the legendary Connie Mack and the Philadelphia Athletics in 1944 when just a sophomore in high school. Fox remained in the Philadelphia system playing at the major league level for brief periods in 1947 and 1948. Fox was called up to the big show for good as he played a full year for Philadelphia in 1949. Fox appeared in 88 games that year and collected 63 hits in 247 plate appearances. On October 19, 1949, Chicago obtained Nellie from the Athletics in exchange for catcher Joe Tipton. No one in Chicago foresaw the quality ballplayer that Fox would become. Fox earned a starting job in Chicago in 1950 and soon thereafter became a perennial American League All-Star. Fox consistently maintained a batting average which hovered at or above .300 and was usually among the league leaders in hits. Fox led the league in number of hits in 1952, 1954, 1957 and 1958.

Fox had amazing bat control and rarely walked away from the plate with the bat in his hand. Nellie averaged approximately 625 plate appearances per season and struck out an average of only 15 times a year. Fox led the league in fewest strikeouts during the season an amazing seven times. Nellie displayed his durability by playing in a total of 628 consecutive games, a major league record for a second baseman. Fox established another major league record in 1958 by leading the league in total fielding chances accepted by a second baseman for seven consecutive years. His teammates and coaches were the ultimate evaluators of Fox's influence and impact on the team. Jim Landis recalled, "Nellie was a terrific leader in a quiet and professional way." Don Gutteridge, Fox's infield coach, remembered Nellie as, "The leader in the infield which was the strength of our club in 1959. Fox did not have natural physical ability. He was not fast and he lacked arm strength. What he did was make all of the plays. Nellie worked harder and produced more than anyone. He really kept everyone on their toes." Landis added that, "We would watch Nellie play hard-he was not a holler guy-the younger guys would really pick that up. Nellie was very strong in the character department, a tremendous person, not cocky, no baloney." The tributes to Fox were well deserved and very appropriate.

In the game that followed the celebration of Nellie Fox, Chicago prevailed 5-4 for its 28th one-run victory of the year. Donovan, in his second start after coming off the disabled list, was sent to the showers by Washington's two-run flurry in the sixth inning. Staley relieved Donovan and was credited with his seventh victory as Chicago scored two runs in its half of the sixth. The Sox added an insurance run in the seventh as Bubba Phillips singled in Jim Landis with his third hit of the game. That run turned into the game-winner as Washington scored one run off of Turk Lown in the eighth inning to make the score 5-4. Phillips and Romano each had two RBIs for Chicago. The White Sox maintained their two and 1/2 game lead as Cleveland blanked Baltimore, 5-0.

Barry Latman stepped up for Chicago on Saturday, August 22, and came through with another clutch performance as he white-washed the Senators 1-0. Every bit of Latman's five-hit, eight-strikcout effort was needed as Washington's Russ Kemmerer pitched nearly as well. Kemmerer deserved a better fate as he pitched three hit, one run ball and still lost the game. In the second frame, Sherman Lollar walked, stole second, and advanced to third on a wild pitch. Lollar scampered home with the game's only run when Bubba Phillips followed with a sharp single to left. Despite the Chicago win, the gap between the White Sox and the Indians remained the same as Cleveland dropped Baltimore 4-2 on the strength of Woody Held's grand slam home run.

It was also a memorable day in the history of our country. Hawaii officially became the fiftieth state to join the Union of the United

States of America. Earlier in the year, on January 3 , after many years of dedicated effort, Alaska was granted statehood and officially became the nation's forty-ninth state. Alaska and Hawaii became the first states to join the Union since 1912, when both Arizona and New Mexico were officially granted statehood.

The White Sox drew their largest home crowd thus far this season as Sunday's doubleheader against the New York Yankees brought out 44,520 fans. Early Wynn and Bob Shaw were selected by manager Lopez to tame the Yankees on this sweltering afternoon. The Yankees got to Early Wynn in the seventh inning of the opener for two runs. Those runs would prove to be the game-winners as Wynn was tagged with his eighth loss of the year. Gerry Staley was hammered by the Yankees for four runs in the eighth inning to put the game out of reach. Art Ditmar went the distance for New York for the 7-1 victory.

In the day's second game, Bob Shaw pitched another gem. The 5-0 blanking of the Bronx Bombers was his second shutout of the year. Shaw's six-hit, six-strikeout masterpiece placed his season record at 13-4, the best winning percentage in the league. The nine scoreless frames lowered Shaw's earned run average to 2.78, second best in the league. The White Sox scored all of their runs in the seventh inning. The key blow was Sherman Lollar's lead-off home run, which proved to be the game-winner. Lollar's 19th round tripper of the season landed in the second row of the upper deck in left field. Ralph Terry took the loss for the Yankees. The Cleveland Indians continued their surge by dropping Boston 1-0 and 6-2 in a twin bill to move within one and 1/2 games of first place.

On Monday, August 24, the White Sox bested New York 4-2. Ray Moore won his first start of the season in this his eighth attempt. Moore received three and 1/3 innings of three-hit, no-run relief help from Turk Lown as Moore improved his record to 3-8.

Jim Landis had three hits for Chicago. Aparicio scored two runs and stole his 41st and 42nd bases of the year. Lollar had one hit, but it was a big one as his fifth inning double drove in the winning run of the game. Mickey Mantle had a terrible day at the plate. He struck out four times, including his game ending whiff. The White Sox lead swelled to two games in the pennant race as Cleveland was idle.

Boston arrived in town for the final time of the season. Before the game between Boston and Chicago on Tuesday, August 25, the White Sox announced that they had acquired former National League home run king Ted Kluszewski from the Pittsburgh Pirates. Kluszewski played first base, batted left-handed, weighed 225-pounds, and stood six-feet, two-inches tall. In his eleven years in the National League, Big Ted had accumulated over 1,600 hits of which 255 were home runs. Kluszewski had driven in 950 runs in the 1,499 career games that he had played. His best year was 1954 when he played for Cincinnati and led the National League in home runs (49) and in RBIs (141). Kluszewski hit over .300 in seven of his eleven major league campaigns. His career peaked in 1954 through 1956 as he was selected to the National League All-Star team each of those years. Since that time " Big Klu" had been hobbled by a sore back. In developments related to the trade, Chicago released Harry Simpson. Simpson was immediately claimed by Pittsburgh. Chicago also sold infielder Bobby Sagers to a club in the Pittsburgh farm system. The White Sox were confident that Kluszewski would provide some much needed power to their attack for the final pennant run.

Boston's Frank Sullivan led Dick Donovan and the Chicago White Sox 4-2 after eight and 1/2 innings of play. With one out in Chicago's last at bat, Al Smith's routine ground ball skipped erratically over the head of Boston shortstop Don Buddin for a single.

Three singles by Norm Cash, Jim Rivera and Johnny Romano followed to tie the score at 4-4. In the 10th inning, Billy Goodman doubled home Sherman Lollar with the game-winner. Earlier in the game, Norm Cash had homered for Chicago's second run. Turk Lown pitched the 10th inning for his eighth victory of the season. Chicago continued to find a way to win close ball games as they prevailed in its 30th one-run decision of the campaign. The win allowed Chicago to maintain its two-game lead over Cleveland.

The Cleveland Indians were charging hard and continued to put pressure on the White Sox as they beat New York for their eighth consecutive victory. Rocky Colavito slammed his 38th home run of the year in the fifth inning to provide the final 5-4 margin of victory over Ryan Duren and the fourth-place Yankees. As the White Sox continued their series with Boston on Wednesday night, August 26, Bill Veeck initiated another promotional event. Chicago celebrated "Al Smith Night" as every individual with Smith, Smythe, or any surname close to Smith was granted free admission to the left field grandstand. The Smiths showed up 5,253 strong and unfortunately witnessed a contest dominated by Chicago's incredible bungling. Chicago jumped out to a 2-1 advantage, but in the seventh inning Al Smith dropped a Vic Wertz fly ball to left center field. This miscue, in plain view of all the Smiths, opened the floodgates for four Boston runs. Turk Lown allowed two more gift runs in the eighth inning as a result of his own throwing error. Chicago rallied for three runs in its half of the eighth on Jim Rivera's three-run double. But it was too little, too late as Chicago fell 7-6. The loss by Chicago cut its lead over the Tribe to one game.

As a general rule our family did not eat out often. Fast-food alternatives were concepts of the future. The favorite spots in the neighborhood for carry-out meals were either hamburger joints or pizza places. For hamburgers, I preferred "Wonder Burgers" first and "Gussies'" second. The Wonder Burger was owned and operated by Bill Grant. The small grille was located on the north side of 111th Street a short distance from Kedzie Avenue. Bill Grant toiled endless hours at this business turning out delicious hamburgers and Curly-Q french-fries. The Wonder Burger became a Mount Greenwood dining institution, moving twice during the ensuing years, always retaining a quality and consistency that was enhanced by my childhood memories. Gussies' was located on the south side of 111th Street and although slightly closer to home, a distant second in the competition for our family dining-out dollars. There was no substitute for a sack of Wonder Burgers and a basket of hot fries to provide sustenance as I listened to White Sox games on the radio. Late night runs for a take-out pizza from "Ray's" or "The Pizza House" were standard fare for my father on a Friday or Saturday night. The thin-crust, Italian sausage variety smothered with a thick blanket of cheese was a particular favorite. I, however, did not acquire a taste for this south side Chicago delicacy until I allowed pizza to pass over my palate during the Kennedy and Nixon presidential debate in 1960. I became a devoted life-long fan at that moment.

During the final game of the current homestand, I enjoyed a meal of Wonder Burgers as Barry Latman posted his seventh victory of the season in a 5-1 triumph over Boston. Latman needed two-out relief help from Gerry Staley to finish the ballgame. Latman lost the shutout in the ninth inning as Ted Williams stroked his 10th home run of the year into the upper deck in right field. Chicago led all the way and received multiple hit games from Fox (3), Landis (2), Romano (2) and Kluszewski (2) as they hammered three Boston pitchers for 12 hits. Kluszewski got his first start for Chicago at first base. Romano's single in the third scored Fox and

Landis with the game-winning runs. The Indians were idle as they awaited Chicago's arrival. The Chicago victory increased its lead over Cleveland to one and 1/2 games.

Chicago next traveled to Cleveland for a four-game weekend showdown at Municipal Stadium against the Indians. The result of this crucial series was expected to greatly influence the outcome of the American League pennant race in 1959. The red hot Indians trailed the South Siders by one and 1/2 games and were sporting an eight game winning streak. Cleveland's weather was also experiencing a hot streak as the temperature soared above 90 degrees. Despite the heat and humidity, the City of Cleveland was in a frenzy in anticipation of the weekend activities.

Friday night's game on August 28 matched Cleveland's Jack Harshman and Chicago's Bob Shaw as mound opponents. Harshman had won his last three starts and Shaw his last two. A crowd of 70,398 jammed Municipal Stadium to watch the game, and possibly the season, unfold for these two clubs. In the fourth inning, the White Sox were first to draw blood. Singles by Al Smith, Jim McAnany and Luis Aparicio coupled with Bob Shaw's sacrifice produced two Chicago runs. McAnany and Aparicio got the RBIs. In the Cleveland half of the fourth, the Tribe answered with a pair of their own. Minoso singled and was forced out at second on Tito Francona's infield ground ball. Francona scored when Colavito doubled off the glove of third baseman Bubba Phillips. Aparicio recovered the ball and threw wildly to Kluszewski covering second, which allowed Colavito to score as well.

Like a heavyweight fight, Chicago counter punched with a single run in the fifth. A Nellie Fox walk and Jim Landis double to right put runners on second and third and sent Cleveland starter Harshman to the showers. Jim "Mudcat" Grant relieved Harshman and enticed Lollar to hit a weak pop fly to center. Kluszewski was walked to fill the bases. Al Smith hit a grounder to second base. Kluszewski stopped in the middle of the base path, as second sacker Baxes threw to first to nip Smith as Fox scored. Kluszewski was then thrown out at second by Vic Power's return throw to end the inning. The 3-2 lead was short-lived however. Shaw opened the fifth inning by walking Fitzgerald on a full count and then struck out Grant as he attempted a sacrifice bunt. A Minoso single advanced Fitzgerald to second base. Fitzgerald then scored on a Vic Power single before Shaw could retire the side. Both teams went down silently in the sixth.

Shaw appeared to be getting stronger. Nellie Fox, a year-long catalyst for Chicago, opened the seventh with a single off Grant. The next batter, Jim Landis, drove Grant's first pitch to left advancing Fox. Chicago cleanup hitter, 35-year-old Sherman Lollar, stepped to the plate with Fox at second and Landis on first. Lollar scorched a blast to left center field. Minnie Minoso raced back to the fence and appeared to catch the ball. However, the ball skipped out of his glove and over the five-foot wire screen for a devastating three-run home run, Lollar's 20th of the campaign. The overflow crowd was stunned. Years later Bob Shaw recalled, "That game was the point in the season where we felt we would win it all." Kluszewski followed with a single and Locke relieved Grant. Pinch runner Torgeson scored later in the inning on a fielder's choice to make the score 7-4. Shaw shut down the Tribe over the final two frames to preserve the victory. Chicago's lead grew to two and 1/2 games over the Indians.

On August 29, Dick Donovan took the mound for Chicago opposing young Jim Perry in the second game of this crucial series. Donovan had been ineffective since returning from the disabled list. He had pitched three games, losing one and getting a no-decision in the other two. Cleveland's rookie right-hander, Jim

Perry, was 10-5 on the season. The "Ladies Day" crowd of 50,290 was treated to a dandy of a ballgame. The contest was a scoreless duel through six innings. Donovan was magnificent, experiencing only one Indian scoring threat in the second inning. In the second frame, Donovan walked Jim Baxes to open the inning. After a strikeout of George Strickland, Woody Held singled to center field. Landis bobbled the ball as Baxes streaked to third and Held pulled into second. Fitzgerald was walked to load the bases with one out. Jim Perry pounded a hard ground ball to Goodman at third. Goodman's quick throw to the plate forced Baxes for the second out of the inning. Power ended the threat by grounding out to Torgeson at first.

Although the Sox made noise, things did not get interesting until the seventh inning. Landis, who had three hits on the day, led off the inning by beating out a high bouncer to short for a single. Lollar and Goodman followed by each flying out. Torgeson then singled sharply to left center. Minoso raced over and grabbed the ball, but bobbled it as he tried to nail Landis at third. Chicago third base coach Tony Cuccinello took advantage of the defensive lapse and waved Landis home. Landis made a perfect fade away slide to beat the relay throw from Strickland. The unearned run was a result of Minoso's second game-deciding miscue of the series. In the Chicago eighth inning, Jim Rivera singled, moved to third on Aparicio's single and scored on Fox's sacrifice fly for an insurance run. The score remained 2-0 as Donovan dominated the Tribe for his first shutout of the season. The five hit performance pushed Donovan's season record to 8-6, with perhaps his biggest victory of the year, if not the biggest victory of his Chicago career. The win pushed the White Sox to a three and 1/2 game lead over Cleveland.

A large crowd of 66,586 turned out to see if Cleveland could reverse its fortunes in Sunday's twin bill. Wynn and Latman were selected to oppose Cleveland's Cal McLish and Gary Bell. In the opener, Early Wynn allowed a total of seven hits and three runs. He also struck out five and walked three before departing after facing one hitter in the eighth inning. Wynn had trailed 2-0 after five frames, but Chicago rallied with five runs in the sixth inning as Early Wynn's lead-off home run ignited Chicago's offense. Following Wynn's 402 foot blast, Aparicio reached first on an infield single, and then proceeded to steal second. After a base on balls to Fox, Landis doubled, sending Aparicio home and Fox to third base. Ted Kluszewski was walked intentionally to load the bases. McLish then hit Sherman Lollar with a pitch to force in a run. Billy Goodman followed with a single to center field to drive in what proved to be the game-winning run. McLish was pulled from the game in favor of Bobby Locke. Locke proceeded to walk Al Smith forcing in the final run of the inning. Cleveland scored one run in the eighth inning and Chicago tallied a run in the ninth to close out the scoring. The final score was Chicago 6 and Cleveland 3. Aparicio, Landis, Lollar, Goodman, Wynn and Torgeson had a RBI for Chicago in the game. Gerry Staley pitched the final two frames in relief as Wynn earned his 17th victory of season. McLish lost for only the seventh time on the year.

In the nightcap, Chicago continued its humiliation of the Indians by handing Cleveland a 9-4 pounding. Chicago pummeled Cleveland starter Gary Bell and relievers Grant, Garcia and Smith for 11 hits and nine runs. Chicago scored three in the second, two in the third, two in the fifth, and single runs in eighth and ninth. Cleveland could only come close once during the day as Rocky Colavito's three-run home run in the fourth inning drew Cleveland to within two of Chicago. Billy Goodman continued his timely hitting with three hits and two RBIs. Al Smith knocked in three runs on two hits, including his 12th home run of the year. Smith's two-run shot in the fifth inning provided the game-winning runs. Latman won his eighth game of the year with the aid of four innings of stellar relief work from Turk Lown. Lown had a record of eight victories against only two defeats on the season while appearing in 51 games.

Turk Lown along with Gerry Staley were a godsend to the Chicago pitching staff in 1959. The experienced veterans consistently provided strong relief work for manager Al Lopez. Omar Joseph "Turk" Lown was born in Brooklyn, New York on May 30, 1924. His major league career began as a starting pitcher with the Chicago Cubs in 1951. After establishing a record of 16-27 as a starter through 1953, the Chicago Cubs used Lown predominantly in relief. Lown played with the Chicago Cubs through May 8, 1958 when he was traded to Cincinnati for Hersh Freeman. Lown appeared in only 11 games with Cincinnati, losing two without a win. On June 23, 1958, the Chicago White Sox claimed Lown, aged 34, on waivers. Al Lopez and Ray Berres felt that the big right-hander had a strong arm but had run upon difficult times in the National League through use of too many pitches. Lown used the blooper, slow curve, slider and screwball. Lopez felt that Lown's fastball could match that of any pitcher in the league. The first time Lown faced Mickey Mantle he threw three fast balls past him. As Lown focused on throwing smoke, his effectiveness as a reliever grew.

In this crucial four-game series against the Tribe, Chicago stepped up in all phases of its game. The starting pitching for Chicago was tremendous. In 30 innings of work, they gave up only 10 runs on 23 hits. The four starters struck out 17 while walking only nine. In contrast, the Cleveland starters pitched a total of 20 and 2/3 innings, yielding 20 hits and 15 runs. They walked 11 South Siders and struck out 10. Harshman, Perry, McLish and Bell had a combined earned run average of 6.09 compared to 3.00 for the Chicago foursome of Shaw, Donovan, Wynn and Latman. The Chicago relief tandem of Gerry Staley and Turk Lown were only called upon twice. They responded by shutting the mighty Cleveland attack completely down. In a combined six innings of work, the pair gave up no runs, six singles, one walk and two strikeouts. Cleveland's relievers Grant, Locke and Harshman were called on to pitch 15 and 1/3 innings and they gave up a collective nine runs and 16 hits, while walking three and striking out five.

Defensively the edge also went to Chicago. Both teams committed three errors, with Cleveland turning three double plays to Chicago's two. But perhaps the most crucial play in the series was the defensive lapse by Cleveland left-fielder Minnie Minoso when, in the seventh inning of the series opener, Sherman Lollar's blast to left center caromed off Minoso's glove and over the wall. The White Sox never looked back after that point.

Chicago out hit Cleveland 36 to 29. Chicago had eight extra base hits to Cleveland's five. Chicago neutralized Cleveland's power game as each team had three home runs. Lollar, Smith and Wynn went deep for Chicago while Held had two home runs and Colavito had one for the Tribe. Of course, the White Sox outscored the Indians by an overwhelming margin of 24-10. Chicago stranded 27 base runners during the series while Cleveland left 28 men on base.

Chicago thoroughly thrashed the Indians and practically crushed their pennant hopes as the four-game sweep placed Chicago five and 1/2 games ahead of the Tribe. Chicago had only 25 games left on its schedule as they swaggered out of Cleveland with the look of a champion. The White Sox were greeted by a crowd of thousands at Chicago's Midway Airport on their return to the Windy City on Sunday evening, August 30.

The White Sox completed the month of August with 21 wins and only 9 losses. Their overall season record stood at 80-49. Chicago was now 31 games over .500. They outdistanced second-place Cleveland by five and 1/2 games. Detroit was in third place,15 and 1/2 games off the pace. The Yankees were in fourth, 16 and 1/2 out. Baltimore, Boston, Kansas City and Washington trailed at 18, 19, 21 and 28 and 1/2 games behind, respectively. The final month of the season would determine if Cleveland had the fight to come back.

CHAPTER SIX

The American League Flag

ON SEPTEMBER 1, 1958, JUST ONE SHORT YEAR EARLIER, CHICAGO had just completed a very successful month of baseball. Chicago's August 1958 record was 20 victories and 10 losses. However, in 1958, Chicago required that type of August performance to climb from fourth place into second place. Chicago's record of 69-60 on September 1, 1958, while good for second place in the American League, still left them trailing the front-running New York Yankees by 10 and 1/2 games. The 1959 version of the White Sox finished the month of August with a slightly better 21-9 record. Chicago's overall record through the month of August of 80-49 (a winning percentage of .620) placed them five and 1/2 games ahead of the second-place Cleveland Indians.

In the tight race for the National League crown, San Francisco lost one game from its lead as Los Angeles left-hander Sandy Koufax struck out 18 Giants en route to a 5-2 decision. Wally Moon stroked a three-run, ninth inning, home run over the friendly left field screen in the Los Angeles Coliseum for the game-winner. Los Angeles trailed San Francisco by a game and Milwaukee was two and 1/2 games behind the league leader. Pittsburgh turned the three-team race into a foursome as they crept to within three and

1/2 games of the front-runner.

Chicago's run for the flag in September found them playing 12 games in the friendly confines of Comiskey Park and the remaining 13 contests on the road. The White Sox completed their September roster expansion with the addition of five youngsters from their Indianapolis affiliate in the American Association and one from Sacramento. Ron Jackson and Johnny Callison, who were both on the 1959 opening day roster, returned to the club. Jackson continued to perform well at the minor league level, as he swatted 30 home runs and drove in 93 for Indianapolis. Callison recovered his batting eye and finished the American Association campaign hitting .290. Outfielder Joe Hicks, hitting .305 for Indianapolis, joined J. C. Martin, a left-handed hitting first baseman/third baseman and Gary Peters, a promising left-handed pitcher, for their first trip to the major leagues. Joe Stanka, a right-handed pitcher from Sacramento, also joined the parent club.

The third place Tigers opened the three-game series with Chicago on September 1, as Detroit manager Jimmie Dykes sent Jim Bunning to the hill and Al Lopez countered with Bob Shaw. Bunning was on his game Tuesday night. Detroit touched Shaw for single runs in the first and third innings and two runs in the fifth. Bunning, pitching with the precision of a surgeon, held Chicago scoreless. Kluszewski with two singles and Aparicio with one had the only base hits that Chicago could manage in the 4-0 setback. The idle Cleveland Indians picked up a half game in the standings with the Chicago loss.

Dick Donovan and Barry Latman started for Chicago in Wednesday's twilight-night doubleheader. Donovan pitched a sparkler in the opener to earn his ninth victory of the season. He tamed the Tiger bats, allowing four hits and two runs in eight innings as Chicago prevailed 7-2. Gerry Staley pitched the ninth inning. The hitting star for Chicago, once again, was Sherman Lollar with two doubles and four RBIs. Landis scored the winning run in the third inning as he stretched his pop fly to shallow right field into a triple and scampered home when the throw from the outfield skipped away from Detroit's third baseman. Chicago handed Frank Lary his ninth loss of the year in 26 decisions.

The crowd of 43,286 was still celebrating the opening game win when the Tigers reached Chicago starter Barry Latman for two first inning runs in the nightcap. Detroit scored again as Frank Bolling drove in his third run of the game with a double in the fifth inning. Latman was removed in favor of Joe Stanka. Chicago's South Siders made the fans go wild, as they exploded in the bottom of the fifth inning for 11 runs. The runs were scored with the aid of 10 base hits, a walk, and a hit batsman. In the inning Chicago had eight singles, an Al Smith upper-deck, leadoff home run and a Nellie Fox base-clearing triple. Fox had four RBIs in the inning and Al Smith had two RBIs. Aparicio and Kluszewski joined the hit parade with three hits each during the contest. Kluszewski had slapped 11 singles in 26 at bats since joining Chicago. Joe Stanka was the beneficiary of the outburst as he earned his first major league victory. Staley was called upon again to mop up with one and 1/3 innings of no-hit relief. Pennant fever was running rampant as the White Sox lead, once again, grew to five and 1/2 games. Cleveland's win over Kansas City allowed them to lose only a half game in the standings on the night.

The White Sox expected a crowd in excess of 45,000 on Friday night as the Indians arrived in Chicago for another crucial three-game series. Early Wynn was slated to face Cleveland's Jim Perry as Chicago attempted to psychologically, if not mathematically, eliminate second-place Cleveland from the pennant race.

A crowd of 45,510 did come through the turnstiles on Friday

night, September 4, in support of their south side heroes. The noise in the stadium was unbelievable, as the largest home audience of the year settled in to observe the drama. The first inning was scoreless. The White Sox broke through for two runs in the bottom of second as the crowd noise escalated. Singles by Billy Goodman and Al Smith put runners at first and third. McAnany singled sharply scoring Goodman and sending Smith to third. Aparicio then laced a single to center that scored Smith with Chicago's second run. The score remained 2-0 until Cleveland's second baseman, Jim Baxes, slammed an Early Wynn offering high down the left field line and into the upper deck in the fifth inning. The home run broke Wynn's scoreless spell. Wynn proceeded to walk Ed Fitzgerald and yield a single to Jim Perry. Minoso stepped to the plate with the tying run in scoring position and tagged Wynn's first pitch, sending a drive to deep right center field. Landis raced back and made a run-saving catch as he crashed into the bullpen wall, 415 feet from the plate, to end the Cleveland threat. The score of the game stood at 2-1 entering the eighth inning. After two were out, Early Wynn ran into trouble. Nemesis Minnie Minoso hit a screaming double to right center field. Tito Francona followed with a single to left. Minoso was running all the way as Chicago left-fielder Al Smith grabbed Francona's hit on one bounce. Smith came up throwing and nailed Minoso at the plate with a perfect one hop strike to Lollar to end another Cleveland threat.

The White Sox scratched out another run in the eighth inning. Kluszewski and Lollar opened the inning with singles. Torgeson, running for Kluszewski, scored as left-fielder Francona bobbled Lollar's single. The unearned run pushed the Chicago advantage to 3-1. After the heart-stopping theatrics of the eighth inning, Gerry Staley was called upon to relieve Early Wynn. Cleveland would not go down easily as Rocky Colavito greeted Staley with a double off the wall in left center field. After retiring Woody Held on a fly to left, Staley gave up a single to George Strickland as Colavito strolled home with Cleveland's second run. Staley struck out Baxes and enticed pinch hitter Elmer Valo into a routine pop fly to end the ballgame. Early Wynn was awarded his 18th victory of season as Chicago's first place lead grew to six and 1/2 games.

The spectacular defensive plays by Al Smith and Jim Landis turned the game for Chicago. Landis' play in center field had been fabulous all year. Jim Landis was a centerpiece for Chicago in its "strength down the middle" equation. His speed, glove work and throwing ability made Landis one of the most valuable defensive players in the league. Landis also turned the corner as an offensive ballplayer in 1958 as he appeared in 142 games and increased his batting average to .277. He improved in the power department as his 145 hits included 23 doubles, seven triples and 15 home runs. Landis was always a threat to steal or take the extra base once he got aboard. James Henry Landis was born in Richmond, California on March 9, 1934. Landis signed a contract to play professional baseball with the Chicago White Sox while attending Contra Costa Junior College. Signed by Bob Mattick and Hollie Thurston for a bonus of $2,500, the six-foot, one-inch, 175-pound, right-hander played for Chicago's Wisconsin Rapids franchise in 1952. A converted third baseman, Landis learned the fine points of playing center field from Sox roving outfield instructor Johnny Mostil. In 1953, Landis earned league most valuable player honors as he hit .313 for Colorado Springs of the Western League. After a stint in the service of Uncle Sam, Landis returned to Colorado Springs and hit .429 to start the season. He was soon promoted to Memphis, where he struggled against tougher pitching and finished the year with a .257 batting average. In 1957, his first year at the major league level, the rookie center fielder was overpowered at the plate and hit just .212 while appearing in 96 games with 274 official plate appearances. In 1958, Landis modified his batting stance, returning to a crouch position which enabled him to see the breaking ball more effectively. This adjustment, along with growing confidence that he belonged in the major leagues, resulted in 1958 being a breakthrough year for Landis. Landis vindicated Al Lopez's judgment in sticking with his young defensive wizard with his level of play in 1958 and 1959.

Entering Saturday's action, the White Sox had beaten Cleveland 14 times (including the last five meetings), while losing only five. Chicago's domination over its closest rivals had everything to do with its lofty first place position. Bob Shaw started for Chicago against Cal McLish for Cleveland. Jim Landis staked Shaw to a two-run lead in the third inning. Chicago loaded the bases on a single by McAnany, a walk to Aparicio and a single by Fox. Landis' sharp single to right field scored two runs before Kluszewski hit into an inning ending double play. Cleveland scored a run in the third on a double by Held and an infield bouncer by Strickland. The Indians took the lead in the fifth as Francona rocked Shaw for a two-out, two-run home run into the center field bullpen. Dick Brown reached Shaw for an upper deck home run to leadoff the seventh inning. After giving up a single to Gary Bell, Shaw was relieved by Turk Lown. Bell scored on a Francona single. The total line on Shaw's disappointing performance was five runs on six hits in six complete innings.

With Chicago trailing 5-2, rookie Joe Stanka came out of the bullpen and was promptly reached for a Woody Held eighth-inning home run. In the ninth inning, Chicago rallied as Billy Goodman singled and Al Smith slammed his 14th home run of the year to left center field. One batter later, pinch hitter Johnny Romano connected for his fifth home run of the season, an upper deck shot to left to draw Chicago within one at 6-5. However, the game ended that way as Cleveland's McLish won his 17th game of the year and Bob Shaw was tagged with his sixth loss.

John Anthony " Honey" Romano was another of the White Sox up-and-coming stars of the future. Romano, born August 23, 1934 in Hoboken, New Jersey, received his first major league exposure in 1958. Romano played in only four games for Chicago, garnering two hits in seven at bats. In 1959, Lopez had at times placed regular catcher Sherman Lollar at first base, and used the five-foot, 11-inch, 205-pound right-handed Romano behind the plate. Romano had also been used very effectively as a pinch hitter during the season.

The South Siders' "Magic Number" was sixteen. Any combination of White Sox victories and Cleveland losses totaling sixteen would clinch the American League flag for Chicago. On Sunday, September 6, Cleveland threatened in the third inning against Dick Donovan as George Strickland and Vic Power both singled. With runners on second and third, Jim Piersall hit a fly ball to Jim McAnany in left. McAnany caught Piersall's drive and gunned down Strickland at the plate to complete the double play, ending the Cleveland threat. Chicago opened the scoring in the fifth inning on singles by Aparicio, Fox and Landis. Landis' infield hit scored Aparicio with Chicago's first run. Donovan cruised into the ninth inning with a 1-0 lead, as he looked for his second shutout in a row. But it was not to be. Chicago's lead was trimmed to 4 and 1/2 games as Vic Power's double in the ninth drove in Francona and Held with the tying and winning runs. The victory went to Jim "Mudcat" Grant, his first win over Chicago after absorbing six defeats.

The Kansas City Athletics returned to Comiskey Park for their final visit of the season. The big Labor Day doubleheader pitted

Chicago's Billy Pierce and Barry Latman against Ned Garver and John Tsitouris. Pierce was exceptional in his return from the injured list. Pierce held the Athletics to one run on five hits through seven innings. He departed after seven with a 2-1 lead, which Turk Lown was able to hold over the final two frames. The Pale Hose scored their runs in the third inning on consecutive singles by Fox, Landis and Kluszewski. Pierce was credited with his 13th victory of the campaign.

In the second game, Latman lasted one inning and Ray Moore, his relief, lasted another two and 1/3 innings as Kansas City jumped out to a 4-0 lead. The White Sox roared back with a run in the second and six in the third to take the lead. In the big third inning, Aparicio singled to left, Landis doubled, Kluszewski hit a homer to right, Romano walked, and Al Smith and Jim Rivera homered. The score was Chicago 7, Kansas City 4. Gerry Staley took the mound for Chicago with one out in the fourth inning. Kansas City came back to score two runs in that inning to pull within one at 7-6. The Sox retaliated with two in the bottom of the fourth on a single by Fox, the game-winning triple by Landis and Ted Kluszewski's sacrifice fly. In the sixth inning Chicago added three more runs on a single by Fox, another Landis triple and Kluszewski's second home run of the game. The final score was 13-7 in favor of Chicago as Gerry Staley was awarded the victory, his eighth of the year. Chicago's "Magic Number" shrunk to 14 as Cleveland maintained the pressure with a doubleheader sweep of the Detroit Tigers, 15-14 and 6-5.

Early Wynn pitched Chicago to a thrilling 10 inning, 3-2 victory on Thursday night, September 8. The game was the finale in Chicago's season series with the Kansas City Athletics. For the season, the South Siders managed to beat the Athletics 12 times while dropping 10. En route to the series sweep against Kansas

City, Chicago set an all-time home attendance record of 1,340,439 besting the 1,328,234 total established in 1951. The Athletics got to Wynn in the top of the ninth as they scored twice to take the lead. Chicago refused to lose as they scored the tying run in the ninth inning on Al Smith's run-scoring single to left. In the Chicago tenth, Jim Rivera, a late inning defensive replacement, led off the inning with a double. After Wynn struck out, Rivera scored with a head-first slide into the plate on an Aparicio single to left. Chicago's "Magic Number" shrunk to 13, as Wynn won his 19th game of the season. At this point in the season all other teams in the league except the Indians had been mathematically eliminated from the race.

Manual Joseph "Jungle Jim" Rivera stood six-feet tall and weighed 196-pounds. The left-handed hitting outfielder was traded from the White Sox to the St. Louis Browns in 1951 in the deal that brought Sherman Lollar to Chicago. On July 28, 1952, Rivera returned to Chicago along with catcher Darrell Johnson as the White Sox dealt outfielder Ray Coleman and the versatile J. W. Porter to the St. Louis Browns. In 1958 Rivera played in 116 games for Chicago and managed only a .225 batting average. However, among his 62 hits he clubbed nine home runs, eight doubles, and four triples. The New York City native was a sound defensive player. In 1958 Rivera's speed on the base paths placed him second in the league in steals with 21. Rivera was recognized as one of the hardest workers on the club and an excellent man in the clubhouse.

On Wednesday, September 9, Chicago traveled to the nation's capital for a two-game set with the Washington Senators. The White Sox split the series with Washington, winning the opener 5-1 as Bob Shaw racked up his 15th victory with a complete game, seven hit performance. Aparicio, Landis, Rivera and Al Smith each had one RBI in the game. Smith's second hit of the day drove in Kluszewski with the game-winning run in Chicago's four-run seventh inning uprising. The "Magic Number" was reduced to 12 with the win. Cleveland swept a doubleheader from Baltimore 3-2 and 4-1 to hang on.

In the second game of the brief series on Thursday, Washington's Camilo Pascual won his 15th game of the year for this last-place club. Chicago starter Dick Donovan absorbed his eighth loss of the season against nine victories in the 8-2 setback. Chicago completed its season series with the Washington Senators winning sixteen games while losing only six. Baltimore beat Cleveland behind Hoyt Wilhelm's three-hit, nine-strikeout pitching performance. Cleveland's loss reduced Chicago's "Magic Number" to eleven.

The grind of the pennant race took its toll on the Pale Hose. Despite excellent pitching performances from Billy Pierce, Barry Latman and Gerry Staley, the White Sox dropped a pair to the Orioles in Baltimore on Friday night, September 11. Chicago's lead in the race with Cleveland was reduced to four games. In the first game of the twin bill Billy Pierce was touched for a Bob Neiman home run in the third, a run-scoring double by Gus Triandos in the sixth, and Willie Tasby's solo home run in the seventh. Chicago could manage only three hits off Baltimore starter Jack Fischer as they were shutout 3-0. In the nightcap, the Sox were whitewashed by Baltimore rookie Jerry Walker as the 20-year-old went sixteen innings for the 1-0 victory. The South Siders got help from the lowly Washington Senators as they topped Cleveland 5-4. Any combination of Chicago victories and Cleveland defeats totaling ten would now clinch the pennant for Chicago.

The National League pennant race tightened on Friday, as the league-leading San Francisco Giants dropped a 1-0 decision to last place Philadelphia. Los Angeles swept Pittsburgh 5-4 and 4-0 in a doubleheader to pull within a half game of the lead and the Milwaukee Braves thrashed Cincinnati 10-2 to close within one of San Francisco.

Early Wynn stopped Baltimore on Saturday, September 12, to earn his 20th victory of the season. Wynn's complete game, 6-1 triumph halted Chicago's losing streak at three and balanced the club's final season record against Baltimore at 11-11. This was the fifth season that Early had achieved the 20-win plateau and the first time since coming over to Chicago. Chicago broke out of its hitting slump, accumulating 10 hits, led by Kluszewski's three. Kluszewski and Landis had two RBIs each on the day. The game-winning run was scored in the second inning when Al Pilarcik lost Bubba Phillips' fly ball in the sun for a double, to allow Big Klu to trot home from second. In addition to Jim Landis' two RBIs, the speed merchant stole home in the seventh inning. Landis was playing despite a sore and infected leg. Chicago's lead over Cleveland remained at four games as the Tribe beat Washington 7-2.

John Melvin "Bubba" Phillips was another valuable player on Chicago's roster. The West Point, Mississippi native and former college football star was traded to Chicago on November 30, 1955. Phillips came over from Detroit in exchange for Virgil Trucks. The five-foot nine-inch, 180-pound right-hander divided his time between the outfield (38 games) and third base (47 games) in 1958. He was slowed for two months in 1958 by a broken bone in his right foot. Phillips had many timely hits for Chicago during the year and played solidly at third base. Phillips could also play center field, and was scheduled to do so in the upcoming series in Boston as Landis was sidelined with a leg injury.

With its "Magic Number" at nine, Chicago traveled to Boston's Fenway Park for a brief two game encounter with the Red Sox. To date Chicago had won six of the nine games played at Fenway in the 1959 season. The fabled left field wall, known as the "Green Monster," stood only 315 feet from home plate and was 37 feet tall. The wall turned routine pop fly balls into home runs and line drives that are potential home runs into singles. The wall jutted out to an irregular shaped junction in center field, 420 feet from home plate. The right field wall stood a mere 302 feet from home and was a haven for left-handed power hitters. The short right field fence came into play as the normally light-hitting Chicago third baseman, Billy Goodman, drove in the deciding runs in Chicago's 3-1 victory in the opener. Goodman lifted the game-winning two-run home run into the White Sox bullpen beyond the right field wall in the top of the fourth inning. Bob Shaw, with relief help from Billy Pierce in the eighth and Turk Lown in ninth, was rewarded with his 16th victory of the season, 3-1.

Meanwhile in New York, Cleveland lost two games to the Yankees to drop five and 1/2 games behind Chicago. The Yankees won the opener 2-1 on the strength of Mickey Mantle's 11th inning two-run blast and the second game 1-0 behind the pitching of Duke Maas. The combination of two Cleveland losses and the Chicago victory reduced the Sox "Magic number" to six.

Goodman had been a consistent .300 hitter since breaking into major league baseball in 1947 as a member of the Boston Red Sox organization. In 1950, his .354 batting average was strong enough to capture the American League batting title. William Dale Goodman was acquired by Chicago along with Tito Francona and Ray Moore in a trade with Baltimore on December 3, 1957. Chicago sent Larry Doby, Jack Harshman, Russ Heman and Jim Marshall to the Orioles in the trade. The five-foot, 11-inch, 165-pound utility infielder was born in Concord, North Carolina. Goodman proved his versatility with Chicago in 1958 as he played

111 games at third base and at least one game at every other infield position. Goodman batted .299 in 1958 in 425 plate appearances and his 127 hits included 15 doubles and five triples.

Nikita S. Khruschev, the Russian Premier, was scheduled to visit the United States on Tuesday, September 15. The Russian leader was making an extended tour of America at the invitation of President Eisenhower. On July 25, at the American National Exhibit in Moscow, Vice President Richard M. Nixon bumped into Khruschev in front of the kitchen exhibit of an American model home. The two leaders engaged in an impromptu debate concerning the technological superiority of their own country over the other's. The dialogue, which was captured by one of the first video tape cameras, became more heated as the two contrasted the merits of capitalism versus communism.

As a precursor to the Premier's visit to America in September, Moscow shocked the world with an incredible breakthrough. Soviet scientists launched a rocket that succeeded in hitting the moon. The moon shot, which was scheduled to coincide with Khruschev's visit, appeared to most Americans as clear evidence that Russian technology had vaulted ahead of that of the United States in the race for space. The lunar rocket traveled a distance of approximately 252,710 miles scoring a direct hit on the surface of the moon. Until this pennant race, most Chicago White Sox faithful thought it would be much easier for man to land a rocket on the moon than it would be for the White Sox to bring an American League flag to Comiskey Park.

On Monday, September 14, the Chicago rocket came back to earth with a crash as Boston handed the Sox a 9-3 drubbing. Dick Donovan took the loss as he, Gerry Staley, Gary Peters, Turk Lown and Ken McBride were all ineffective. Boston scored six runs in the sixth and three in the seventh to put the game out of reach. The loss evened Donovan's season record at 9-9. In the overall season series with Boston, Chicago won 14 while losing eight. Chicago's "Magic Number" remained at six as Cleveland beat the New York Yankees 8-5.

Chicago completed its eastern road swing with a two game series in historic Yankee Stadium. The "House That Ruth Built" had a seating capacity of 67,000 and for only the second time in over a decade would not play host to a World Series game. Yankee Stadium with its non-symmetrical dimensions, sported a left field foul pole that stood only 301 feet from home plate. The fence in left field quickly slanted out to a distance of 466 feet in dead center field. The expansive area in left center was often referred to as "Death Valley." Most mortal right-handed power hitters found the barrier unreachable. The right field foul line was a short 296 feet from the plate. The "Home Run" porch in right field had made this an outstanding target for Yankee left-handed power hitters, past and present.

In another one-run thriller, the White Sox outscored the Yankees 4-3 for Chicago's 34th one-run victory of the season. Billy Pierce bested the Yankees for his 14th win of the year despite departing the game in the eighth inning as his back stiffened up. Pierce was ambushed by Mickey Mantle's two-run homer in the first inning to fall behind 2-0. The White Sox battled back with one run in the fourth and two runs in the top of the eighth. Chicago scored a run in the ninth on a Norman Cash pinch hit sacrifice fly to go up 4-2. The extra run was needed as Mantle connected again this time off Shaw for his second home run of the game. The ninth inning blast represented the eighth time in Mantle's career that he had hit a home run from both the left and right side of the plate in the same game. Jim Rivera made a spectacular, diving, shoestring catch on Elston Howard's line drive for the second out of the inning and his quick throw to second base doubled up pinch runner Bobby Shantz for the final out of the game. Nellie Fox had three hits and Sherman Lollar had two hits and two RBIs to spearhead the Chicago attack. Chicago's lead was back to five and 1/2 games and its "Magic Number" became four as Cleveland dropped a heart breaker to the Red Sox 1-0.

The White Sox ended their season competition with the Yankees at 13-9 as they lost the Wednesday afternoon contest 3-1 to Jim Coates and the Bronx Bombers. Early Wynn failed in his bid for victory number 21 as the Yankees overcame a 1-0 deficit with three runs in the sixth inning. The White Sox managed only four hits on the day, two each by Billy Goodman and Al Smith. Slumping Cleveland lost again to Boston, 6-5, as Chicago's "Magic Number" dwindled to three.

Chicago had seven games remaining on its schedule. Two three-game series with Detroit were sandwiched around a September 22 game with the Indians in Cleveland. On Friday night, September 18, Bob Shaw battled Tiger ace Jim Bunning before a crowd of 37,352 at Comiskey Park. The two right-handers were locked in a scoreless duel until the bottom of the fifth inning. Chicago catcher, Sherman Lollar, led off the inning with his 21st home run of the year to hand Shaw the 1-0 advantage. Shaw made the run stick as he won his 17th game of the year with a five-hit, 1-0 shutout, his third shutout of the season. Lollar's drive into the seats in left was his 15th game-winning RBI of the season.

Sherman Lollar had been a bedrock performer since arriving in Chicago on November 27, 1951. The White Sox obtained Al Widmar and Tom Upton along with Lollar from the Bill Veeck-owned St. Louis Browns. To get this trio, Chicago gave away Joe DeMaestri, Dick Littlefield, Gus Niarhos, Gordon Goldsberry and Jim Rivera. Lollar was not known for his foot speed, but was considered one of the best defensive backstops in the game. Lollar was well respected for his ability to handle pitchers and call an effective ballgame. John Sherman Lollar, born August 23, 1924 in Durham, Arkansas, started his major league career in Cleveland in 1946. He had a brief stay with the New York Yankees, getting into the 1947 World Series where he had three hits in four plate appearances, including two doubles. Lollar was traded from the Yankees to the St. Louis Browns in 1949. The six-foot, one-inch, 185-pound right-hander was a steady, if not spectacular, offensive performer in his years with the White Sox and was a perennial All-Star during the 1950s. In 1958, Lollar established personal career records for home runs (20), and RBIs (84) while hitting .273. In 1959, Lollar had not only provided veteran leadership behind the plate, but had been responsible for more game-winning clutch hits than anyone else on the club.

Chicago's "Magic Number" stood at two. Cleveland's slim chances of catching Chicago stayed alive as they crushed seventh-place Kansas City 11-2. Cleveland's field general, Joe Gordon, resigned after the game as a result of his ongoing feud with the club's general manager, Frank Lane. Lane had openly criticized Gordon's managerial decisions as the Indians had fallen behind the White Sox in the American League pennant race. Speculation was that Lane would name 53-year-old Leo Durocher to take Gordon's place at the helm in 1960. The outspoken Lane indicated that he was considering several candidates to manage the club the following year.

A young golfer charged upon the scene at the United States Amateur Golf Championship at the Broadmoor Golf Club in Colorado Springs, Colorado. Jack Nicklaus, a junior at Ohio State University, beat out reigning champion, Charles Robert Coe for the title. At the age of 19 years and 8 months, Jack Nicklaus became the youngest champion in over 50 years in the 59th year of competition.

The White Sox were edged by Detroit on Saturday, September 19, 5-4. Dick Donovan was tagged with his 10th loss of the year. The White Sox were never ahead in the game and trailed 5-2 going into their final at bat. Norman Cash stroked his fourth home run of the year to make the game appear close. The pinch hit shot into the right center field bleachers was good for two runs and the final 5-4 margin. Overall the White Sox had a sloppy day on the mound, in the field, and on the basepaths. Cleveland picked up a game on Chicago as they again dismantled Kansas City, 13-7.

The White Sox played their last regular season home game of the year on Sunday as 27,784 fans were aboard to determine if the Pale Hose could clinch at least a tie for the American League flag. If Chicago derailed Detroit and Cleveland lost to Kansas City, the South Siders would clinch the pennant. The White Sox season attendance soared to a record 1,422,862, an incredible 625,411 increase in fans through the turnstiles over 1958. Sunday was not to be the day as Chicago lost to Detroit again by a count of 5-4 and Cleveland edged the Athletics 4-3. The "Magic Number" for Chicago remained at two and its lead over Cleveland was reduced to three and 1/2 games. Pierce was ineffective and was knocked out in the fifth inning after giving up six hits and all five Detroit runs. Aparicio stole his 54th base of the season and Lollar slammed his 22nd homer of the campaign in the losing cause. Lollar was also hit on the right hand by a pitch thrown by Jim Bunning in the late innings.

As the Chicago White Sox traveled to Cleveland for their Tuesday night battle of all battles, the race in the National League was coming to a head. Los Angeles, fresh from a three-game sweep of the front-running San Francisco Giants, had moved into a dead heat with the Milwaukee Braves for the lead. Los Angeles and

Milwaukee had identical records of 83-66. San Francisco trailed both teams by one game. Each of the three teams had five games remaining in their season. The Dodger games were all on the road, with two against seventh-place St. Louis and three at sixth-place Chicago. Milwaukee was scheduled to play a three-game series at home against last-place Philadelphia and two on the road at Pittsburgh. San Francisco was to play its remaining games on the road, two at Chicago and three at St. Louis.

Chicago's record over Cleveland to that point in the 1959 season was 14 wins and seven losses. The White Sox were 8-2 when playing in Cleveland. Early Wynn, Chicago's scheduled starter, had beaten Cleveland five times already during the year while losing only once. Jim Perry was selected to start for Cleveland in this must win game. Perry had lost both of his previous starts against Chicago. A crowd of 54,293 settled into the ball yard on September 22 to witness this heavyweight contest. Both sides went out in order in the first inning. In the Cleveland half of the second inning, Minoso reached first base after being hit by an Early Wynn inside fastball. Russ Nixon followed with a single to center field as Minoso raced into third base. Rocky Colavito hit a fly ball down the line in left, which Al Smith gathered in. Minoso tagged and attempted to score, but Smith's perfect strike to catcher Johnny Romano beat the sliding Minoso for the second out. Held fouled out to Kluszewski to end the inning.

Jim Rivera opened the Chicago third inning with a fly to right field that was caught easily by Colavito. Bubba Phillips became Chicago's first base runner as he blooped a single to center field. Early Wynn hit a short pop fly that shortstop Woody Held caught in shallow left field for the second out of the inning. The dimensions of the playing field in Cleveland's Municipal Stadium were 320 feet down both the left and right field lines and 410 to center field. Chicago's next batter, Luis Aparicio, measured that distance as he hit an opposite field drive that caromed off the wall at the 320 foot mark in right field for a double. Colavito relayed the ball to Held, whose throw was too late to nip Phillips at the plate. With one run across, Nellie Fox walked and Billy Goodman smashed a double down the right field line to score Aparicio for Chicago's second run. Kluszewski received an intentional pass from Perry before Romano became the final out of the inning on a ground ball to short.

In the fifth inning Cleveland retaliated. Held walked to open the frame. Wynn fanned pinch hitter Chuck Tanner on a 3-2 fastball. Rookie Gordon Coleman followed with a single that Aparicio knocked down behind second base. Piersall sliced a single to deep left center field, scoring Held and sending Coleman to third. Vic Power ended the inning by rapping into an Aparicio, to Fox, to Kluszewski double play. The score favored Chicago, 2-1.

Jim "Mudcat" Grant was called out of the Cleveland bullpen to pitch the sixth inning. Romano greeted Grant with a deep drive to center field that Piersall flagged down for the first out of the inning. Al Smith stepped to the plate and pulled a long drive over the wire screen in left for a home run to push the Chicago advantage to 3-1. Chicago's next batter, Jim Rivera, uncorked a shot over the 365 foot barrier in right center for a home run. The back-to-back haymakers gave Chicago the lead at 4-1. Phillips followed with a first pitch single to left. Grant then settled down to retire the side by coaxing Early Wynn and Aparicio into force plays.

Cleveland responded in their half of the sixth inning with a run. Francona opened the inning with a single to center field. Smith hauled in Minoso's drive for the first out of the inning. Russ Nixon singled to right as Francona loped to third. Phillips, playing center field for the injured Jim Landis, raced deep to pull down Colavito's long drive. Francona was able to tag at third and score without a throw for the Indians second run. Early Wynn was tiring and manager Al Lopez called upon Bob Shaw to relieve. Lollar, in spite of a sore and swollen right hand, replaced Battey behind the plate. Shaw induced Woody Held to hit a ground ball to Billy Goodman at third. Goodman's throw forced Nixon at second for the final out of the inning.

The White Sox were retired without incident in the seventh. Jim Landis came in to play center field as Bubba Phillips replaced Billy Goodman at third. Shaw had trouble in the seventh as Piersall and Powers singled to start the inning. Shaw retired Francona on a hard grounder to Fox as both runners advanced. With the tying run at second and another runner on third, Shaw dispensed with pinch hitters Elmer Valo and Jack Harshman. Neither club scored in the eighth inning. The White Sox went down silently in the ninth as Shaw struck out, Aparicio grounded out to second and Fox flied out to left.

Held popped up to Nellie Fox at second base to start the Indians ninth inning. After Shaw got two strikes on Baxes, the Cleveland infielder lined a shot off the pitcher's glove for a single. Jack Harshman lined a single to right sending pinch runner Ray Webster to third. Piersall then hit a smash which Fox knocked down at second. All hands were safe. Al Lopez went to the mound and summoned 39-year-old Gerry Staley from the bullpen. Staley, making his 65th appearance of the campaign, came in to face the dangerous Vic Power. On September 6 in Chicago, Power had come to the plate in a similar situation. In the ninth inning of that ballgame he clubbed a two-run double off Dick Donovan to give the Indians a 2-1, come-from-behind victory. Staley took the ball from Lopez. As he conferred with Lopez and Lollar, he surveyed the field. Staley threw a few warm up tosses and rubbed the ball as he glanced around the infield. The sign received from Lollar was for

Staley's money pitch-the hard sinker. Lollar set up on the lower outside portion of the plate. Staley stretched and threw his best pitch to the perfect spot, low and on the outside corner. Power swung at the offering and hit a hard ground ball to the left side of the infield. Aparicio glided over, gloved the ball, took three steps, grazed the bag at second and rifled a throw to Kluszewski at first to complete the game ending double play. One pitch, two outs, the "Magic Number" was zero.

The Chicago dugout emptied as the players and coaches mobbed Staley. The White Sox had finally clinched their first American League pennant in 40 years. Not since the 1919 Chicago "Black Sox" had the flag flown over Chicago's south side. Early Wynn picked up his 21st victory of the season and sixth over Cleveland. The heart-stopping victory added an exclamation point to Chicago's dominance of the Tribe in 1959.

The temperature stood at 80 degrees at 10:02 P M in Chicago on Thursday night, September 22, 1959. Without notice, the air raid sirens, which were strategically placed around the city to warn of enemy air attack, split the night air. Citizens all over the city poured into the streets to determine the cause for the alarm. Switch boards lit up and the volume of calls completely paralyzed the Bell Telephone System. Panic and joy hit the streets of Chicago simultaneously. Panic came from those uninformed souls who truly felt the city was under Russian attack. Joy and celebration came from those who had been glued to the Chicago White Sox and Cleveland Indian game on their radios and television sets.

Even though City leaders were soundly criticized for the panic they unleashed by setting off the air raid warning system, the panic was doused with the knowledge that all was done in celebration of the fantastic feat of Chicago's own White Sox. The players celebration in the visitors clubhouse at Municipal Stadium in

Cleveland was broadcast to the citizenry of Chicago via WGN Television. The play-by-play broadcast of the game was handled by Jack Brickhouse and Lou Boudreau. The celebration of the fans continued all night and into the morning. Forty years of pent-up baseball frustration was being released into the sultry night air. A contingent of 25,000 celebrating partisans made their way to Chicago's Midway Airport where the team's charter flight touched down at 2:05 A M. Among the 25,000 present to greet their conquering heroes were Mayor Richard Daley and Chicago White Sox president and owner Bill Veeck. Aparicio led the players from the plane to the cheers of the maddening throng. The "Go-Go" chant which had been shouted throughout Chicago during the course of the year filled the night air with a deafening roar. The celebration had just begun.

In the National League, the pennant chase was still not complete. Milwaukee dropped Pittsburgh 5-3. Rookie George Altman slammed a two-run home run in the ninth inning to push the Chicago Cubs past San Francisco 5-4. Los Angeles lost to the seventh-place St. Louis Cardinals in an 11-10 slugfest. When the dust cleared, Milwaukee led the Los Angeles Dodgers by one game and the San Francisco Giants by two.

Before departing for Detroit for the final three games of the regular season, the City of Chicago sponsored a parade and ceremony honoring the American League champion White Sox. The parade started at Wacker Drive and State Street and moved south on State to Adams, then west on Adams to LaSalle Street, then north on LaSalle to City Hall. The parade proceeded through a constant blizzard of ticker tape and confetti. The procession was led by Mayor Daley, Chuck Comiskey and Bill Veeck. The players followed, trailed by a hearse labeled "Dead Indian."

The race in the National League became a two team affair as the

Chicago Cubs beat San Francisco again, effectively eliminating the Giants from the race. Milwaukee lost to Pittsburgh and Los Angeles trumped the St. Louis Cardinals to deadlock both clubs with a record of 84-67. The Dodgers were scheduled to play the Cubs and the Braves were hosting the Phillies as both teams pressed for the privilege of facing the White Sox in the World Series.

The White Sox used the final three-game series in Detroit to rest several of their key players and to give much-needed major league experience to their youngsters and nonstarters. Sammy Esposito, J. C. Martin, Norm Cash, Johnny Romano and Joe Hicks all saw action as the White Sox allowed three ninth-inning runs to fall to the Tigers 6-5. Billy Pierce was battered in his two innings of work for three runs on five hits. Chicago rallied for three runs in the third as Pierce departed with the score knotted 3-3. Chicago scored two ninth inning runs on a Bubba Phillips single to surge ahead 5-3. It was short-lived as Gerry Staley gave up three ninth inning runs as he was tagged with his fifth loss of the year. Sherman Lollar was sent back Chicago for treatment of his right hand, which he injured the previous Sunday when he was struck by a Jim Bunning pitch. In the National League race, Milwaukee dropped a 6-3 decision to the Phillies as Los Angeles beat Chicago, 5-4.

On Saturday, September 26, Early Wynn won his 22nd decision of the year as he pitched five innings and gave up three Detroit runs. Chicago scored four in the first inning and one run in both the fifth and six innings. Callison's grand slam home run closed out the scoring for Chicago in the eighth. Earl Battey also went deep for Chicago, a solo home run in the sixth, which was the game-winner. Chicago won by a final score of 10-5. Gerry Staley broke a White Sox record for number of appearances by a pitcher as he played in his 67th game of season. In later years, Staley recalled, "In 1959 I warmed up in the bullpen during either 114 or 115 games, actually pitching in 67."

Also on Saturday, Milwaukee beat the Phillies 3-2 to pull even with the Los Angeles Dodgers who were hammered by the Chicago Cubs 12-2.

On Sunday afternoon at Detroit's Briggs Stadium, the American League champions ended the regular season on a positive note. Bob Shaw won his 18th of the year as the South Siders whipped Detroit 6-4. Shaw pitched five innings, giving up five Detroit hits and two runs to earn the victory. Chicago scored five runs in the first inning, the last two coming on Jim Rivera's game-winning home run into the upper deck in right field. Aparicio stole his 55th and 56th bases of the year to tie him with Wally Moses for Chicago's all-time season base stealing record. The victory completed Chicago's season competition with the Detroit Tigers with Chicago winning 13 while losing only 9.

Milwaukee clipped Philadelphia 5-2 as Bob Buhl won his 15th game of the year. The Dodgers kept pace by blasting the Chicago Cubs 7-1. The teams were deadlocked at 86-68 on the year. The dead heat would necessitate a best two out of three game playoff for the National League pennant. The first playoff game would take place in Milwaukee's County Stadium, with the second game to be played in the Los Angeles Coliseum. The third game, if necessary, would also be played in Los Angeles. This was the first time since 1951, and the third time in the history of the National League, that a playoff was required to determine the National League participant in the World Series. In 1951, Bobby Thomson hit a game-ending home run, which became known as the "Shot Heard 'Round The World," to rally the then New York Giants past the Brooklyn Dodgers for the 1951 National League crown.

Chicago's amazing run for the 1959 American League pennant came to an end. Chicago completed the regular season with 94 victories and 60 losses. They had won the American League crown by five games over the second-place Cleveland Indians, who had finished the year with a 89-65 record. The New York Yankees finished in third place, with a record of 79-75, a total of 15 games behind Chicago. The Detroit Tigers finished fourth, at 76-78, 18 games off the lead. Boston wound up in fifth place, with a record of 75-79, a full 19 games behind Chicago. Baltimore tailed off at the end of the year to finish with a record of 74-80, 20 games off the pace. The Kansas City Athletics finished at 66-88, which placed them in seventh place, 28 games behind the league leader. And for the third consecutive year the Washington Senators finished in the cellar, a miserable 31 games behind Chicago with a record of 63-91.

The White Sox had a few days of idle time as they awaited the outcome of the National League playoff which would determine their World Series opposition. If they turned on the radio in their spare time, they were entertained by top ten hits such as *The Battle of New Orleans* by Johnny Horton, *Lonely Boy* by Paul Anka, *A Big Hunk of Love* by Elvis Presley, *The Three Bells* by The Browns and another great hit by Bobby Darin, *Mack The Knife*. If television was their pleasure, they could watch a host of new shows which debuted in 1959. *Bonanza* rode onto the scene with Lorne Greene as Ben Cartwright, and his sons played by Michael Landon, Dan Blocker and Pernel Roberts. Clint Eastwood starred in *Rawhide* as Rowdy Yates. *The Many Loves of Dobie Gillis* featured Bob Denver as beatnik Maynard G. Krebs. *The Twilight Zone* and *The Untouchables* became instant successes.

CHAPTER SEVEN

National League Playoff

THE MILWAUKEE BRAVES AND THE LOS ANGELES DODGERS FINISHED the regular season in a dead heat for the 1959 National League flag. The two-time National League Champion Braves had finished first in 1957 under Fred Haney with a 95-59 record en route to beating the New York Yankees for the World Series crown. In 1958 the Braves again won the National League pennant with a 92-62 record before falling to the Bronx Bombers in the World Series rematch. In 1959 their record slipped further to 86-68 as they faced the surprising Dodgers in this best two out of three game playoff. Warren Spahn and Lew Burdette had won a league-leading 21 games apiece to form an awesome one-two punch in the Braves' starting rotation. Henry Aaron had a tremendous year at the plate, leading the league in hitting at .355 while compiling a solid power year with 39 home runs and 123 RBIs. Eddie Matthews, the Braves left-handed hitting, third baseman led the senior circuit in home runs with 46 while accounting for 114 RBIs and hitting at a .306 clip.

The Dodgers completed 1958, their first year in Los Angeles, with a very disappointing 71-83 record, netting them a seventh place finish, only one notch above the cellar dwelling Philadelphia Phillies. Without major changes from the club they fielded in 1958, the Dodgers rose from that seventh-place finish to tie the mighty Milwaukee Braves for the top spot in the league. The Dodgers received excellent, but not spectacular, pitching from Don Drysdale, Johnny Podres, Sandy Koufax, Roger Craig and Danny McDevitt. The surprise of the season was the relief work of rookie Larry Sherry. Sherry, a perennial loser in the minor leagues, was called up to the parent club on July 3 from its St. Paul affiliate in the American Association. The six-foot, one-inch tall right-hander proceeded to finish the regular season by stringing together six consecutive victories out of the bullpen. During that streak, he compiled an earned run average of less than one. Sherry had been dominant in the Dodgers' push for the National League pennant. The 24-year-old rookie had been a Los Angeles Fairfax High School teammate of Chicago's Barry Latman. Veterans from the Brooklyn Dodger glory days, Duke Snider, Charlie Neal, Gil Hodges and Jim Gilliam, had good seasons. Wally Moon, a December 4, 1958 acquisition from the St. Louis Cardinals had a solid year as well. Moon hit .302, with 19 home runs and 74 RBIs. He did a great job of adapting his hitting style to take advantage of the friendly left field screen in the Los Angeles Coliseum. Catcher John Roseboro provided outstanding defense as did rookie shortstop Maury Wills. Wills took over the starting role at shortstop in midsummer and provided an immediate infusion of energy to the team.

The first game of the playoff series commenced on Monday, September 28, at Milwaukee's County Stadium. The second play-off game and the third, if necessary, would be played in Los Angeles. The crowd was a sparse 18,297 on the damp, rainy afternoon. The start of the contest was delayed 47 minutes because of rain. The Braves sent Carlton Willey to the mound to oppose Dodger starter Danny McDevitt. The entire game was played under the lights due to the rain-darkened afternoon skies. Charlie

Neal, the second man to bat for the Dodgers, singled sharply off second baseman Bobby Avilla's glove. Neal advanced to second on Wally Moon's tap to the mound. Norm Larker followed with a single to right that scored Neal to put the Dodgers in front 1-0. In the bottom of the second inning, the rain picked up again. Dodger starter McDevitt walked Johnny Logan on four pitches after one man was out. Del Crandall followed with a line drive single to left advancing Logan to second base. Billy Bruton drove Logan home with the tying run as he singled to right center field. With runners at first and second, Braves pitcher Carlton Willey came to the plate. McDevitt quickly went to a 2-0 count on the Braves pitcher. Walter Alston, the Dodger manager, pulled the plug on McDevitt and summoned his rookie relief phenom, Larry Sherry, from the bullpen. Sherry worked the count to 3-2 before inducing Willey into a routine bouncer to shortstop Maury Wills. The normally dependable Wills muffed the ball for an error and the bases were loaded. Bobby Avilla, the next hitter, hit a scorching ground ball to Wills' right. The shortstop made a spectacular play as he snagged the ground ball and forced Willey out at second base. Crandall raced home with the second run of the inning. As the rain grew harder, Matthews grounded out to end the inning. The Braves surged to a 2-1 advantage.

In the top of the third inning, the Dodgers came back to tie the score. Neal singled to right after one out before Moon forced him at second for the second out of the inning. Larker slapped a ball up the middle that Avilla barely knocked down behind second and all runners were safe. Veteran Gil Hodges then lined a single to left as Moon raced home to knot the score at 2-2. There was no further scoring until the sixth inning. Johnny Roseboro led off in the top of the sixth for the Dodgers. Willey worked the count on the Dodger catcher to 2-1. On the next offering, Roseboro slammed a long drive to right field. Hank Aaron raced back to the wall and watched helplessly as the ball fell into the fifth row of the bleachers, 375 feet from home plate. The solo shot gave the Dodgers a 3-2 lead that Larry Sherry made stick. Sherry went seven and 2/3 innings and held the Braves to only four singles. Sherry had excellent control and a baffling assortment of pitches. His repertoire included a fastball, curve and his out pitch—the slider. Larry mastered the slider in the winter of 1958 in the Venezuelan League. That pitch coupled with a much improved command of all his pitches, transformed Sherry into a very capable major league pitcher. The Braves only threat after the sixth was squelched as Don Demeter made a great catch against the wall in center field as Billy Bruton led off the ninth inning with a 390 foot blast to the furthest reaches of the playing field. The Dodgers had won the opening round in the Braves' own back yard. Chicago White Sox manager, Al Lopez, looked on from the stands. Lopez had foregone the season ending road trip to Detroit so that he could personally scout the Braves and Dodgers as potential adversaries for the upcoming World Series.

The two National League clubs headed to the airport for the six-hour flight to Los Angeles for the second game of the series. The game was scheduled for the Los Angeles Coliseum on Tuesday afternoon. Milwaukee manager Fred Haney selected 21 game winner Lew Burdette to start for the Braves as Walter Alston picked Don Drysdale to take the mound for the Dodgers. Drysdale had posted 17 victories to pace the Dodgers' staff in 1959.

The crowd of 36,528 watched as big Don Drysdale got into trouble immediately in the first inning. He walked Eddie Matthews after one out. Henry Aaron then slammed a Drysdale offering low off the fence in left. As Matthews steamed into third, Aaron raced for second base. Duke Snider's throw to second was in time to nail

Aaron, but umpire Augie Donatelli ruled Aaron safe as Neal missed the tag. The Braves' cleanup hitter, Frank Torre, singled to left to plate both Matthews and Aaron. The Braves had a lightning quick two-run lead. The Dodgers countered in the first inning as Charlie Neal drove a triple to right center field. Wally Moon then singled to center to drive in Neal and pull the Dodgers to within one run.

As the two teams exchanged punches, the Braves scored another run in the second to answer the Dodgers. Johnny Logan singled, then advanced to third on Lew Burdette's single to center and scored when Duke Snider's throw from the outfield skipped past Gilliam at third. In the bottom of the fourth inning, Charlie Neal continued his torrid hitting as he lofted a home run over the left field screen to lead off the frame, shaving the lead to 3-2. In the fifth inning, the Braves responded after one out when Eddie Matthews clubbed his 46th home run of the year to stretch the Braves lead to two. The tremendous blast sent Don Drysdale to the showers and gave Matthews the National League home run title. Matthews broke his tie with Chicago shortstop Ernie Banks, who had ended his season with 45 round-trippers. The Braves scored another run in the eighth inning as Del Crandall tripled off the left field screen and scored on Billy Bruton's sacrifice fly. Through eight innings, Lew Burdette had kept the Dodgers at bay. Podres, Churn, Koufax and Labine followed Drysdale to the mound through the ninth.

The Dodgers were faced with a 5-2 deficit as they opened the last half of the ninth inning. Wally Moon, Duke Snider and Gil Hodges opened the inning for the Dodgers with consecutive singles to load the bases. Don McMahon relieved Burdette for the Braves and faced only one batter, Norm Larker, who singled to the screen in left to score Moon and Snider, closing the gap to 5-4. Fred Haney called upon staff ace Warren Spahn to quell the uprising. Pinch hitter Carl Furillo drove a deep fly to right that Aaron flagged down with a fine running catch. Hodges tagged at third and scored easily to tie the score at 5-5. Maury Wills followed with a single that drove Spahn from the mound. Joey Jay entered the game for the Braves and got the last out of the inning as Hank Aaron gathered in Junior Gilliam's tremendous drive to deep right field. The Dodgers dramatic comeback forced the sudden death affair for the Braves into extra innings.

The Dodgers threatened in the 11th inning, but could not score after loading the bases. Stan Williams pitched the 10th, 11th and 12th inning for the Dodgers holding the Braves hitless. However, Williams experienced some tense moments as he walked the bases loaded in the 11th before retiring the Braves. In the bottom of the 12th, Braves reliever Bob Rush retired Wally Moon and Stan Williams to open the inning before walking Gil Hodges. The Dodgers second string catcher, Joe Pignatano, then singled sharply to left as Hodges stopped at second. Carl Furillo, the 37-year-old veteran, was the next hitter. After falling behind in the count to Rush, one ball and two strikes, Furillo slashed a drive up the middle that shortstop Felix Mantilla flagged down behind the bag. As Furillo made a headlong slide into the bag at first, Mantilla's off balance throw skipped past first baseman Frank Torre as Gil Hodges chugged home with the deciding run. Mantilla had moved over to shortstop from second base to replace Johnny Logan, who was injured in the seventh inning of the game in a collision at second. Furillo was credited with a single, as the Dodgers became the first club in National League history to climb from seventh place one season to win the pennant the next. The Dodgers had won the 13th National League pennant in the history of the franchise.

As the Dodgers and their fans celebrated, the Braves accepted defeat like professionals. The scene was now set for the World

Series. Both the Chicago White Sox and the Los Angeles Dodgers were surprise winners in 1959. The amazing season saw a changing of the guard as the mighty New York Yankees and Milwaukee Braves had fallen from the American and National League thrones.

CHAPTER EIGHT

The World Series

THE BASEBALL WORLD WAS FOCUSED ON CHICAGO'S COMISKEY PARK as the 56th World Series commenced on October 1, 1959. The Chicago White Sox and the Los Angeles Dodgers, two surprise participants in this year's post season classic, were both confident of their ability to prevail. Both clubs displayed an amazing grit during the season in their ability to win close ballgames. The Pale Hose had won 35 of 50 one run contests. Their National League counterparts had been only slightly less spectacular as they won 33 of 55 games decided by one run. The White Sox World Series eligible roster included Aparicio, Fox, Kluszewski, Landis, Lollar, Phillips, Smith and Rivera as starters. Wynn, Shaw, Donovan, Pierce, Staley and Lown comprised Chicago's starting rotation and bullpen. Players off the bench included Arias, Battey, Cash, Esposito, Goodman, Latman, McAnany, McBride, Moore, Romano and Torgeson.

The Dodgers countered with a mixture of post season hardened veterans from the team's glory days in Brooklyn and a fine crop of youngsters. Hodges, Neal, Wills, Gilliam, Larker, Snider, Moon and Roseboro were slated to start for the Dodgers. Craig, Podres, Drysdale, Koufax and Sherry were the core of the Dodgers mound staff and the bench was manned by Churn, Demeter, Essegian, Fairly, Furillo, Klippstein, Labine, McDevitt, Pignatano, Repulski, Williams and Zimmer.

In World Series competition prior to 1959, the American League had won 35 World Championships and the National League 20. In the history of the post season classic, the New York Yankees had dominated by winning a remarkable 18 World Series titles. The White Sox had prevailed as World Champions in 1906 and 1917. Perhaps Chicago's most infamous appearance in the post season classic was its defeat in 1919. That series allegedly was "thrown" by the Sox, who became forever known as the "1919 Black Sox." The Dodgers were frequent participants in the World Series but had only managed to bring a World Championship to the franchise once, in 1955, while still in Brooklyn.

The great City of Chicago had practically shut down its commerce and industry in anticipation of its first World Series in 40 years. Elaborate plans were made so that ingress and egress to the ball yard at 35th Street and Shields Avenue would be smooth and trouble free. Certain streets in the neighborhood of Comiskey Park were turned into one-way thoroughfares to facilitate the process. Shuttle buses were scheduled to run every 10 minutes to bring fans from the downtown Loop area to the Park. Additional parking was provided, as the recently acquired right of way for the future north-south expressway was converted to public parking. This expressway, when completed, would be named the Dan Ryan Expressway. Mr. Dan Ryan was currently serving as president of the Cook County Board and was a guest in Mayor Richard Daley's Comiskey Park box for the opening game of the World Series.

The White Sox were well rested. Manager Lopez had foregone the last White Sox road trip to Detroit to scout both the Braves and Dodgers who were finishing their regular season play in

Milwaukee and Chicago, respectively. Both clubs were ready for the games to begin.

On Thursday, October 1, 1959, the day dawned at 6:49 a.m. with a temperature of 53 degrees. A tremendous throng of 48,013 partisan fans made their way to the yard. Dignitaries from across the spectrum of sports, politics and entertainment were on hand. Mayor Richard Daley and his family were present in their usual box. Illinois Governor Stratton was also present for the opener. Television sets all over the city were tuned to WGN-TV to watch Jack Brickhouse and Vin Scully broadcast the game. The entire series was to be televised in color for the first time in history. Large screen televisions were set up in hotels, bars, offices and store windows all over town for the benefit of fans unable to attend the game in person. In our school, even Mrs. Murphy was prepared to give us periodic updates on the game's progress. At 1 p.m. as the game started, the air was clear and a slightly chilly 63 degrees.

Early Wynn, Chicago's veteran 22-game winner, took the mound for the White Sox. As the capacity crowd went wild with every pitch, Wynn opened the first inning by coaxing Dodger leadoff hitter Jim Gilliam to ground out to Aparicio. The Dodgers could only manage an infield single by Charlie Neal and a walk to Duke Snider as Wynn retired the side without allowing a run. The White Sox drew first blood in the bottom of the first inning. Fox walked, Landis singled and Kluszewski followed with a single to score Fox. Sherman Lollar then hit a sacrifice fly to deep right center field to score Landis with Chicago's second run. The Sox were up on Roger Craig and the Dodgers 2-0 after one inning. Both teams went down in order in the second frame. After Wynn retired the Dodgers in the third, the White Sox came to bat.

Chicago's first man up in the third was Luis Aparicio. Craig retired the speedster Aparicio on a liner to Larker in right field.

Nellie Fox then hammered a double into the right field corner. Landis stroked a single for his second hit of the day as Fox scampered home with Chicago's third run of the game. Big Ted Kluszewski hit a towering drive that found the first row of the lower right field bleachers for a home run. The two-run blast handed the White Sox a 5-0 lead and sent Roger Craig to the showers. Chuck Churn replaced Craig as Sherman Lollar came to the plate. Lollar lofted an easy fly ball to left center field. Wally Moon and Duke Snider converged on the ball and collided as the ball dropped to the turf with Snider being charged with the error as Lollar reached second base. Goodman made the Dodgers pay for the gaffe as his single drove home Lollar. Al Smith followed with a double as Goodman scored on Snider's throwing error. Jim Rivera hit a sharp ground ball to Charlie Neal, who threw wildly to the plate in a futile attempt to nail Smith. Wynn completed the onslaught with a run scoring double to deep left center field. The White Sox pushed their lead to 9-0 as they scored seven runs on six hits with the help of three Dodger errors. The weak hitting Chicago White Sox had powered their way to an insurmountable lead as the ballpark shook with the roar of the crowd.

The White Sox scored two runs in the fourth inning as Kluszewski hammered a tremendous drive off of the facing of the upper deck in right field for his second home run of the day and a single-game World Series record-tying five RBIs. Labine, Koufax and Klippstein followed Churn to the mound and effectively shut down the Chicago attack for the remainder of the day. Early Wynn continued his mastery of the Dodgers as he allowed no runs on six hits, while striking out six over seven complete innings. But Wynn's elbow stiffened in the eighth inning and season long bullpen sensation Gerry Staley came on in relief to pitch two scoreless innings. The game ended mercifully for the Dodgers as they absorbed the humiliating 11-0 thrashing. The victory was Early Wynn's first in post season competition. Wynn had started Game Two of the 1954 World Series for the Cleveland Indians and pitched well, but was charged with the loss as the Indians fell to the New York Giants by a score of three to one.

Talk of a four-game sweep flooded the City of Chicago. Were the Dodgers mentally and physically exhausted from their pennant run and their pulsating playoff battle with the Milwaukee Braves? That possibility was discussed everywhere, but not in either clubhouse. Both teams recognized that the Dodgers simply had a bad day. The White Sox knew that the Los Angeles Dodgers were a very formidable opponent. The Los Angeles ball club had built up confidence by overcoming crushing defeats like this many other times throughout their season.

The second game of the series would turn out to be pivotal in the overall outcome of the conflict. The 1 p.m. start on October 2, 1959 took place under sunny skies and a pleasant 71-degree temperature. The crowd of 47,368 was amused as the normally adept Nat "King" Cole fumbled through the lyrics of our National Anthem. Right-hander Bob Shaw took the mound for Chicago. The 26-year-old Shaw's regular season record was a sparkling 18-6, with an earned run average of 2.69. His southpaw mound opponent was the 1955 World Series hero, Johnny Podres. The little left-hander's season record was 14 and 9, with an earned run average of 4.11. In the bottom of the first inning, Chicago jumped on Podres for two runs. Aparicio doubled to open the inning, then Fox sent a deep fly ball to right field sacrificing Aparicio to third. Landis walked to put men at the corners with only one out. Dodger second baseman Charlie Neal bobbled a hot ground ball off the bat of Kluszewski but recovered in time to get the lumbering giant at first. Landis advanced to second on the play as Aparicio scored

Chicago's first run. Sherman Lollar singled off the glove of third baseman Jim Gilliam, as Landis scampered home with the second run of the inning.

The score remained Chicago 2, Los Angeles 0 until two were out in the top of the fifth inning. Charlie Neal hit Shaw's first offering, a belt-high slider deep into left field. Al Smith sprinted to the warning track and drifted back to the wall. As Smith looked up, the ball cleared the fence and disappeared into the crowd as a cascade of cold beer descended on his head. Smith recently reflected upon the incident, "At first I was mad, but field umpire Rice was on top of the action and said he saw the play all the way and felt it was an accident. I cooled off quickly. I later met the fella who spilled the beer. He was a nice guy, an executive in business." The home run enabled the Dodgers to draw to within one run of the White Sox.

The score remained unchanged until the Dodger half of the seventh inning. Lightning struck once again after two were out. Dodger manager Walter Alston called upon Chuck Essegian to pinch hit for Johnny Podres. Shaw fell behind Essegian in the count, three balls and one strike when Shaw came in with a slider that remained high in the strike zone. Essegian hammered the offering deep into the upper deck in left center field to tie the score 2-2. Shaw had uncharacteristically made two big mistakes to Neal and Essegian as he was having trouble keeping his pitches low in the strike zone. The next hitter, Jim Gilliam, walked on five pitches as Al Lopez got Turk Lown and Billy Pierce up in the Chicago bullpen to be ready should Shaw falter any further. Charlie Neal, whose home run two innings earlier had provided the Dodgers first run of the series, was the next man to come to the plate. Neal took Shaw's first pitch for a called strike, but deposited the second one into the Chicago White Sox bullpen. The 420 foot shot put the Dodgers in the lead at 4-2 and chased Bob

Shaw from the game. Turk Lown came on to end the inning without further damage.

With Podres gone from the game, Alston called upon his rookie relief ace, Larry Sherry, to work his magic on the Chicago bats. Sherry had been almost untouchable in relief during the Dodgers' drive to the National League pennant. He quickly retired Aparicio, Fox and Landis in the bottom of the seventh. Lown followed suit by retiring the Dodgers in order in the top of the eighth inning.

The bottom of the eighth inning was to be the pivotal half inning in the 1959 World Series. Game One hero Ted Kluszewski reached Sherry for a single to center field to open the inning. Sherman Lollar followed with a hard single off the glove of Jim Gilliam at third base proving that Sherry indeed might be vulnerable. With runners at first and second and no one out, manager Lopez sent Earl Torgeson into the game to pinch run for the slow-footed Kluszewski. Al Smith, the next batter, attempted to move both runners along with a sacrifice bunt but failed on his first attempt. After taking Sherry's second pitch for a called strike, the sacrifice bunt was abandoned. After working the count to 3-2, Smith hammered the ball to the wall in left center field. As it appeared that Moon or Demeter might have a chance to catch the ball, Torgeson hesitated as he rounded third and Lollar came to a complete stop at second. Third base coach Tony Cuccinello, watching the ball all the way, waived Torgeson home. Not fully realizing that Lollar had stopped his momentum at second, Cuccinello continued to waive Lollar to the plate. Moon played the carom off the wall perfectly and his throw hit cut off man Maury Wills. Wills strong, accurate throw to home nailed Lollar by 10 feet. Smith hustled into third base as Lollar was tagged out at the plate. The gamble of aggressively taking the extra base had paid off for Chicago throughout the year. However, Lollar's hesitation and Cuccinello's aggressiveness were punished by the Dodgers' perfect defensive execution. Goodman, pinch hitting for Bubba Phillips, went to bat with the tying run 90 feet away with only one out. The normally reliable contact hitter struck out. Jim Rivera, the next man up, promptly fouled out to catcher John Roseboro to end the inning and effectively the game.

Chicago went down easily in the ninth as Cash, Aparicio and Fox all grounded out. With the 4-3 Dodger victory, the series was tied at one game each. It appeared that the momentum of the series had been taken away from Chicago when Lollar was tagged out at the plate. Both Cuccinello and Lollar were labeled as goats for the rally-killing gaffe. Al Smith, the man who slammed the double that had initiated the play had a somewhat different slant on the inning recalling recently that, "Lollar and Cuccinello were blamed for blowing the play, but Cuccinello was an aggressive coach. He won many ball games for us in 1959 with his aggressive approach to running the bases. I went to third on the play hoping I could draw a throw and let the tying run score. The real problem was that we had the tying run on third base in that inning with only one out and couldn't score. We had two more chances to score the tying run and couldn't do it. That's the real reason why we lost that ballgame."

As the World Series moved to Los Angeles, the odds at the wagering window also took an about-face. The odds makers now favored the Dodgers to win the best of seven series 11 to 10. At the conclusion of the 11-0 Chicago route of the Dodgers in the opener, these same odds makers had picked Chicago as an 11-5 favorite to win the series.

While Chicago dropped the second game of the series to the Dodgers at Comiskey Park, work crews were being organized to convert the Los Angeles Coliseum from its football configuration into a baseball field. The University of Southern California football team played in the Coliseum on Friday evening and handed Ohio

State a 17-0 thumping. Major work was required to prepare the Coliseum for Sunday afternoon's contest. As the mound was installed, it appeared abnormally high due to its sharp contrast with the matted sod of the board-flat infield. The 42-foot high, 142-foot long wire-mesh screen was reinstalled atop the short left field wall. This screen was the National League version of Fenway Park's fabled "Green Monster." The dimensions of this Coliseum, masquerading as a baseball diamond, were quite unusual. The left field foul pole was a mere 251 feet from home. The wall broke out gradually to 320 feet and then more sharply to 390 feet in far left center field. The wire-mesh screen stretched from the foul pole to the 320 foot mark. The farthest point to the wall was 420 feet in center field. The right center field power alley was 375 feet from the plate and the foul pole down the right field line was 333 feet away. The Dodgers had hammered 147 home runs as a team during the regular season in 1959, with the majority being hit in the Coliseum.

Al Lopez selected Dick Donovan to pitch the third game of the series for Chicago on Sunday afternoon, October 4. Donovan finished the regular season with a record of nine wins and 10 losses, with an earned run average of 3.65. Alston countered with Don Drysdale who had experienced an up and down year as well. Drysdale finished the regular season at 17-13 with a 3.46 earned run average. The largest crowd in World Series history, 92,394 strong, turned out on this bright, hot afternoon. The shirtsleeve-clad throng provided a daunting background of white, that impaired both the fielders' and batters' ability to quickly pick up the path of the hit or pitched ball. Donovan and Drysdale were locked in a scoreless duel through six and 1/2 innings. Drysdale gave up 11 hits but no runs. Chicago's lack of ability to hit with men on base coupled with John Roseboro's ability to throw out would-be base stealers kept Chicago off the scoreboard. Roseboro had gunned down Aparicio, Fox and Rivera as Chicago attempted to challenge the Dodger catcher's ability to control the basepaths. Donovan pitched near flawless baseball through six, yielding only a second-inning single to Gil Hodges. That hit dropped in front of left-fielder Al Smith as he was slow to pick up the path of the ball against the background of white shirts.

After one out in the seventh inning, Donovan ran into trouble as Charlie Neal slammed a single off the screen in left field for the Dodgers' second hit. Wally Moon grounded out to Fox as Neal reached second. Then Donovan's control deserted him as he walked both Larker and Hodges to fill the bases. The loss of control caused manager Lopez to dispatch Donovan to the showers in favor of Chicago's relief ace, Gerry Staley. Pinch hitter Carl Furillo came to bat for Demeter. After taking a called strike, Furillo slapped a ground ball to the shortstop side of second base that skipped over Aparicio's out-stretched glove for a single. Neal and Larker scored to give the Dodgers a two-run lead. It appeared that Aparicio got a bad jump on the ball. Aparicio, like many other fielders on both teams, had a difficult time following the flight of the ball off the bat due to the stark white background created by the combination of the shirt-sleeve crowd and the blazing afternoon sun. In addition, the ball may have hit a pebble in the rocky infield as it appeared to hop over Aparicio's glove at the last second.

In the top of the eighth inning, Kluszewski and Lollar led off with back-to-back singles. Larry Sherry was summoned to relieve Drysdale and added to his existing problem by hitting Billy Goodman in the knee with a two-strike pitch. The bases were loaded with no one out. Al Smith hit into his second double play of the game as Kluszewski scored. Rivera then fouled out to catcher John Roseboro to end the inning. Once again, Chicago failed to hit with men on base in a crucial situation. The Dodgers responded with one run in the bottom of the eighth inning as Charlie Neal doubled to score Maury Wills. Chicago was retired harmlessly in the ninth inning as the game ended Los Angeles 3, and Chicago 1. Drysdale was credited with the victory and Donovan took the loss despite an excellent pitching effort.

Chicago now faced a 2-1 series deficit. Both Chicago losses could have gone either way. The White Sox lack of timely hitting proved fatal in both defeats. Their inability to score a runner from third base, with one out, in the eighth inning of Game Two in Chicago was critical. In Game Three, Chicago stranded 11 men on base while only scoring one run. Early Wynn was selected to start Game Four for Chicago and the Dodgers' Game One starter, Roger Craig, was also selected to take the mound. Chicago's players were hopeful of regaining the offensive touch that they exhibited in scoring 11 runs in the opening game of the series.

Game Four on October 5 was another closely-fought contest played before a crowd of 92,650. Both teams were held scoreless until the third inning. The Dodgers got to Early Wynn after two were out in the bottom of the third, scoring four runs on five singles by Moon, Larker, Hodges, Demeter and Roseboro. The Sox contributed to their own demise by making two errors. Jim Landis was charged with an error as his strong throw to third base hit a sliding Wally Moon. The ball bounced away as Moon raced home. Later in the inning, Aparicio dropped a throw from Rivera that allowed Demeter to make it safely to second base. The poor visibility created by the sea of white shirts in the crowd once again had an effect on the game. Al Smith got a late jump on a routine fly ball hit by Hodges, that fell in front of him for a single. Under normal circumstances, Smith would have caught the ball and the Dodger inning would have ended with just one run scoring. Lown relieved Wynn and nailed down the final out of the frame, but not before

Chicago had fallen behind 4-0.

Roger Craig held the White Sox in check until the seventh inning, while Lown and Billy Pierce were doing the same to the Dodgers. Craig had given up six hits and four walks through six innings as Chicago stranded eight men on the bases. The Pale Hose continued to be plagued by their inability to come up with the timely hit with men on base. The top of the seventh inning for Chicago began as pinch hitter Earl Torgeson bounced out to Charlie Neal at second. Landis next singled to center field. After an Aparicio sacrifice, Nellie Fox's two-out single kept the inning alive. Kluszewski came through with a single to center, scoring Landis for Chicago's first run. Craig got one strike on Sherman Lollar, the fifth man in Chicago's batting order, but on the next pitch Lollar turned on a low slider and sent it down the left field line, and into the 29th row of the bleachers beyond the 42-foot high screen. The three-run shot tied the game at four all. Lollar, Chicago's regular season home run leader, had hit his first round tripper of the series. Billy Goodman ended the rally by striking out for the third time on the day.

Gerry Staley pitched the bottom of the seventh inning for Chicago and retired the Dodgers in order. Larry Sherry came on in the eighth inning to pitch for Los Angeles and retired the side, giving up a walk to Staley. Veteran first baseman Gil Hodges opened the eighth inning by smashing a fly ball to left center field on a Gerry Staley sinker. The ball landed 10 rows deep into the bleachers at the 320-foot mark, just to the right of the 42-foot screen. The home run would have been a routine out in just about every other ball park in the major leagues. Instead, it provided Los Angeles with the 5-4 victory as the Sox did not produce a run in the ninth. Staley was charged with the loss and Larry Sherry earned the victory as the Dodgers stretched their Series lead to a seemingly insurmountable three games to one.

In the 1958 World Series, the New York Yankees were in a similar position as they trailed the Milwaukee Braves three games to one. The Yankees took the field in New York for the fifth game of that series with their backs against the wall. Bob Turley, the great Yankee pitcher, took command and hurled a five hit, 7-0 shutout to enable the Yankees to live another day. The series moved back to Milwaukee and the Yankees proceeded to beat the Braves 4-3 in the ten-inning, sixth game. The Bronx Bombers then completed their miraculous comeback by breaking open a 2-2 ballgame with a four-run eighth inning in game seven. Chicago was hopeful that they could replicate that performance. Bob Shaw, Chicago's Game Two starter, was tabbed for the task by Al Lopez. Sandy Koufax, the young, fireballing lefty was given the ball by Walter Alston.

The teams were scoreless through three innings with both Shaw and Koufax pitching well, as another record crowd of 92,706 looked on. In the Chicago fourth, Fox and Landis opened the inning with back-to-back singles. Lollar, batting cleanup, hit a sharp grounder to Charlie Neal at second. Neal, without looking at Fox streaking for the plate, never hesitated as he turned the double play, stepping on the bag at second and firing the ball to Hodges at first. Fox scored, providing Chicago with a 1-0 lead. Through seven innings Koufax pitched brilliantly, giving up just one run on only five hits, while striking out six. But Shaw had better results, yielding seven hits and no runs through seven frames. The Dodgers had stranded eight base runners. In the seventh inning, with two outs and two men on base, Al Lopez called time out to make a defensive substitution, bringing Jim Rivera in the game to play right field and moving Al Smith to left to replace McAnany. Charlie Neal, the next batter hammered a deep drive to right center field. Lopez's defensive change proved to be a stroke of managerial genius, as Rivera made a spectacular one-handed, over the shoulder catch of

Neal's drive to preserve the White Sox lead.

Stan Williams pitched the eighth inning for the Dodgers, as starter Sandy Koufax had been lifted for a pinch hitter when the Dodgers had threatened in the seventh. In the Dodgers' half of the eighth inning, Shaw ran into trouble. Wally Moon led off the inning with a pop fly to center field that fell in front of Landis as he completely lost the ball in the sun. After Larker flied out, Hodges singled to center and advanced to second when Landis attempted to throw Moon out at third. Pierce replaced Shaw and walked pinch hitter Rip Repulski intentionally to load the bases. Lopez summoned Dick Donovan to face pinch hitter Carl Furillo with one out and the bases jammed with Dodgers. Displaying nerves of steel, Donovan coaxed Furillo to pop out to third base-man Bubba Phillips for the second out of the inning and then retired Don Zimmer on a routine fly ball to Al Smith in left field to end the threat. Both Chicago and Los Angeles went down in order in the ninth, preserving the 1-0 White Sox victory behind the great clutch pitching of Bob Shaw and Dick Donovan. Shaw currently remembered the day as, "One of the most important highlights of my major league career. In later years Sandy Koufax proved to be one of the greatest pitchers of our time." Chicago was still alive and had renewed confidence as they flew back to the Windy City for the sixth game of the World Series.

Exactly one week after the White Sox had humbled the Dodgers in the series opener, 47,653 fans gathered on October 8 in Comiskey Park to see if their heroes could prevail once more. Early Wynn was called upon again to preserve Chicago's hope of a World Championship. Johnny Podres was selected to pitch for the Dodgers. Chicago faced sudden death for the second game in a row. Under overcast skies and the threat of rain, the drama played out quickly. In the third inning, Duke Snider slammed an Early

Wynn offering into the bleachers in lower left field to give the Dodgers a 2-0 advantage. Then in the top of the fourth inning, the flood gates opened and Los Angeles scored six runs on six hits, one walk and one error, against three Chicago pitchers. Wynn was reached for singles by Larker and Wills and a double by Johnny Podres. Wills and Podres both had a RBI as Wynn took a seat on the bench trailing 4-0. Dick Donovan, the relief hero of Game Five, proceeded to throw gasoline on the Dodger inferno. After walking Gilliam, Donovan allowed a double to Charlie Neal, scoring Podres and Gilliam as the lead grew to six. Wally Moon hit Donovan's next pitch into the lower right field stands for a two-run homer as the Dodgers advantage grew to an insurmountable 8-0. Turk Lown relieved Donovan and retired Snider and Demeter on ground balls to end the inning.

Dodgers starter Johnny Podres opened the bottom of the fourth inning by retiring Fox on a foul pop fly before nailing Jim Landis in the head with a fastball. Although Landis jumped up immediately, Podres was clearly rattled as he walked the next batter, Sherman Lollar. Ted Kluszewski gave Chicago a glimmer of hope as he unloaded his third home run of the series into the upper deck in right field to put Chicago on the scoreboard. Podres was replaced by Larry Sherry, after walking Al Smith on five pitches. The rookie, Sherry, allowed two more runners to reach base before retiring the side without further damage. Chicago never posed another serious threat as Larry Sherry earned his second victory of the series. In the ninth inning, as rain clouds darkened the Chicago skyline, pinch hitter Chuck Essegian slammed a Ray Moore offering into the lower left field stands to close out the scoring at 9-3. In the last of the ninth, Goodman, Cash and finally Aparicio went down meekly to end Chicago's magnificent season, two victories short of the coveted prize.

Many factors influenced the ultimate outcome of the series. Chicago's failure to get key hits with men on base certainly contributed to its demise. Conversely, the Los Angeles Dodgers were able to get the key home run or the seeing-eye single at just the right moment. The play in the eighth inning of the second game when Sherman Lollar was thrown out at the plate, diffusing a critical Chicago rally, could also be viewed as a turning point in the series. Larry Sherry's dominating pitching performance was clearly a deciding factor. Sherry had a hand in all four Dodger victories, saving two and winning two. The Dodgers turned the tables on the White Sox by stealing five bases against Lollar, as Chicago mustered only two thefts on Roseboro. The Dodgers turned seven double plays to only two for the White Sox. The overall team earned run average in the series favored Los Angeles (3.23) compared to Chicago (3.46).

Alas, offensive statistics for both teams were remarkably similar. The Dodgers scored 21 runs and hit seven home runs while the White Sox scored 23 runs, 11 of which were scored in the first game blowout, and hit four home runs. The team batting averages over the series were identical at .261.

The offensive stars for Los Angeles were Charlie Neal and Gil Hodges. In addition, Chuck Essegian and Carl Furillo came through with clutch hits in pinch hitting roles. Neal had 10 hits in 27 at-bats, including two doubles and two home runs. He knocked in six runs and his batting average of .370 was second on the team to Gil Hodges. Neal's two home runs and three RBIs in pivotal Game Two were decisive in Los Angeles' 4-3 victory. Gil Hodges hit .391 for the series and drove in two runs. His nine hits in 23 at-bats included a triple and a game-winning home run. Hodges solo shot in the eighth inning of Game Four gave the Dodgers a 5-4 victory and what proved to be an insurmountable 3-1 lead in the series. Furillo's pinch hit two-run single in the seventh inning of Game Three was the game winner. Chuck Essegian hit two pinch hit home runs. The first tied the second game of the series at 2-2 and provided the platform for Charlie Neal's game-winning home run. The second ended the scoring in the sixth and final game of the series.

On the mound, Larry Sherry's accomplishments were acclaimed as he was voted the World Series Most Valuable Player. He appeared in all four Dodger victories winning two and saving the other two, while posting a .071 earned run average. In 12 and 2/3 innings pitched, he gave up eight hits and only one earned run while striking out five. After 40 years Ray Berres, the Chicago head pitching coach, indicated that "Sherry was clearly the difference in the series. Back in Chicago after the World Series, I received a bottle of fine Sherry in the mail from a fan. It came with a note to remind me just how good Larry Sherry had been in the Series."

When a team loses the World Series, no one feels like a hero. Chicago did however have its stars. Ted Kluszewski led the way with a .391 batting average, 10 RBIs, and three home runs. Kluszewski's two home run, five RBIs heroics in Game One of the series spearheaded Chicago's 11-0 domination of the Dodgers. Aparicio (.308 average, three RBIs, eight hits), Fox (.375 average, nine hits) and Landis (.292 average, seven hits) all lived up to expectations. Bob Shaw and Early Wynn, Chicago's regular season pitching mainstays, each won one game and lost one game.

The 56th World Series was a financial success. The paid attendance for the six games was a record 420,784, with the gate receipts totaling $2,628,809.44. Television and radio revenue gathered in an additional $3,000,000. The Los Angeles Dodgers winning players pool aggregated $375,186.59, with a full individual player's share totaling a record $11,231.18. The losing Chicago

White Sox received individual full player shares of $7,275.17.

The 1959 Chicago White Sox brought the American League flag to the south side of Chicago for the first time in forty years. With that championship, they brought lifelong memories to the players, coaches and fans. Jim Landis reflected on that team and that era when he said of his teammates of 1959: "To be a part of something like that was really special. It's hard to find people and relationships like that in the outside world." Not only did Landis feel that way about his teammates, but he also had admiration and fond memories for many of his foes. Landis added, "It was an absolute thrill to get a hit off Koufax in the World Series. People realize what a great career Koufax had, but don't understand what a great person he is. I played winter ball with Koufax in San Juan, Puerto Rico. During that time we fished together and he would come over for breakfast and have scrambled eggs. Years later, I attended a Hall of Fame induction ceremony. Someone came up behind me and gave me a big hug, and asked where my wife was because he wanted some scrambled eggs. It was Sandy. I hadn't seen Koufax in several years and he took the time to seek me out and visit with me. Sandy is a fine person, whose mere presence can take over a room filled with dignitaries." At the induction ceremony for Nellie Fox into the Hall of Fame, Jim recalled a telling incident, "I was in the Hall of Fame town and walked into an old Woolworth's store. In that store, a group of kids were gathered and five New York Yankees were standing around talking with the kids and giving them free autographs. Hank Bauer, Moose Skowron, Whitey Ford, Don Larsen and Phil Rizzuto were signing autographs and giving these kids all the time they wanted." Jim's comments properly framed the character of the men who played and loved the game. The magic of that era infused several generations of fans, including myself, with a lifelong love for the game of baseball.

CHAPTER NINE

The Game-Winners

DURING THE REGULAR SEASON, THE CHICAGO WHITE SOX HAD MANY
different players step to the forefront in game-deciding situations,
but as a team, Chicago finished well behind the league leaders in
most offensive categories. The White Sox had an overall .250 team
batting average, placing them sixth in the field of eight American
League teams. During the regular season, Chicago scored 669 total
runs, had 620 RBIs and 1,325 base hits. Once again these totals
placed them sixth in the league in each of these offensive measures
of performance. The team total base count of 1,928 was seventh in
the eight team field. Chicago finished dead last in home runs with
97. They were the only team in both major leagues to finish the
season with fewer than 100 home runs.

The White Sox finished among the league leaders in offensive
statistics related to speed and discipline at the plate. They led the
league in stolen bases with 113, with 56 attributed to perennial
league-leader Luis Aparicio. The closest club to Chicago in thefts
was Boston with a total of 68. Chicago led the league in triples
with 46. The Pale Hose total of 220 two-base hits placed them
fourth among the eight teams. Chicago tied Detroit for league best
in getting on base via the walk with 580 and held the dubious

honor of having the most batters (49) hit by a pitch. Chicago showed its discipline at the plate by leading the league in fewest times striking out with 634. The White Sox made the most out of their offensive talents combining discipline at the plate with timely hitting and speed to win many close ballgames.

SHERMAN LOLLAR

Chicago catcher Sherman Lollar led the way for the White Sox with fifteen game-winning hits. Lollar commenced his game-winning dramatics in Chicago's third game of the season, as his single beat Detroit 5-3. Lollar's history of clutch hits was spectacular in 1959 as his game-winning dramatics included eight home runs. All were important to Chicago's success during the season, but perhaps Lollar's three-run shot against Cleveland on August 28 was the most important. That home run provided the initial victory in Chicago's four-game sweep of the Indians in Cleveland. Chicago entered that series with a one and 1/2 game lead over Cleveland and left town with what proved to be an insurmountable 5 and 1/2 game advantage.

AL SMITH

Chicago outfielder Al Smith was second only to Lollar in game-winning hits with eleven. The hard-hitting, right-hander won over many of his Comiskey Park detractors in 1959 with his frequent late-inning heroics. Smith was originally obtained from the Cleveland Indians for his veteran leadership and clutch bat work. Smith's achievements were impressive in 1959. Smith's crowning accomplishment was his sixth-inning, game-winning solo home run against Jim "Mudcat" Grant of the Cleveland Indians on September 22. That home run clinched the American League pennant for Chicago in Cleveland's Municipal Stadium.

NELLIE FOX

Nellie Fox, Chicago's inspirational leader, contributed seven game-winning hits to his extensive repertoire of accomplishments during the year. Fox was recognized for his contribution to the club's success in 1959 by winning the American League Most Valuable Player award. Chicago finished one, two, three in the year-end balloting for the coveted award as Fox beat out teammates Luis Aparicio and Early Wynn. Fox's biggest game-winning hit set the course for Chicago's spectacular season of come-from-behind victories. Fox's never give up attitude was perhaps indelibly etched on the personality of the 1959 Chicago club in the opening game of the season. Fox's fourteenth-inning, two-run blast off Don Mossi of the Detroit Tigers made Chicago and Gerry Staley 9-7 winners on that cold afternoon at season's start. The victory ignited Chicago's four-game winning streak to open the 1959 campaign.

BILLY GOODMAN AND BUBBA PHILLIPS

Chicago's third base tandem of Billy Goodman and Bubba Phillips had a combined total of thirteen game-winning hits for the Pale Hose in 1959. Billy Goodman, with seven game-deciding hits, didn't get his first until the 98th game of the season. That took place on July 30 against the New York Yankees as his seventh-inning single enabled Early Wynn to beat the Yankees by a score of 3-1. In the month of August, Billy was on a clutch hitting binge as he was responsible for five game-winners. Billy's most important game-winner came in Chicago's 6-3 triumph over Cleveland on August 30 when his single provided the margin of victory in Chicago's third triumph in their four-game sweep of the Indians.

Bubba Phillips got the majority of the starts at third base for Chicago in 1959. Phillips was responsible for six game-winners during Chicago's pennant drive. Phillips brightest moment of the season came in early May. The Sox, after a hot start to the season, saw their record slip to 11-11, as they dropped the first game of a crucial series to the Cleveland Indians at Comiskey Park. In the next two ball games, Phillips lifted the club on his back. His third inning double on May 9 was the decisive hit in Chicago's 9-5, must win over the Tribe. In the first game of the following day's double header, Phillips refused to let Chicago lose. Phillips' eighth inning leadoff home run tied the game. And after Cleveland surged ahead in the 11th inning, Phillips came through with a single to score the winning run.

JIM LANDIS

In accumulating his seven game-winning hits during the 1959 campaign, Landis hit for the cycle. Landis hit a home run in Detroit on August 13 for the game-winning hit. His triple was decisive in Chicago's 13-7 triumph over Kansas City on September 7. Landis' two doubles beat the Washington Senators on June 11 and again on August 1. Landis' safeties provided the margin of victory in close games against New York on July 17 and Boston on July 21. Jim Landis' clutch hitting complemented the many games he helped win for Chicago with his speed, glove and throwing arm.

JIM MCANANY

Jim McAnany, Chicago's rookie outfielder, joined the club on June 27, 1959. McAnany worked his way into the outfield rotation by making contributions both offensively and defensively. McAnany's bat was hot from the outset. In three successive games, commencing with the July 12 double header against Kansas City, McAnany delivered game-deciding hits. In both ends of that double header, his base clearing triples proved to be game-winners. McAnany followed that performance with a game-deciding single against the Red Sox in the next game Chicago played. In total McAnany had five game-winners in 1959, all within a thirty day period.

TORGESON, ENNIS, ROMANO, APARICIO, RIVERA AND SIMPSON

Earl Torgeson, Del Ennis and John Romano had four game-winning hits each during the course of the season. This group was followed by Aparicio, Rivera and Simpson with three game-deciders apiece. Torgeson clubbed two home runs for game-winners. On April 25, Torgeson ended Cleveland's long winning streak by capping off Chicago's five-run, ninth-inning rally with a pinch hit, three-run home run. On June 4, Earl ended a seventeen-inning affair as his dramatic solo shot off Baltimore's Jerry Walker handed Chicago a 6-5 victory.

Del Ennis made his mark on Chicago's season during his brief stay with the club as he drove in the game-winning run four times during a seven game stretch in mid-May.

Johnny Romano appeared in only 53 games for Chicago in 1959, but made his at-bats count with four game-winners to his credit.

Although Aparicio tallied only three game-winning hits during the campaign, he started the season dramatically. Aparicio provided the margin of victory in two of Chicago's first four games of the season. Aparicio's seventh-inning home run against Detroit on April 11 sealed Chicago's 5-3 victory and he turned the trick again three days later in Chicago's home opening 2-0 victory over Kansas City with his fifth-inning single.

Jim Rivera's three game-winners included the difference maker in Chicago's final game of the season at Detroit on September 27. In that contest, Rivera's first-inning home run was the game-winner.

Although Harry Simpson departed Chicago in the acquisition of Ted Kluszewski, he did provide three game-winning hits during his stay. On June 26, Simpson hit a grand slam home run off a

Bob Turley offering to make Chicago 5-4 winners over the New York Yankees.

Billy Pierce (2), Early Wynn (1), and Bob Shaw (1) helped their own cause during the season with hits that proved decisive in victory.

Chicago received offensive contributions from men up and down the roster. Some of these men played brief but important roles in winning the pennant. Others like Lollar, Smith, Landis, Fox, Aparicio, Goodman, Phillips and McAnany played much larger offensive roles in this intricate mosaic of championship performance. Ray Berres best captured the essence of these collective efforts by saying recently that, "The men would step up and someone would seem to always do the right thing at the right psychological moment." That is how championships are decided.

1959 CHICAGO WHITE SOX GAME-WINNERS

S. LOLLAR	GAME	H/A	TEAM	SCORE	HIT	INNING	WINNER
April 12	3	A	DET	5-3	1B	6	Donovan
May 15	29	A	NY	6-0	SF	1	Pierce
May 20	35	A	BALT	5-2	SF	4	Donovan
June 28	70	H	NY	9-2	HR	6	Wynn
June 28	71	H	NY	4-2	HR	1	Donovan
July 4	76	A	KC	7-4	HR	7	Shaw
July 16	85	A	BOS	4-3	2B	8	Donovan
July 22	92	H	BOS	5-4	1B	8	Lown
Aug 12	110	A	DET	11-6	HR	5	Staley
Aug 14	112	A	KC	5-1	HR	7	Shaw
Aug 23	121	H	NY	5-0	HR	7	Shaw
Aug 24	122	H	NY	4-2	2B	5	Moore
Aug 28	126	A	CLEV	7-3	HR	7	Shaw
Sept 2	132	H	DET	11-4	1B	5	Stanka
Sept 18	148	H	DET	1-0	HR	5	Shaw

A. SMITH	GAME	H/A	TEAM	SCORE	HIT	INNING	WINNER
April 30	16	H	NY	4-3	HR	11	Pierce
May 12	26	A	BOS	4-3	HR	12	Arias
June 10	54	A	WASH	4-1	3B	1	Wynn
June 14	58	A	BALT	3-2	1B	10	Donovan
July 3	75	A	DET	6-5	HR	10	Lown
July 24	93	H	BALT	2-1	HR	9	Pierce
July 26	95	H	BALT	4-1	HR	4	Wynn
July 28	97	H	NY	4-3	HR	8	Pierce
Aug 30	129	A	CLEV	9-4	HR	5	Latman
Sept 9	139	A	WASH	5-1	1B	7	Shaw
Sept 22	151	A	CLEV	4-2	HR	6	Wynn

N. FOX	GAME	H/A	TEAM	SCORE	HIT	INNING	WINNER
April 10	1	A	DET	9-7	HR	14	Staley
May 10	25	H	CLEV	5-0	1B	1	Wynn
June 3	47	H	BALT	6-1	3B	5	Pierce
June 14	57	A	BALT	9-6	1B	8	Wynn
July 5	78	A	KC	4-3	1B	10	Lown
July 11	81	H	KC	8-3	2B	5	Latman
Aug 18	115	H	BALT	6-4	2B	8	Staley

B. GOODMAN	GAME	H/A	TEAM	SCORE	HIT	INNING	WINNER
July 30	98	H	NY	3-1	1B	7	Wynn
Aug 2	101	H	WASH	3-2	1B	9	Lown
Aug 7	106	A	WASH	4-1	1B	3	Shaw
Aug 9	108	A	WASH	9-0	ERR	1	Wynn
Aug 25	123	H	BOS	5-4	2B	10	Lown
Aug 30	128	A	CLEV	6-3	1B	6	Wynn
Sept 13	144	A	BOS	3-1	HR	4	Shaw

B. PHILLIPS	GAME	H/A	TEAM	SCORE	HIT	INNING	WINNER
May 9	23	H	CLEV	9-5	2B	3	Moore
May 10	24	H	CLEV	5-4	1B	11	Pierce
July 9	79	H	CLEV	4-3	HR	6	Pierce
Aug 21	118	H	WASH	5-4	1B	7	Staley
Aug 22	119	H	WASH	1-0	1B	2	Latman
Sept 12	143	A	BALT	6-1	2B	2	Wynn

J. LANDIS	GAME	H/A	TEAM	SCORE	HIT	INNING	WINNER
June 11	55	A	WASH	3-1	2B	9	Pierce
July 1	73	A	CLEV	6-5	SF	9	Latman
July 17	87	A	NY	2-0	1B	9	Wynn
July 21	91	H	BOS	2-1	1B	7	Donovan
Aug 1	100	H	WASH	2-1	2B	9	Staley
Aug 13	111	A	DET	9-0	HR	1	Wynn
Sept 7	137	H	KC	13-7	3B	4	Staley

J. MCANANY	GAME	H/A	TEAM	SCORE	HIT	INNING	WINNER
July 12	82	H	KC	5-3	3B	1	Moore
July 12	83	H	KC	9-7	3B	5	Shaw
July 14	84	A	BOS	7-3	1B	4	Pierce
July 31	99	H	WASH	7-1	1B	2	Latman
Aug 5	104	A	BALT	2-0	1B	2	Latman

E. TORGESON	GAME	H/A	TEAM	SCORE	HIT	INNING	WINNER
April 25	12	A	CLEV	8-6	HR	9	Lown
June 4	48	H	BALT	6-5	HR	17	Shaw
June 7	51	H	BOS	9-4	SF	2	Donovan
June 23	65	H	WASH	4-1	1B	2	Wynn

D. ENNIS	GAME	H/A	TEAM	SCORE	HIT	INNING	WINNER
May 13	27	A	BOS	4-0	1B	1	Shaw
May 14	28	A	BOS	14-6	HR	5	Wynn
May 16	30	A	NY	4-3	1B	11	Lown
May 18	33	A	WASH	9-2	2B	1	Wynn

J. ROMANO	GAME	H/A	TEAM	SCORE	HIT	INNING	WINNER
May 25	43	H	DET	4-3	1B	9	Lown
Aug 2	102	H	WASH	9-3	2B	5	Shaw
Aug 9	107	A	WASH	4-3	ERR	8	Staley
Aug 27	125	H	BOS	5-1	1B	3	Latman

L. APARICIO	GAME	H/A	TEAM	SCORE	HIT	INNING	WINNER
April 11	2	A	DET	5-3	HR	7	Wynn
April 14	4	H	KC	2-0	1B	5	Pierce
Sept 8	138	H	KC	3-2	1B	10	Wynn

J. RIVERA	GAME	H/A	TEAM	SCORE	HIT	INNING	WINNER
April 17	7	H	DET	6-5	2B	8	Arias
April 26	13	A	CLEV	6-5	SF	4	Wynn
Sept 27	154	A	DET	6-4	HR	1	Shaw

H. SIMPSON	GAME	H/A	TEAM	SCORE	HIT	INNING	WINNER
June 5	49	H	BOS	5-2	2B	8	Staley
June 26	69	H	NY	5-4	HR	9	Shaw
July 25	94	H	BALT	3-2	1B	17	Lown

CHAPTER TEN

The Pitchers

QUALITY PITCHING WAS A SIGNIFICANT FACTOR IN CHICAGO'S RISE TO the top of the American League in 1959. Chicago led the league in team earned run average with a 3.29 overall mark. Chicago's starting pitching was rock solid as Early Wynn and Bob Shaw had tremendous seasons. The Sox bullpen was anchored by Gerry Staley and Turk Lown, who both had career years. Each pitcher on the staff stepped up and played a meaningful role at some point in the season. Veterans Billy Pierce and Dick Donovan had sub-par years gauged against their own high standards. In spite of this, both Pierce and Donovan stepped forward and notched important victories for the club at crucial points in the season. Barry Latman had a very solid rookie season but veteran Ray Moore could never get on track during the course of the year. Rudolfo Arias pitched well in early season relief work. Ken McBride, Gary Peters, Claude Raymond, Don Rudolph and Joe Stanka all made cameo appearances for Chicago in 1959 as well.

EARLY WYNN

Early Wynn, the 39-year-old veteran, had a spectacular season for the Pale Hose. Wynn, thought to be on the downside of an illustrious career, rebounded in 1959 to lead the Chicago White Sox to the American League flag. In doing so, Wynn was recognized as the best pitcher in the major leagues as he captured the Cy Young Award, beating out Sam Jones of the San Francisco Giants and teammate and road roommate Bob Shaw.

Wynn pitched a remarkable 256 innings during his 37 starting assignments. He compiled 22 victories against only 10 defeats and pitched 14 complete games. Wynn allowed 106 runs on 202 hits, including 20 home runs. The hard throwing right-hander struck out 179 batters while walking 119. His earned run average was a sparkling 3.16.

In Wynn's 37 starts during the season, Chicago prevailed as a team in 27 of those contests. Wynn dominated his old team, the Cleveland Indians, compiling six victories and only one loss against the second-place finishers. Wynn had five starts against Baltimore (3-1), Washington (4-1), New York (3-2), and Kansas City (1-3). In his six starts against the Boston Red Sox, Wynn was 2-2. Against Detroit, Wynn was undefeated in his four starting assignments with a 3-0 record.

Wynn pitched five shutouts during the season. On May 1, Wynn beat the Boston Red Sox 1-0 as he gave up only one hit, striking out 14 Red Sox hitters and slamming a home run himself for Chicago's only run. On May 10, Wynn allowed only four hits in whitewashing Cleveland 5-0. Wynn shut down the Yankees in New York on July 17, 2-0, while yielding only two hits. Early Wynn pitched back-to-back three-hit shutouts against Washington (9-0) on August 9, and Detroit (9-0) on August 13. Of the many crucial games won by Wynn during the year, perhaps the biggest took place on September 22. On that day, Wynn pitched Chicago to a pennant clinching 4-2 victory over Cleveland in front of 54,293 hostile fans in Cleveland's Municipal Stadium.

BOB SHAW

Bob Shaw began 1959 in the Chicago bullpen and was utilized early in the season as a short and long relief specialist. Shaw made 14 relief appearances before getting his first start of the season against Boston on May 13. From that point on, Shaw appeared primarily as a starter. In his 26 starts, Shaw won 15 games while losing six. Shaw led the league in 1959 with an overall winning percentage of .750, as his season record was 18 and 6.

Shaw started 12 games in Comiskey Park and 14 on the road. Shaw faced Detroit (2-3), Washington (4-0) and New York (3-0) five times each. He was undefeated against Kansas City (3-0) in three starts, and Boston (2-0) in two starts. Shaw had trouble with the Orioles (0-2), as he was winless in his four starting assignments. He pushed his season victory total to 18 with wins in relief over Kansas City on April 22, Baltimore on June 3, and Kansas City once again on July 3. Shaw also had three saves for the year.

The emergence of Bob Shaw was a key factor in Chicago's pennant drive. Shaw completed eight of the 26 games that he started. Although Shaw's entire season was a highlight, perhaps his most important victory was on August 28. On that day, Chicago commenced a crucial four-game series against the red-hot second-place Cleveland Indians. A crowd of 70,398 jammed Cleveland's cavernous Municipal Stadium to witness the series opener, as Shaw twirled a complete game, seven-hit, 7-3 masterpiece over the Tribe. The victory initiated a four-game sweep that demoralized the Indians and thrust Chicago into a 5 and 1/2 game lead in the pennant race. Shaw pitched two complete game shutouts during the season, the first against Boston on May 13 (4-0, five hits), and the second on August 23 against the New York Yankees (5-0, six hits).

Overall in 1959, Shaw pitched 231 innings and gave up 72 runs on 217 hits, including 15 home runs. Bob Shaw struck out 89 opponents while walking 54. His season earned run average was 2.69, best among Chicago's starters. Shaw was recognized for his magnificent effort by being selected third in the post season Cy Young Award balloting for the best pitcher in the major leagues.

BILLY PIERCE

By his standards, the crafty veteran left-hander had an off year. Pierce was plagued by hip and back injuries from mid-August through early September. Pierce started 33 games for Chicago and completed 12 of them. Of the 33 starts, he won 14 of those decisions and lost 15. He faced the Yankees (4-3) seven times. He had trouble with the Kansas City Athletics as his six starts resulted in only two wins and four losses. Pierce took the mound against Detroit (0-3), and Baltimore (2-2) five times each. He posted a solid record of 3-1 in his four starting assignments against Cleveland. Billy Pierce was the starting pitcher against Boston (2-1), and Washington (1-1), three times. Pierce shutout Kansas City 2-0 on a six hitter in Chicago's fourth game of the season. He also whitewashed the New York Yankees and Whitey Ford on May 15, 6-0. Pierce's best game of the season was a one-hit masterpiece over the Washington Senators on June 11 as Chicago prevailed 3-1. On August 6, Pierce pitched 16 innings against Baltimore and came up empty with a 1-1, curfew-induced, tie.

In his injury-plagued, up and down season, Pierce was responsible for a number of important victories. Billy pitched a total of 224 innings, giving up 98 runs on 217 hits, including 26 home runs. Pierce struck out 114 and walked 62, as he posted a 3.62 earned run average.

DICK DONOVAN

Dick Donovan started 29 ballgames for Chicago during the 1959 season, completing five of them. In the games that Donovan started the Chicago White Sox won 17 and lost 12. Donovan was credited with 9 of those victories and 10 losses. In the ten ballgames that Donovan started and departed without a decision, Chicago prevailed in eight. In a testament to the depth of Chicago's bullpen, five different relievers were credited with those victories.

Donovan was called upon to start 16 games at Comiskey Park and 13 games on the road. In his 29 starting assignments, Donovan faced Boston (3-2) seven times, Cleveland (1-3) and Detroit (2-1) five times each, Washington (0-3) and Baltimore (2-0) four times each, Kansas City (0-1) three times, and New York (1-0) once. Donovan's most effective stretch during the season was May 20 through July 21. During that span Donovan started 13 games and Chicago won 10 of those, with Dick getting credit for six of the 10 victories. Donovan experienced shoulder problems after his July 21 start against Boston and didn't return to action until August 16. Donovan's finest effort of the season was on August 29 in Cleveland's Municipal Stadium in the second game of a crucial four-game series against the second-place Indians. Donovan beat Jim Perry as he pitched a complete game, five-hit shutout, with the 2-0 victory elevating Chicago's lead over Cleveland to 3 and 1/2 games.

In 1959, Donovan pitched 180 innings, yielding 171 hits, 15 home runs and 84 runs. Donovan struck out 71 and issued 58 bases on balls. His 3.65 earned run average ranked him fifteenth in the league among qualifiers.

BARRY LATMAN

Hard throwing right-hander Barry Latman won eight while losing five in his 21 starting assignments in 1959. During the season, he hurled five complete games. Chicago was victorious in 14 of the 21 games that Latman started. Latman was handed the starting assignment for 12 home games and nine games on the road. He faced Cleveland (2-0), Kansas City (1-1) and Baltimore (1-2) four times each. He opposed Washington (3-0) and Boston (1-1) three times apiece. He had no record in his two starting assignments against Detroit, and was beaten 6-2 in his only start against the Yankees on July 19.

In the period from July 31 through September 7, Latman started nine times for Chicago and the team won eight of those decisions. Latman earned five of his season victories during that span, including a 2-0, three-hit shutout of Baltimore on August 5 and a 1-0, five-hit shutout of Washington on August 22.

On the season, Latman pitched a total of 156 innings, giving up 138 hits, 15 home runs and 71 runs, while striking out 97 and walking 72. Latman's earned run average for the season was 3.75.

GERRY STALEY

Gerry Staley appeared in a club record 67 games in 1959 and pitched an amazing 116 innings, all in relief. Staley won eight games, lost five, and had 14 saves. He was second in the league to Turk Lown in saves. Staley gave up 39 runs on 111 hits, including only five home runs. Staley struck out 54 batters and walked 25. His earned run average of 2.25 was the best on the club. Staley started the season by winning Chicago's 14 inning, opening day victory over Detroit. His four and 2/3 innings of four-hit, no-run relief work stopped the Tigers in their tracks. In the month of August alone, Staley won five games, three over the Washington Senators and one each over Baltimore and Detroit. Staley's most memorable appearance took place in Chicago's September 22 pennant clinching victory over Cleveland. On that day, Staley relieved Bob Shaw with one out and the bases loaded with Indians in the bottom of the ninth inning. He threw one pitch to Vic Power who promptly grounded into the game ending, pennant clinching double play. In 1959, Staley and his road roommate, Turk Lown, combined to form one of the most devastating relief tandems in the American League.

TURK LOWN

Turk Lown had his best overall season in the major leagues in 1959. Lown appeared in 60 ballgames, pitching 93 innings of relief. Lown had an earned run average of 2.89 as he gave up 32 runs on 73 hits, including 12 home runs. He struck out 63 batters and walked only 42. Lown established a record of nine wins, two losses and 15 saves. His total number of victories in relief and games saved were both tops in the American League.

Lown had at least one victory in relief against every club in the American League. His longest outing of the year was on July 25, as he pitched the final six innings of Chicago's 17 inning, 3-2 victory over Baltimore in Comiskey Park. Three different times during the course of the season Lown pitched on three consecutive days.

CHAPTER ELEVEN

Post 1959

THE PLAYERS ON THE 1959 CHICAGO WHITE SOX CLUB WERE expected to be the nucleus of championship teams of the future. Little did these men realize when they walked off the field in Comiskey Park on October 8, 1959, that neither this group nor any future group of ballplayers would bring another American League championship to Chicago in the twentieth century. The players themselves would go their separate ways, some finishing their careers with Chicago, but most moving on to other clubs.

Bill Veeck's fingerprints became more visible as the 1960 club was designed more for power, while attempting to retain the elements of speed and team defense that exemplified the 1959 team. The most notable changes to the starting lineup were the acquisitions of Roy Sievers to play first base, Gene Freese to play third base and Minnie Minoso to patrol left field. In 1960 Sievers responded by hitting 28 home runs, knocking in 93 runs and hitting .295. Freese hit 17 home runs, 79 RBIs and maintained a .273 batting average. Minoso hit .311 with 20 home runs and 105 RBIs. Gone were key elements in Chicago's 1959 youth program, including Bubba Phillips, Norman Cash, Ron Jackson, Johnny Callison, Earl Battey and John Romano. Billy Goodman, Ted Kluszewski,

Earl Torgeson, Jim McAnany and Jim Rivera were reduced to relatively insignificant roles in 1960. In part due to injuries, Sherman Lollar's numbers tailed off dramatically to only seven home runs and 46 RBIs compared to 22 home runs and 84 RBIs in 1959.

As a team, the 1960 Chicago White Sox scored more runs, hit more doubles, hit more home runs, hit for a higher batting average, had a higher slugging average and stole more bases than the 1959 American League champions. In the field, the 1960 club made fewer errors, more double plays, and had a better overall fielding average than the 1959 team.

Changes also took place in the makeup and performance of the pitching staff for the 1960 season. Barry Latman was gone. Frank Bauman, Russ Kemmerer and Herb Score were added to the staff. Early Wynn and Bob Shaw combined for 26 victories and 25 losses, compared to their combined 40 victories and 16 defeats in 1959. New additions to the starting rotation and relief corps, Bauman, Kemmerer and Score had a total of 24 wins and 19 losses between them. Turk Lown also faded in 1960. His save total slipped to five from 15 in 1959, and his earned run average ballooned to 3.88 from the 2.89 standard he set in the prior year. In the aggregate, the 1960 staff had fewer complete games, more walks, fewer strikeouts, fewer shutouts, fewer saves and a higher earned run average than its 1959 counterparts.

The cumulative effect of those offensive and defensive changes earned the Pale Hose an 87-67 season record during the 1960 campaign. The seven game deterioration in their victory total netted Chicago a third place finish, 10 games behind the New York Yankees and two games behind the second place Baltimore Orioles. The 1960 season was the first season that manager Al Lopez had finished lower than second place in his major league managing career. In 1961, the slide continued with Chicago finishing in fourth place. Its 86-76 record placed them behind New York, Detroit and Baltimore. A fifth place finish in 1962 reflected the continued downward fortunes of the team.

LUIS APARICIO

Aparicio had three more good years for Chicago. He led the league in stolen bases for five more seasons, giving him an incredible string of nine stolen base titles in succession. Aparicio was traded to Baltimore along with Al Smith on January 14, 1963. Chicago received Hoyt Wilhelm, Ron Hanson, Pete Ward and Dave Nicholson in return. While in Baltimore, Aparicio played in the 1966 World Series as Baltimore became World Champions by beating the Los Angeles Dodgers in four consecutive games. After five years in Baltimore, on November 26, 1967, Aparicio was dealt back to Chicago along with Russ Snyder and John Mateus for Don Buford, Bruce Howard and Roger Nelson. On December 1, 1970, Chicago dealt Aparicio to the Boston Red Sox for Mike Andrews and Louis Alvarado. Luis Aparicio's 18-year major league career, which ended in 1973, spanned a total of 2,599 games. In that time, Aparicio went to the plate 10,230 times, accumulated 2,677 hits, scored 1,335 runs, and stole 506 bases. Defensively, he had 4,548 career put outs and 8,016 assists while committing only 366 errors. Aparicio was elected to the Major League Baseball Hall of Fame in 1984.

RAY BOONE

The major league career of Ray Boone spanned 14 seasons. During that time, Boone appeared in 1,373 games and established a .275 career batting average. Boone accumulated 1,260 hits in his 4,589 at bats, including 151 home runs. Boone drove in 737 runs and scored 645 runs. Boone appeared in the 1948 World Series as a member of the American League Champion Cleveland Indians. Boone was traded by Chicago to the Kansas City Athletics early in the 1959 season. In August of 1959, the Milwaukee Braves acquired Boone on waivers from Kansas City. Boone had the distinction of playing for the Chicago White Sox and the Milwaukee Braves in 1959, but did not make it to the World Series. Milwaukee traded Boone to Boston on May 17, 1960 for Ron Jackson. Ray Boone ended his major league career in 1960. Boone's son, Bob Boone, also had a long and successful major league career. Currently, Ray Boone has two grandsons playing at the major league level.

NORMAN CASH

Hard-hitting Norman Cash was traded to the Cleveland Indians on December 6, 1959. On that day, Cash was packaged with John Romano and Bubba Phillips for Minnie Minoso, Jack Striker, Don Ferrarese and Dick Brown. Chicago gave up budding young talent for proven but aging veterans. On April 12, 1960, Cleveland traded Cash to Detroit. In Detroit Cash flourished as a power-hitting first baseman during the remaining years of his 17 season major league career. In 2,089 games, Cash accumulated 1,820 base hits including 377 home runs in 6,705 at-bats. During that time frame, Norm scored 1,046 runs while driving in 1,103 runs. While in Detroit, Cash participated in the 1968 World Series, batting .385 and driving in five runs. Cash won the American League batting title in 1961 with an average of .361. Norman Cash finished his major league career with Detroit in 1974 and died on October 12, 1986.

SAM ESPOSITO

Sammy Esposito enjoyed a 10-year major league career appearing in 560 games, predominantly as a utility infielder. Esposito was credited with 792 official plate appearances. After departing Chicago in 1963, Esposito was picked up by the Kansas City Athletics and finished his career that year.

NELSON FOX

Nelson Fox earned the American League Most Valuable Player award for his 1959 performance, in what was perhaps the best all-around season of his career. Fox was also recognized in 1959 as the outstanding player in the American League by the prestigious *Sporting News*. He beat out teammate Luis Aparicio for both honors. Fox remained with the Chicago White Sox until December 12, 1963 when he was traded to the Houston Colt 45's for Jim Golden, Danny Murphy and cash. Fox's illustrious major league career spanned 19 seasons. He batted 9,232 times and accumulated 2,663 hits while striking out a remarkable 216 times. Fox's career batting average was .288 as he led the league in plate appearances in 1952, 1955, 1956, 1959 and 1960. Fox accumulated more hits than anyone in the American League in 1952, 1954, 1957 and 1958. His walk to strikeout ratio was an outstanding four to one. In the 2,367 games in which Fox played, he scored 1,279 runs and drove in 790 runs himself. Fox established an overall .984 fielding average as he was credited with 6,102 put outs and 6,385 assists. Fox ended his playing career with Houston in 1965. Nelson Fox died on December 1, 1975. The perennial American League All-Star was elected to the Major League Baseball Hall of Fame posthumously in 1997.

BILLY GOODMAN

Billy Goodman remained with Chicago White Sox until the 1962 season. He was acquired at that time by the expansion Houston Colt 45's. Goodman enjoyed a 16-year major league career during which time he established a .300 career batting average. Goodman accumulated 1,691 hits in 5,644 plate appearances. The highlight of Goodman's career was 1950 when he won the American League batting title, hitting .354 while playing for the Boston Red Sox. Goodman ended his playing career in Houston in 1962 and died on October 1, 1984.

JOE HICKS

Joe Hicks' career lasted five seasons. Hicks appeared in 212 games and accumulated 92 hits in 416 at-bats. He was picked up by the Washington Senators in 1961, and ended his career with the New York Mets in 1963.

RON JACKSON

Ron Jackson was traded to the Boston Red Sox on November 3, 1959 for pitcher Frank Bauman. The next season Boston traded Jackson to the Milwaukee Braves on May 17 for Ray Boone. Although Jackson's career spanned portions of 7 seasons, he appeared in only 196 games and had only 474 official plate appearances.

TED KLUSZEWSKI

Big Ted Kluszewski remained with Chicago through the 1960 season. Kluszewski's 15-year major league career came to an end with the expansion California Angels in 1961. During that time, he appeared in 1,718 games predominantly with the Cincinnati Redlegs in the National League. Chicago's World Series batting hero had 5,929 career plate appearances during which time he accumulated 1,766 hits, including 279 home runs. The big left-hander also hit for average, establishing a .298 career mark. Ted Kluszewski died on March 29, 1988.

J. C. MARTIN

J. C. Martin, the youngster that was called up to Chicago in September of 1959, remained with the club through July 22, 1967. On that date, he was dealt to the New York Mets along with Bill Southworth for veteran Ken Boyer. The Mets traded Martin to the Chicago Cubs on March 29, 1970 for Randy Bobb. While with the New York Mets, Martin was a member of the 1969 World Champion Miracle Mets that upset the power-house Baltimore Orioles in the World Series. Martin's career spanned 14 seasons and 905 games and he accumulated 487 hits in 2,189 at bats. His playing career ended in 1972.

BUBBA PHILLIPS

In the winter of 1959, Phillips was traded to Cleveland in the same transaction that sent Romano and Cash to the Indians. After three years in Clevcland, Phillips was traded to the Detroit Tigers on November 11, 1962 for Gordon Seyfried and Ron Nisckwitz. His 10-year major league career ended in 1964. During that time, Phillips accumulated 835 hits in 3,278 official plate appearances spanning 1,062 games. Bubba Phillips died on June 22, 1993.

EARL TORGESON

Earl Torgeson remained with Chicago through the early part of 1961. Torgeson's 15-year major league career ended in 1961 after a brief stint with the New York Yankees. In 1948, while with the National League Boston Braves, Torgeson appeared in the World Series and had seven hits in 18 plate appearances as Boston fell to the Cleveland Indians. In his career, Torgeson appeared in 1,668 games and had 4,969 at bats. His hit total of 1,318 base hits included 149 home runs. Earl Torgeson passed away on November 8, 1990.

JOHNNY CALLISON

As the Chicago White Sox quickly abandoned their youth movement, they traded Johnny Callison to the Philadelphia Phillies on December 9, 1959. Chicago obtained veteran third baseman Gene Freese from Philadelphia. After a 10-year stretch with the Phillies, Callison was traded to the Chicago Cubs on November 11, 1969 for Dick Selma and Oscar Gamble. On January 1, 1972, Callison was sent to the New York Yankees in exchange for Jack Aker. Johnny Callison's major league career lasted 16 seasons. During that time, he appeared in 1,886 games and had 6,652 career at bats. Callison accumulated 1,757 hits, including 226 home runs on his way to a .264 career batting average. He finished his career in 1973 with the New York Yankees.

DEL ENNIS

Del Ennis' 14-year major league career ended with his mid-season 1959 release by the Chicago White Sox. The majority of Ennis' playing career was spent with the Philadelphia Phillies. While with the Phillies, he played in the 1950 World Series. During Ennis' stellar career, he appeared in 1,903 games establishing a .284 batting average. His 7,254 career at bats produced 2,063 hits. The power hitter hammered 288 home runs while driving in 1,284 runs. Del Ennis died February 8, 1996.

JIM MCANANY

Jim McAnany, Chicago's 1959 rookie sensation, could never match the brilliance of the summer of 1959. McAnany was shipped to the Los Angeles Angels in the 1961 expansion draft and was immediately traded to the Chicago Cubs on April 1, 1961 for Lou Johnson. McAnany's career spanned a portion of five seasons as he appeared in only 93 games. He had 210 of his 241 career plate appearances in 1959.

JIM LANDIS

Jim Landis remained on Chicago's south side until January 20, 1965. In a three-way trade with the Kansas City Athletics and Cleveland Indians, Jim was destined for Kansas City along with Mike Hershberger and Fred Talbot for Rocky Colavito. On December 1, 1965, after just one season, the Athletics shipped Landis to Cleveland for Phil Roof and Joe Rudi. On January 4, 1967, Landis was traded to the Houston Astros along with Jim Weaver and Doc Edwards for Lee Maye and Ken Retzer. On June 29, 1967, Houston traded Landis to the Detroit Tigers for 1959 World Series hero Larry Sherry. Landis completed his 11-year major league career with the Boston Red Sox in 1967. Landis appeared in 1,346 major league games and had 1,061 hits in 4,288 plate appearances. Landis, one of the better defensive center-fielders of his era, had a .989 fielding average. He had 2,927 career put outs and 69 assists while committing only 32 errors.

DON MUELLER

Mueller was injured in 1959 and appeared in only four ball games for the Chicago White Sox. His major league career came to an end that year after 12 campaigns. In his career, Mueller appeared in 1,245 ball games, batting 4,364 times. His hit total of 1,292 resulted in a lofty .296 career batting average. In 1954, Mueller played with the New York Giants as they thrashed the Cleveland Indians in four straight games to win the World Series title. Mueller played in all four games of that series and compiled a .389 batting average in 18 plate appearances.

JIM RIVERA

"Jungle" Jim Rivera was known as an exciting ballplayer during his 10-year major league career. Rivera's trademark was his spectacular head-first slides on the basepaths. He appeared in 1,171 games, scoring 503 runs and stealing 160 bases. Rivera established a career .256 batting average by getting 911 hits in 3,552 official at bats and had some pop in his bat, as he hit 83 home runs while driving in 422 runs. Rivera's last season in Chicago was 1960, and he finished his major league career in 1961 with the Kansas City Athletics.

HARRY SIMPSON

Harry "Suitcase" Simpson played for five different clubs during his eight-year major league career. During that time he had two stints with the Kansas City Athletics. After moving to the Pittsburgh Pirates in the Ted Kluszewski transaction in late 1959, Simpson's career came to a close. Simpson appeared in a total of 888 games with 2,829 plate appearances and collected 73 home runs in his 752 total hits. His career batting average was .266. Harry Simpson died on April 3, 1979.

LOU SKIZAS

Lou Skizas never made it back to the major leagues after he was sold by the White Sox to Cincinnati's Havana, Cuba affiliate in 1959. His brief major league career encompassed four seasons, 239 games, 725 official at bats, 196 hits, a .270 batting average and 30 home runs.

AL SMITH

Al Smith remained in Chicago for three more solid seasons after 1959. On January 14, 1963 he was traded to the Baltimore Orioles along with Luis Aparicio. In December of 1963, Baltimore traded Smith to the Cleveland Indians along with $25,000 for Willie Kirkland. In addition to his appearance in the 1959 World Series with Chicago, Smith played in the 1954 World Series while in his second season with Cleveland. Smith completed his 12-year major league career with the Boston Red Sox in 1964. During his career, Smith had 1,458 base hits, including 164 home runs in 1,517 games. In 5,378 official plate appearances, Smith established a .272 batting average.

LARRY DOBY

Larry Doby had a 13-year major league career that ended with his cameo appearance with the Chicago White Sox in 1959. Doby became the first black baseball player in the American League when he joined the Cleveland Indians in late 1947. Doby led the league in home runs and runs scored in 1952 and again in home runs, and RBIs in Cleveland's 1954 American League pennant winning season. Prior to that, Doby was instrumental in bringing a World Championship to the Cleveland Indians in 1948. In his 1,533 career games, Doby established a .283 batting average along with 1,515 hits, 253 home runs and 1,011 strikeouts in 5,348 official at bats. Doby knocked in 969 runs and scored 960 runs himself. In 1998, Larry Doby was elected to the Major League Baseball Hall of Fame.

EARL BATTEY

Earl Battey was traded to the Washington Senators on April 4, 1960. Battey was packaged with Don Mincher and $150,000 cash in exchange for slugging first baseman Roy Sievers. Battey, noted for his defensive ability, blossomed as an all-around ballplayer with the Washington Senators and Minnesota Twins. Battey played in the 1965 World Series, getting three hits and two RBIs as the Twins lost to the Los Angeles Dodgers. He went on to perform for 13 major league seasons, appearing in 1,141 games. In 3,586 official at bats, Battey had 969 hits, including 104 home runs. He had a .270 batting average, scored 393 runs and had 449 RBIs.

CAMILO CARREON

Cam Carreon was another of Chicago's 1959 late season call ups. The catcher remained with Chicago through January 20, 1965. In the same three-way trade with Cleveland and Kansas City, Carreon was packaged with Rocky Colavito in exchange for Tommy John, Tommy Agee and Johnny Romano. Carreon was picked up by the Baltimore Orioles for the 1966 season and ended his eight-year career that year. In 354 games, Carreon had 986 official at bats. He turned those opportunities into 260 hits and a .264 batting average. Camilo Carreon passed away on September 2, 1987.

SHERMAN LOLLAR

Sherman Lollar ended his 18-year major league career with the White Sox in 1963. Lollar was Mr. Clutch for the Sox in 1959 and steady throughout the 1,752 games he played during his career. Lollar's .264 career batting average was the result of 1,415 hits in 5,351 at bats. Lollar slammed 155 home runs, scored 623 runs and knocked in 808 runs during that time. Sherman Lollar died in the fall of 1977.

JOHNNY ROMANO

Johnny Romano departed Chicago on December 6, 1959 along with Norman Cash and Bubba Phillips in the trade with Cleveland. He returned to Chicago for two seasons on January 20, 1965. In December 1966, Chicago dealt Romano and Lee White to the St. Louis Cardinals in exchange for Walt Williams and Don Dennis. Romano's career spanned a decade. He appeared in 905 games, with 2,767 plate appearances. His offensive accomplishments include a .255 batting average, 706 hits, 129 home runs, 355 runs scored and 417 RBIs. Romano's career ended in 1967 with the St. Louis Cardinals.

RUDOLFO ARIAS

Rudolfo Arias was in the major leagues for only one season. He appeared in 34 games, won two and lost none, with two saves. His earned run average was 4.09. In his 44 innings pitched, he gave up 49 hits, walked 20 and struck out 28.

DICK DONOVAN

Dick Donovan departed the White Sox after the 1960 campaign for the Washington Senators. In the winter of 1961, Donovan was shipped to the Cleveland Indians. Donovan, Gene Green and Jim Maloney were exchanged for Jimmy Piersall. Donovan's 15-year major league career ended in Cleveland in 1965. During the course of his career, Donovan appeared in 345 games and completed 101 of them, including 25 shutouts. His 3.67 career earned run average was established in over 2,017 innings pitched. Donovan yielded 1,968 hits during that time while striking out 880 and walking 495. Dick Donovan passed away in 1998.

BARRY LATMAN

On April 18, 1960, Barry Latman was traded to the Cleveland Indians for Herb Score. On December 2, 1963, Latman and Joe Adcock were traded to the Los Angeles Angels for Leon Wagner. On December 15, 1965, Latman was sent to the Houston Astros for minor league catcher Ed Pacheco and cash. Latman's 11-year major league career ended in 1967. Latman appeared in 344 games, winning 59 and losing 68. His career earned run average was 3.91. Barry Latman pitched a total of 1,219 innings, giving up 1,130 hits and 489 bases on balls and striking out 829.

KEN MCBRIDE

Ken McBride remained in Chicago one more season after 1959 and then was acquired by the expansion Los Angeles Angels in 1961. He remained with that club until his retirement in 1965. McBride won 40 games and lost 50 in his seven-year major league career and posted a 3.79 earned run average in 807 innings pitched.

TURK LOWN

Turk Lown completed his 11-year major league career in 1962 as a member of the Chicago White Sox. Lown's career marks included 55 wins, 61 losses, a 4.12 earned run average, 504 game appearances, and 1,032 innings pitched. Lown gave up 978 hits, while walking 590 and striking out 574. Lown also had 73 saves in his career. His bullpen work in 1959, in tandem with his roommate Gerry Staley, was one of the key factors in Chicago's pennant drive.

RAY MOORE

Ray Moore remained in Chicago for just two months into the 1960 season. On June 13, 1960 Moore was sold to the Washington Senators for cash. He remained with Washington until he completed his 11-year major league career in 1963. In 365 games, Moore established a 4.06 earned run average. He won 63 games while losing 59. Moore pitched 24 complete games and had five shutouts. In his 1,072 innings pitched, he gave up 935 hits and 560 bases on balls and struck out 612 batters. Moore also saved 46 games during his career. Ray Moore died on March 2, 1995.

GARY PETERS

Gary Peters' cameo appearance with the White Sox in 1959 was just the beginning as he went on to be a mainstay of the Chicago pitching staff during the decade of the 1960s. In his 14-year major league career, Peters won 124 games and lost 103. His 3.25 earned run average over 2,081 innings pitched was punctuated by 79 complete games and 23 shutouts. Peters struck out 1,420 while walking 706. Peters, an excellent hitter, slammed 19 career home runs. He was traded to the Boston Red Sox on December 13, 1969 with Don Pavletich for Syd O'Brien and Gerry Janeski. Peters ended his career with the Red Sox in 1972.

BILLY PIERCE

Billy Pierce had an outstanding 18-year major league career. Pierce remained in Chicago until November 30, 1961, when he was traded to the San Francisco Giants. In 1962, Pierce finished with a 16 and six record in his 23 starts for the Giants. In the 1962 World Series, Pierce had one win and one loss as San Francisco fell to the New York Yankees. Pierce led the American League in complete games from 1956 through 1958. He led the league in strikeouts in 1953 and in wins in 1957. In his career, the left-handed workhorse won 211 games and lost 169. He pitched a total of 193 complete games and had 38 shutouts. In his 3,306 innings pitched, Pierce struck out 1,999 batters, gave up 2,989 hits and walked 1,178. Pierce had an excellent career earned run average of 3.27.

DON RUDOLPH

Don Rudolph was traded to Cincinnati in 1959 for Del Ennis. His six-year career continued with stops in Cleveland and Washington. Rudolph left baseball in 1964 after pitching 450 innings and winning 18 games and losing 32.

CLAUDE RAYMOND

Claude Raymond had a 12-year career that included stops in Milwaukee, Houston, Atlanta and Montreal. He departed Chicago

221

after the 1960 season. Raymond appeared in 449 ball games, won 46, lost 53 and had 83 saves. His 3.66 earned run average was established during 721 innings pitched. Raymond finished his career in Montreal in 1971.

BOB SHAW

Bob Shaw came out of nowhere to make a significant and deciding difference to Chicago's drive for the 1959 pennant. Shaw remained with the Chicago White Sox until June 10, 1961 when he was traded to the Kansas City Athletics along with Stan Johnson, Wes Covington and fellow 1959 hero Gerry Staley. In the trade, the White Sox received Ray Herbert, Don Larsen, Andy Carey and Al Pilarcik. Bob Shaw's 11-year major league career ended in 1969 after stops with the Milwaukee Braves, San Francisco Giants, New York Mets and Chicago Cubs. During his career, Shaw appeared in 430 games, completing 55, winning 108, and losing 98. Shaw pitched 1,778 innings and had a 3.52 earned run average. He gave up 1,837 hits and 511 bases on balls and struck out 880.

GERRY STALEY

Gerry Staley had an outstanding year out of the bullpen for Chicago in 1959. The tandem of Staley and Lown provided relentless relief work during the entire year. Staley remained in Chicago until June of 1961 at which time he was shipped to the Kansas City Athletics with Bob Shaw. Staley's career ended in 1961. During his 15-year major league career, Staley won 134 games, lost 111 and saved 61. He began his career as a starter and was credited with pitching 58 complete games. He appeared in 640 games overall and pitched 1,981 innings. Staley struck out 727, walked 529, gave up 2,070 hits and had a career earned run average of 3.70.

JOE STANKA

Joe Stanka pitched only one season in the major leagues. In 1959 he won one ballgame. He pitched only five innings, yielding two hits, walking four and striking out two.

EARLY WYNN

Early Wynn had a tremendous year in 1959. Wynn was recognized as the most outstanding pitcher in both the American and National League as he was awarded the post season Cy Young award. Wynn was voted the American League's best pitcher in 1959 by the prestigious "Sporting News." Wynn's major league career spanned 23 seasons. He finished his stay in Chicago in 1962, one victory shy of the magic 300 victory plateau. In 1963, Wynn earned his 300th major league victory while pitching for the Cleveland Indians. Wynn pitched 4,564 innings while appearing in 691 games. He pitched an astounding 290 complete games which included 49 shutouts. Wynn won 300 and lost 244 games during his career. He gave up 4,291 hits, struck out 2,334, and walked 1,775. Early Wynn led the league in victories in 1954 and 1959; earned run average in 1950; innings pitched in 1951, 1954 and 1959; strikeouts in 1957 and 1958; and shutouts in 1960. Early Wynn was elected to the Major League Baseball Hall of Fame in 1972. Early "Gus" Wynn died in 1999.

1959 CHICAGO WHITE SOX GAME STATISTICS

Date	Record W	Record L	Game	Opponent	Home/ Away	Attendance	Time of Game	Starting Pitcher White Sox	Starting Pitcher Opponent	Winning Pitcher
10-Apr	1	0	1	DET	A	38,332	4.25	Pierce	Bunning	Staley
11-Apr	2	0	2	DET	A	5,529	2.29	Wynn	Foytack	Wynn
12-Apr	3	0	3	DET	A	11,228	2.42	Donovan	Lary	Donovan
14-Apr	4	0	4	KC	H	19,303	1.55	Pierce	Terry	Pierce
15-Apr	4	1	5	KC	H	4,713	2.49	Latman	Grim	Grim
16-Apr	4	2	6	KC	H	3,211	2.21	Wynn	Garver	Garver
17-Apr	5	2	7	DET	H	2,656	2.24	Donovan	Narleski	Arias
18-Apr	5	3	8	DET	H	7,159	2.42	Moore	Hoeft	Hoeft
21-Apr	5	4	9	KC	A	6,569	1.57	Pierce	Grim	Grim
22-Apr	6	4	10	KC	A	7,446	3.12	Wynn	Garver	Shaw
24-Apr	6	5	11	CLEV	A	28,498	3.12	Donovan	Score	Robinson
25-Apr	7	5	12	CLEV	A	7,290	2.39	Latman	McLish	Lown
26-Apr	8	5	13	CLEV	A	14,358	3.19	Wynn	Ferrarese	Wynn
26-Apr	9	5	14	CLEV	A	0	2.45	Pierce	Bell	Pierce
29-Apr	9	6	15	NY	H	9,952	2.38	Moore	Turley	Turley
30-Apr	10	6	16	NY	H	26,944	3.34	Pierce	Ford	Pierce
01-May	11	6	17	BOS	H	13,022	2.46	Wynn	Brewer	Wynn
02-May	11	7	18	BOS	H	7,718	2.48	Latman	Delock	Delock
03-May	11	8	19	BALT	H	11,208	2.32	Donovan	O'Dell	Loes
05-May	11	9	20	WASH	H	2,087	2.31	Pierce	Stobbs	Stobbs
06-May	11	10	21	WASH	H	1,710	2.36	Wynn	Pascual	Pascual
08-May	11	11	22	CLEV	H	19,170	2.23	Donovan	McLish	McLish
09-May	12	11	23	CLEV	H	6,325	3.02	Latman	Score	Moore
10-May	13	11	24	CLEV	H	24,346	2.59	Pierce	Grant	Pierce
10-May	14	11	25	CLEV	H	0	2.37	Wynn	Garcia	Wynn
12-May	15	11	26	BOS	A	22,012	4.23	Donovan	Delock	Arias
13-May	16	11	27	BOS	A	4,787	2.19	Shaw	Sullivan	Shaw
14-May	17	11	28	BOS	A	3,554	3.08	Wynn	Hoeft	Wynn
15-May	18	11	29	NY	A	27,863	2.37	Pierce	Ford	Pierce
16-May	19	11	30	NY	A	20,890	3.48	Moore	Turley	Lown
17-May	19	12	31	WASH	A	22,240	2.12	Donovan	Ramos	Ramos
17-May	20	12	32	WASH	A	0	2.55	Shaw	Fischer	Shaw
18-May	21	12	33	WASH	A	3,995	2.48	Wynn	Stobb	Wynn
19-May	21	13	34	BALT	A	6,519	2.37	Pierce	O'Dell	O'Dell
20-May	22	13	35	BALT	A	16,036	2.30	Donovan	Harshman	Donovan
22-May	23	13	36	KC	A	2,572	2.05	Shaw	Grim	Shaw
23-May	23	14	37	KC	A	12,416	2.20	Wynn	Daley	Daley
24-May	23	15	38	KC	A	14,985	2.43	Pierce	Herbert	Herbert
26-May	23	16	39	CLEV	H	40,018	2.28	Donovan	Ferrarese	Ferrarese
27-May	24	16	40	CLEV	H	6,883	2.21	Wynn	Bell	Wynn
29-May	24	17	41	DET	H	4,114	2.08	Shaw	Mossi	Mossi
30-May	24	18	42	DET	H	23,621	2.44	Pierce	Lary	Lary
30-May	25	18	43	DET	H	0	2.25	Donovan	Bunning	Lown
31-May	25	19	44	KC	H	11,414	2.32	Wynn	Garver	Garver
01-Jun	25	20	45	KC	H	8,221	2.13	Moore	Daley	Daley
02-Jun	25	21	46	BALT	H	12,482	2.27	Shaw	Wilhelm	Wilhelm

1959 CHICAGO WHITE SOX GAME STATISTICS

Losing Pitcher	W/L	Score WS	Score OP	INN	WS AB	WS R	WS H	WS RBI	OP AB	OP R	OP H	OP RBI
Mossi	W	9	7	14	57	9	17	6	54	7	14	7
Narleski	W	5	3	9	34	5	8	5	34	3	7	2
Lary	W	5	3	9	34	5	8	5	33	3	8	3
Terry	W	2	0	9	26	2	8	2	30	0	6	0
Latman	L	8	10	9	38	8	11	8	37	10	9	10
Wynn	L	0	6	9	32	0	5	0	39	6	11	6
Narleski	W	6	5	9	30	6	7	6	39	5	14	5
Moore	L	2	5	9	31	2	5	2	32	5	12	5
Pierce	L	3	8	9	30	3	4	3	32	8	9	5
Daly	W	20	6	9	40	20	16	18	36	6	9	6
Staley	L	4	6	9	29	4	6	4	29	6	6	5
Brodowski	W	8	6	9	34	8	6	6	34	6	8	4
Ferrarese	W	6	5	9	32	6	8	6	34	5	9	4
Bell	W	5	2	9	34	5	10	5	34	2	8	2
Moore	L	2	5	9	35	2	9	2	32	5	8	4
Duren	W	4	3	11	42	4	13	3	41	3	9	2
Brewer	W	1	0	9	29	1	5	1	27	0	1	0
Latman	L	4	5	9	34	4	8	4	38	5	14	5
Lown	L	2	4	10	32	2	5	2	38	4	10	4
Pierce	L	3	8	9	31	3	6	3	37	8	13	8
Wynn	L	4	6	9	39	4	11	4	34	6	10	6
Donovan	L	1	3	9	29	1	5	1	31	3	3	3
Score	W	9	5	9	29	9	9	9	34	5	11	4
Brodowski	W	5	4	11	37	5	9	5	45	4	13	4
Garcia	W	5	0	9	31	5	13	5	30	0	4	0
Wall	W	4	3	12	44	4	12	4	43	3	9	3
Sullivan	W	4	0	9	39	4	12	4	33	0	5	0
Hoeft	W	14	6	9	42	14	19	13	36	6	11	6
Ford	W	6	0	9	37	6	9	5	31	0	6	0
Ditmar	W	4	3	11	40	4	10	4	37	3	7	3
Donovan	L	2	4	9	31	2	5	1	32	4	7	3
Fischer	W	10	7	9	37	10	13	8	41	7	15	7
Stobb	W	9	2	9	38	9	12	9	32	2	5	2
Pierce	L	1	2	9	33	1	6	1	28	2	4	2
Harshman	W	5	2	9	33	5	11	5	30	2	4	2
Grim	W	2	1	9	31	2	7	1	33	1	4	1
Wynn	L	0	16	9	29	0	4	0	43	16	21	16
Pierce	L	6	8	9	41	6	12	6	35	8	15	8
Donovan	L	0	3	9	27	0	4	0	33	3	7	3
Bell	W	5	1	9	30	5	8	5	29	1	5	1
Shaw	L	1	4	9	32	1	5	1	34	4	9	3
Pierce	L	2	4	9	33	2	9	2	36	4	12	4
Morgan	W	4	3	9	37	4	11	3	36	3	9	3
Wynn	L	1	9	9	29	1	4	1	38	9	12	9
Moore	L	1	3	9	31	1	7	1	35	3	9	2
Shaw	L	2	3	9	32	2	7	2	38	3	12	3

1959 CHICAGO WHITE SOX GAME STATISTICS

Date	Record W	Record L	Game	Opponent	Home/ Away	Attendance	Time of Game	Starting Pitcher White Sox	Starting Pitcher Opponent	Winning Pitcher
03-Jun	26	21	47	BALT	H	3,607	2.10	Pierce	O'Dell	Pierce
04-Jun	27	21	48	BALT	H	3,514	4.37	Donovan	Harshman	Shaw
05-Jun	28	21	49	BOS	H	32,321	3.01	Wynn	Baumann	Staley
06-Jun	28	22	50	BOS	H	10,301	2.26	Moore	Willis	Willis
07-Jun	29	22	51	BOS	H	25,844	2.55	Donovan	Delock	Donovan
07-Jun	29	23	52	BOS	H	0	2.37	Pierce	Sullivan	Sullivan
09-Jun	29	24	53	WASH	A	19,157	2.53	Shaw	Fischer	Clevenger
10-Jun	30	24	54	WASH	A	9,121	2.23	Wynn	Woodeshick	Wynn
11-Jun	31	24	55	WASH	A	6,738	2.28	Pierce	Pascual	Pierce
13-Jun	31	25	56	BALT	A	8,081	2.19	Shaw	Brown	Loes
14-Jun	32	25	57	BALT	A	20,257	2.57	Wynn	Harshman	Wynn
14-Jun	33	25	58	BALT	A	0	2.50	Donovan	O'Dell	Donovan
16-Jun	33	26	59	NY	A	30,097	2.02	Pierce	Ditmar	Ditmar
17-Jun	33	27	60	NY	A	11,078	2.56	Moore	Turley	Turley
18-Jun	33	28	61	NY	A	12,217	2.54	Shaw	Bronstad	Shantz
20-Jun	33	29	62	BOS	A	12,997	2.42	Wynn	Brewer	Brewer
20-Jun	33	30	63	BOS	A	16,967	2.48	Donovan	Casale	Casale
21-Jun	34	30	64	BOS	A	21,094	2.19	Pierce	Wills	Pierce
23-Jun	35	30	65	WASH	H	16,300	2.22	Wynn	Fischer	Wynn
24-Jun	35	31	66	WASH	H	5,370	2.25	Donovan	Kemmerer	Clevenger
25-Jun	36	31	67	WASH	H	4,848	2.15	Latman	Ramos	Latman
26-Jun	36	32	68	NY	H	37,909	3.05	Pierce	Ditmar	Ditmar
27-Jun	37	32	69	NY	H	21,624	2.27	Shaw	Turley	Shaw
28-Jun	38	32	70	NY	H	42,121	2.44	Wynn	Ford	Wynn
28-Jun	39	32	71	NY	H	0	2.29	Donovan	Larsen	Donovan
30-Jun	39	33	72	CLEV	A	23,416	1.53	Pierce	McLish	McLish
01-Jul	40	33	73	CLEV	A	16,992	2.51	Latman	Grant	Latman
02-Jul	40	34	74	DET	A	29,312	3.00	Shaw	Mossi	Mossi
03-Jul	41	34	75	DET	A	11,729	3.13	Wynn	Bunning	Lown
04-Jul	42	34	76	KC	A	18,884	2.36	Donovan	Daley	Shaw
04-Jul	42	35	77	KC	A	0	2.47	Pierce	Coleman	Kucks
05-Jul	43	35	78	KC	A	9,664	2.28	Latman	Garver	Lown
09-Jul	44	35	79	CLEV	H	36,742	2.31	Pierce	Score	Pierce
10-Jul	44	36	80	CLEV	H	41,588	3.00	Wynn	McLish	McLish
11-Jul	45	36	81	KC	H	7,346	2.21	Latman	Garver	Latman
12-Jul	46	36	82	KC	H	18,426	2.37	Donovan	Daley	Moore
12-Jul	47	36	83	KC	H	0	2.51	Shaw	Coleman	Shaw
14-Jul	48	36	84	BOS	A	20,006	3.00	Pierce	Wills	Pierce
16-Jul	49	36	85	BOS	A	17,255	2.40	Donovan	Brewer	Donovan
16-Jul	49	37	86	BOS	A	0	3.00	Latman	Casale	Fornieles
17-Jul	50	37	87	NY	A	42,020	2.37	Wynn	Terry	Wynn
18-Jul	51	37	88	NY	A	27,959	2.31	Shaw	Larsen	Shaw
19-Jul	51	38	89	NY	A	57,057	2.33	Latman	Ford	Ford
19-Jul	51	39	90	NY	A	0	3.00	Pierce	Grba	Grba
21-Jul	52	39	91	BOS	H	28,534	2.27	Donovan	Brewer	Donovan

Pumpsie Green pinch ran for Vic Wertz. Boston became the last team to put a Negro on its roster.

1959 CHICAGO WHITE SOX GAME STATISTICS

Losing Pitcher	W/L	Score WS	Score OP	INN	WS AB	WS R	WS H	WS RBI	OP AB	OP R	OP H	OP RBI
O'Dell	W	6	1	9	32	6	9	5	34	1	8	1
Walker	W	6	5	17	60	6	14	5	62	5	11	5
Wall	W	5	2	9	32	5	10	5	34	2	7	1
Moore	L	2	4	9	32	2	9	2	34	4	8	4
Delock	W	9	4	9	30	9	12	9	36	4	10	4
Pierce	L	2	4	9	34	2	8	2	35	4	10	4
Lown	L	4	7	9	33	4	12	4	32	7	10	7
Woodeshick	W	4	1	9	36	4	10	3	31	1	5	1
Pascual	W	3	1	9	32	3	9	3	27	1	1	1
Staley	L	4	6	9	32	4	7	4	28	6	9	6
Zuverink	W	9	6	9	39	9	16	9	35	6	8	4
O'Dell	W	3	2	10	38	3	6	3	34	2	8	2
Pierce	L	1	5	9	31	1	4	1	31	5	9	4
Moore	L	3	7	9	35	3	9	2	36	7	14	7
Staley	L	4	5	10	39	4	10	4	35	5	9	5
Wynn	L	2	8	9	36	2	8	2	33	8	9	8
Donovan	L	0	9	9	30	0	3	0	38	9	13	8
Wills	W	3	2	9	33	3	7	3	32	2	6	2
Fischer	W	4	3	9	32	4	8	4	32	3	7	3
Donovan	L	2	4	9	32	2	6	2	36	4	9	2
Ramos	W	4	1	9	29	4	5	4	31	1	5	1
Pierce	L	4	8	9	34	4	10	4	37	8	14	8
Turley	W	5	4	9	30	5	9	5	35	4	9	4
Ford	W	9	2	9	34	9	10	9	33	2	9	2
Larsen	W	4	2	9	32	4	9	4	31	2	5	2
Pierce	L	1	3	9	31	1	4	1	29	3	6	3
Grant	W	6	5	9	30	6	6	5	37	5	11	5
Shaw	L	7	9	9	40	7	13	7	32	9	9	8
Morgan	W	6	5	10	38	6	12	5	34	5	6	5
Grim	W	7	4	9	42	7	17	7	34	4	9	4
Pierce	L	3	8	9	34	3	8	3	35	8	13	8
Garver	W	4	3	10	37	4	7	4	38	3	9	3
Score	W	4	3	9	26	4	5	4	32	3	5	3
Wynn	L	4	8	9	34	4	9	4	38	8	17	7
Garver	W	8	3	9	32	8	12	7	29	3	4	3
Daley	W	5	3	9	32	5	9	4	31	3	9	3
Coleman	W	9	7	9	35	9	13	9	43	7	16	7
Wills	W	7	3	9	39	7	13	7	35	3	11	2
Brewer	W	4	3	9	35	4	9	4	29	3	4	3
Moore	L	4	5	9	33	4	10	4	33	5	12	5
Terry	W	2	0	9	25	2	2	2	28	0	2	0
Larsen	W	2	1	9	37	2	11	2	30	1	6	1
Latman	L	2	6	9	31	2	6	2	31	6	10	6
Pierce	L	4	6	9	32	4	3	1	33	6	8	6
Brewer	W	2	1	9	33	2	9	1	33	1	6	1

1959 CHICAGO WHITE SOX GAME STATISTICS

Date	Record W	Record L	Game	Opponent	Home/ Away	Attendence	Time of Game	Starting Pitcher White Sox	Starting Pitcher Opponent	Winning Pitcher
22-Jul	53	39	92	BOS	H	11,847	3.15	Wynn	Casale	Lown
24-Jul	54	39	93	BALT	H	29,274	2.08	Pierce	Wilhelm	Pierce
25-Jul	55	39	94	BALT	H	25,625	4.05	Shaw	O'Dell	Lown
26-Jul	56	39	95	BALT	H	35,207	2.34	Wynn	Portocarrero	Wynn
26-Jul	56	40	96	BALT	H	0	2.23	Latman	Pappas	Pappas
28-Jul	57	40	97	NY	H	43,829	2.22	Pierce	Terry	Pierce
29-Jul	57	40	98	NY	H	43,599	1.45	Shaw	Ford	——
30-Jul	58	40	99	NY	H	30,858	2.35	Wynn	Grba	Wynn
31-Jul	59	40	100	WASH	H	24,278	2.28	Latman	Ramos	Latman
01-Aug	60	40	101	WASH	H	12,374	2.29	Moore	Pascual	Staley
02-Aug	61	40	102	WASH	H	26,866	2.05	Pierce	Kemmerer	Lown
02-Aug	62	40	103	WASH	H	0	3.03	Shaw	Kaat	Shaw
04-Aug	62	41	104	BALT	A	11,746	2.24	McBride	Hoeft	Hoeft
05-Aug	63	41	105	BALT	A	15,321	2.02	Latman	Fischer	Latman
05-Aug	63	42	106	BALT	A	0	2.28	Wynn	Portocarrero	Portocarrero
06-Aug	63	42	107	BALT	A	8,907	4.03	Pierce	O'Dell	——
07-Aug	64	42	108	WASH	A	7,702	2.37	Shaw	Fischer	Shaw
09-Aug	65	42	109	WASH	A	17,472	2.32	McBride	Stobbs	Staley
09-Aug	66	42	110	WASH	A	0	2.27	Wynn	Clevenger	Wynn
11-Aug	66	43	111	DET	A	34,417	2.30	Pierce	Bunning	Bunning
12-Aug	67	43	112	DET	A	12,820	2.55	Latman	Burnside	Staley
13-Aug	68	43	113	DET	A	9,894	2.17	Wynn	Mossi	Wynn
14-Aug	69	43	114	KC	A	11,477	2.02	Shaw	Kucks	Shaw
15-Aug	69	44	115	KC	A	14,497	2.30	Pierce	Daley	Daley
16-Aug	69	45	116	KC	A	13,373	2.44	Donovan	Garver	Garver
18-Aug	70	45	117	BALT	H	34,547	2.59	Wynn	Portocarrero	Staley
19-Aug	70	46	118	BALT	H	14,310	2.47	Shaw	O'Dell	O'Dell
20-Aug	70	47	119	BALT	H	11,084	3.14	Latman	Wilhelm	Wilhelm
21-Aug	71	47	120	WASH	H	37,986	2.52	Donovan	Stobbs	Staley
22-Aug	72	47	121	WASH	H	9,739	2.12	Latman	Kemmerer	Latman
23-Aug	72	48	122	NY	H	44,520	2.27	Wynn	Ditmar	Ditmar
23-Aug	73	48	123	NY	H	0	2.16	Shaw	Terry	Shaw
24-Aug	74	48	124	NY	H	21,923	3.03	Moore	Larsen	Moore
25-Aug	75	48	125	BOS	H	27,002	3.10	Donovan	Sullivan	Lown
26-Aug	75	49	126	BOS	H	22,497	3.06	Wynn	Momboquet	Momboquet
27-Aug	76	49	127	BOS	H	11,703	2.35	Latman	Baumann	Latman
28-Aug	77	49	128	CLEV	A	70,398	2.52	Shaw	Grant	Shaw
29-Aug	78	49	129	CLEV	A	28,109	2.12	Donovan	Perry	Donovan
30-Aug	79	49	130	CLEV	A	66,586	2.56	Wynn	McLish	Wynn
30-Aug	80	49	131	CLEV	A	0	2.37	Latman	Bell	Latman
01-Sep	80	50	132	DET	H	27,218	2.45	Shaw	Bunning	Bunning
02-Sep	81	50	133	DET	H	43,286	2.16	Donovan	Lary	Donovan
02-Sep	82	50	134	DET	H	0	2.42	Latman	Foytack	Stanka
04-Sep	83	50	135	CLEV	H	45,510	2.20	Wynn	Perry	Wynn
05-Sep	83	51	136	CLEV	H	26,920	2.50	Shaw	McLish	McLish
06-Sep	83	52	137	CLEV	H	34,269	2.30	Donovan	Grant	Grant

1959 CHICAGO WHITE SOX GAME STATISTICS

Losing Pitcher	W/L	Score WS	Score OP	INN	WS AB	WS R	WS H	WS RBI	OP AB	OP R	OP H	OP RBI
Kiely	W	5	4	9	33	5	13	5	34	4	7	4
Wilhelm	W	2	1	9	30	2	5	2	32	1	7	1
Loes	W	3	2	17	55	3	12	3	61	2	12	2
Portocarrero	W	4	1	9	30	4	6	4	28	1	2	1
Latman	L	0	4	9	29	0	5	0	32	4	10	4
Terry	W	4	3	9	30	4	9	3	36	3	10	3
——	T	4	4	6	23	4	8	4	21	4	5	4
Grba	W	3	1	9	30	3	6	3	32	1	6	1
Ramos	W	7	1	9	30	7	9	6	32	1	4	1
Hyde	W	2	1	9	28	2	3	2	30	1	4	1
Kemmerer	W	3	2	9	27	3	5	3	32	2	9	1
Kaat	W	9	3	9	35	9	10	9	32	3	6	3
McBride	L	2	3	9	32	2	6	2	30	3	6	3
Fischer	W	2	0	9	30	2	6	2	30	0	3	0
Wynn	L	1	7	9	32	1	5	1	32	7	7	5
——	T	1	1	18	57	1	7	1	64	1	12	1
Fischer	W	4	1	9	36	4	10	4	35	1	8	1
Hyde	W	4	3	9	36	4	10	3	30	3	5	2
Clevenger	W	9	0	9	34	9	11	7	29	0	3	0
Pierce	L	1	8	9	33	1	8	1	32	8	8	8
Burnside	W	11	6	9	34	11	8	11	41	6	14	6
Mossi	W	9	0	9	40	9	14	8	29	0	3	0
Kucks	W	5	1	9	34	5	9	5	30	1	5	1
Pierce	L	1	2	9	32	1	6	1	29	2	6	2
Donovan	L	2	7	9	36	2	9	2	36	7	13	7
Fischer	W	6	4	9	30	6	9	6	32	4	8	4
Shaw	L	1	3	9	32	1	5	1	30	3	6	3
Latman	L	6	7	9	37	6	10	5	38	7	13	6
Stobbs	W	5	4	9	33	5	9	4	37	4	11	4
Kemmerer	W	1	0	9	26	1	3	1	29	0	5	0
Wynn	L	1	7	9	31	1	3	1	39	7	12	7
Terry	W	5	0	9	29	5	7	4	33	0	6	0
Larsen	W	4	2	9	31	4	9	4	30	2	6	2
Fornielies	W	5	4	10	34	5	10	5	38	4	10	4
Wynn	L	6	7	9	37	6	10	6	35	7	7	6
Baumann	W	5	1	9	35	5	12	5	33	1	6	1
Grant	W	7	3	9	36	7	12	7	33	3	7	1
Perry	W	2	0	9	29	2	7	1	32	0	5	0
McLish	W	6	3	9	30	6	6	6	33	3	8	3
Bell	W	9	4	9	35	9	11	9	36	4	9	4
Shaw	L	0	4	9	29	0	3	0	37	4	12	4
Lary	W	7	2	9	32	7	7	5	31	2	4	2
Foytack	W	11	4	9	37	11	14	11	33	4	6	4
Perry	W	3	2	9	32	3	9	2	32	2	7	2
Shaw	L	5	6	9	34	5	10	5	35	6	8	5
Donovan	L	1	2	9	34	1	8	1	34	2	9	2

1959 CHICAGO WHITE SOX GAME STATISTICS

Date	Record W	Record L	Game	Opponent	Home/ Away	Attendence	Time of Game	Starting Pitcher White Sox	Starting Pitcher Opponent	Winning Pitcher
07-Sep	84	52	138	KC	H	26,368	2.03	Pierce	Garver	Pierce
07-Sep	85	52	139	KC	H	0	2.51	Latman	Tsitouris	Staley
08-Sep	86	52	140	KC	H	28,238	2.19	Wynn	Daley	Wynn
09-Sep	87	52	141	WASH	A	9,610	2.19	Shaw	Clevenger	Shaw
10-Sep	87	53	142	WASH	A	6,350	2.23	Donovan	Pascual	Pascual
11-Sep	87	54	143	BALT	A	23,305	1.45	Pierce	Fischer	Fischer
11-Sep	87	55	144	BALT	A	0	3.40	Latman	Walker	Walker
12-Sep	88	55	145	BALT	A	11,904	2.27	Wynn	O'Dell	Wynn
13-Sep	89	55	146	BOS	A	20,720	2.15	Shaw	Sullivan	Shaw
14-Sep	89	56	147	BOS	A	3,676	2.36	Donovan	Momboquet	Momboquet
15-Sep	90	56	148	NY	A	8,714	2.24	Pierce	Ford	Pierce
16-Sep	90	57	149	NY	A	7,550	2.08	Wynn	Coates	Coates
18-Sep	91	57	150	DET	H	37,352	2.12	Shaw	Bunning	Shaw
19-Sep	91	58	151	DET	H	17,287	2.31	Donovan	Foytack	Foytack
20-Sep	91	59	152	DET	H	27,784	2.43	Pierce	Mossi	Mossi
22-Sep	92	59	153	CLEV	A	54,293	2.43	Wynn	Perry	Wynn
25-Sep	92	60	154	DET	A	3,386	2.11	Pierce	Mossi	Mossi
26-Sep	93	60	155	DET	A	4,325	2.14	Wynn	Practor	Wynn
27-Sep	94	60	156	DET	A	13,985	1.56	Shaw	Bruce	Shaw
TOTAL						2,645,726				
AVERAGE						16,960	2.46			

1959 CHICAGO WHITE SOX GAME STATISTICS

Losing Pitcher	W/L	Score WS	Score OP	INN	WS AB	WS R	WS H	WS RBI	OP AB	OP R	OP H	OP RBI
Garver	W	2	1	9	30	2	8	1	32	1	7	1
Tomanek	W	13	7	9	35	13	13	11	39	7	16	7
Daley	W	3	2	10	34	3	9	3	35	2	6	2
Clevenger	W	5	1	9	41	5	6	4	33	1	7	1
Donovan	L	2	8	9	32	2	4	2	34	8	11	7
Pierce	L	0	3	9	27	0	3	0	32	3	10	3
Staley	L	0	1	16	51	0	6	0	52	1	8	1
O'Dell	W	6	1	9	36	6	10	5	33	1	7	1
Sullivan	W	3	1	9	32	3	8	3	32	1	6	1
Donovan	L	3	9	9	36	3	10	3	34	9	9	9
Ford	W	4	3	9	34	4	11	4	33	3	7	3
Wynn	L	1	3	9	30	1	4	1	29	3	6	3
Bunning	W	1	0	9	27	1	4	1	32	0	5	0
Donovan	L	4	5	9	38	4	12	3	35	5	10	5
Pierce	L	4	5	9	32	4	9	4	34	5	8	4
Perry	W	4	2	9	36	4	9	4	34	2	11	2
Staley	L	5	6	9	33	5	6	5	32	6	8	5
Practor	W	10	5	9	42	10	15	10	45	5	7	5
Bruce	W	6	4	9	35	6	8	5	34	4	7	3
TOTAL		669	590	1,454	5,298	669	1,326	622	5,366	590	1,296	553
AVERAGE		4.29	3.78	9.32	33.96	4.29	8.5	3.99	34.4	3.78	8.31	3.55

231

1959 CHICAGO WHITE SOX SEASON PITCHING RECORDS

PITCHER	THROWS	GAMES PITCHED	GAMES STARTED	GAMES COMPLETED	WINS	LOSSES	WINNING AVG.
Arias, Rudolfo	L	34	0	0	2	0	1.000
Donovan, Richard	R	31	29	5	9	10	0.474
Latman, A. Barry	R	37	21	5	8	5	0.615
Lown, Omar	R	60	0	0	9	2	0.818
McBride, Kenneth	R	11	2	0	0	1	0.000
Moore, Raymond	R	29	8	0	3	6	0.333
Peters, Gary	L	2	0	0	0	0	0.000
Pierce, W. William	L	34	33	12	14	15	0.483
Raymond, J. Claude	R	3	0	0	0	0	0.000
Rudolph, F. Donald	L	4	0	0	0	0	0.000
Shaw, Robert	R	47	26	8	18	6	0.750
Staley, Gerald	R	67	0	0	8	5	0.615
Stanka, Joseph	R	2	0	0	1	0	1.000
Wynn, Early	R	37	37	14	22	10	0.688

1959 CHICAGO WHITE SOX SEASON PITCHING RECORDS

INNINGS PITCHED	AT BATS	HITS	HOME RUNS	RUNS	EARNED RUNS	BASE ON BALLS	STRIKE-OUTS	ERA
44	177	49	7	23	20	20	28	4.090
180	692	171	15	84	73	58	71	3.650
156	587	138	15	71	65	72	97	3.750
93	340	73	12	32	30	42	63	2.900
23	87	20	1	11	8	17	12	0.000
90	329	86	10	46	41	46	49	4.100
1	5	2	0	0	0	2	1	0.000
224	858	217	26	98	90	62	114	3.620
4	15	5	2	4	4	2	1	0.000
3	12	4	0	0	0	2	0	0.000
231	873	217	15	72	69	54	89	2.690
116	429	111	5	39	29	25	54	2.250
5	18	2	1	2	2	4	3	0.000
256	937	202	20	106	90	119	179	3.160

1959 CHICAGO WHITE SOX SEASON BATTING RECORDS

PLAYER	BATS	GAMES	AT BATS	TOTAL RUNS	HITS
Aparicio, Luis	R	152	612	98	157
Arias, Rodolfo	L	34	4	0	0
Battey, Earl	R	26	64	9	14
Boone, Raymond	R	70	153	22	41
Callison, John	L	49	104	12	18
Carreon, Camilo	R	1	1	0	0
Cash, Norman	L	58	104	16	25
Doby, Lawrence	L	39	113	6	26
Donovan, Richard	L	31	61	4	8
Ennis, Delmer	R	26	96	10	21
Esposito, Samuel	R	69	66	12	11
Fox, J. Nelson	L	156	624	84	191
Goodman, William	L	104	268	21	67
Hicks, W. Joseph	L	6	7	0	3
Jackson, Ronald	R	10	14	3	3
Kluszewski, Theodore	L	31	101	11	30
Landis, James	R	149	515	78	140
Latman, A. Barry	R	37	47	3	6
Lollar, J. Sherman	R	140	505	63	134
Lown, Omar	R	60	12	1	3
Martin, Joseph	L	3	4	0	1
McAnany, James	R	67	210	22	58
McBride, Kenneth	R	11	6	0	1
Moore, Raymond	R	29	23	0	2
Mueller, Donald	L	4	4	0	2
Peters, Gary	L	2	0	0	0
Phillips, John	R	117	379	43	100
Pierce, W. William	L	34	68	3	13
Raymond, J. Claude	R	3	0	0	0
Rivera, Manuel	L	80	177	18	39
Romano, John	R	53	126	20	37
Rudolph, F. Donald	L	4	0	0	0
Shaw, Robert	R	47	73	7	9
Simpson, Harry	L	46	89	6	18
Skizas, Louis	R	8	13	3	1
Smith, Alphonse	R	129	472	65	112
Staley, Gerald	R	67	13	2	2
Stanka, Joseph	R	2	3	1	1
Torgeson, C. Earl	L	127	277	40	61
Wynn, Early	Both	37	90	11	22

1959 CHICAGO WHITE SOX SEASON BATTING RECORDS

BASES	DOUBLES	TRIPLES	HOME RUNS	STOLEN BASES	RBIS	BATT. AVG
203	18	5	6	56	51	0.268
0	0	0	0	0	0	0.000
25	1	2	2	0	7	0.219
56	6	0	3	2	17	0.268
30	3	0	3	0	12	0.173
0	0	0	0	0	0	0.000
39	0	1	4	1	16	0.240
34	4	2	0	1	13	0.230
15	4	0	1	0	5	0.131
33	6	0	2	0	7	0.219
15	1	0	1	0	5	0.167
243	34	6	2	5	70	0.306
86	14	1	1	3	28	0.250
3	0	0	0	0	0	0.429
7	1	0	1	0	2	0.214
40	2	1	2	0	10	0.297
195	26	7	5	20	60	0.272
7	1	0	0	0	6	0.128
228	22	3	22	4	84	0.265
3	0	0	0	0	0	0.250
1	0	0	0	0	1	0.250
73	9	3	0	2	27	0.276
1	0	0	0	0	0	0.167
3	1	0	0	0	0	0.087
2	0	0	0	0	0	0.500
0	0	0	0	0	0	0.000
144	27	1	5	1	40	0.264
18	1	2	0	0	7	0.191
0	0	0	0	0	0	0.000
68	9	4	4	5	19	0.220
59	5	1	5	0	25	0.294
0	0	0	0	0	0	0.000
10	1	0	0	0	2	0.123
34	5	1	3	0	15	0.202
1	0	0	0	0	0	0.077
187	16	4	17	7	55	0.237
2	0	0	0	0	0	0.154
1	0	0	0	0	1	0.333
99	5	3	9	7	45	0.220
35	7	0	2	0	8	0.244